PRACTICE - ASSESS - DIAGNOSE

180 Days of MATH for Third Grade

Developed by
Jodene Smith

Shell Education

Publishing Credits

Dona Herweck Rice, *Editor-in-Chief*; Lee Aucoin, *Creative Director*;
Don Tran, *Print Production Manager*; Timothy J. Bradley, *Illustration Manager*;
Chris McIntyre, M.A.Ed., *Editorial Director*; Sara Johnson, M.S.Ed., *Senior Editor*;
Aubrie Nielsen, M.S.Ed., *Associate Education Editor*; Juan Chavolla, *Cover/Interior Layout Designer*;
Robin Erickson, *Production Artist*; Agi Palinay, *Illustrator*; Corinne Burton, M.A.Ed., *Publisher*

Shell Education
5482 Argosy Avenue
Huntington Beach, CA 92649-1030
www.tcmpub.com/shell-education
ISBN 978-1-4258-0806-8

Printed by: 51497
Printed in: China

TABLE OF CONTENTS

INTRODUCTION AND RESEARCH

The Need for Practice

In order to be successful in today's mathematics classroom, students must deeply understand both concepts and procedures so that they can discuss and demonstrate their understanding. Demonstrating understanding is a process that must be continually practiced in order for students to be successful. According to Marzano (2010, 83), "practice has always been, and will always be, a necessary ingredient to learning procedural knowledge at a level at which students execute it independently." Practice is especially important to help students apply their concrete, conceptual understanding to a particular procedural skill.

Understanding Assessment

In addition to providing opportunities for frequent practice, teachers must be able to assess students' understanding of mathematical procedures, terms, concepts, and reasoning (Kilpatrick, Swafford, and Findell 2001). This is important so that teachers can adequately address students' misconceptions, build on their current understanding, and challenge them appropriately.

Assessment is a long-term process that often involves careful analysis of student responses from a lesson discussion, project, practice sheet, or test. When analyzing the data, it is important for teachers to reflect on how their teaching practices may have influenced students' responses and to identify those areas where additional instruction may be required. In short, the data gathered from assessments should be used to inform instruction: slow down, speed up, or reteach. This type of assessment is called *formative assessment* and is used to provide a seamless connection between instruction and assessment (McIntosh 1997).

HOW TO USE THIS BOOK

180 Days of Math for Third Grade offers teachers and parents a full page of daily mathematics practice activities for each day of the school year.

Easy to Use and Standards-Based

These activities reinforce grade-level skills across a variety of mathematical concepts. The questions are provided as a full practice page, making them easy to prepare and implement as part of a classroom morning routine, at the beginning of each mathematics lesson, or as homework.

Every third-grade practice page provides 10 questions, each tied to a specific mathematical concept. Students are given the opportunity for regular practice in each mathematical concept, allowing them to build confidence through these quick standards-based activities.

Question	Mathematics Concept	NCTM Standard
1	**Addition or Subtraction**	Understands meanings of operations and how they relate to one another; Computes fluently and makes reasonable estimates; Understands various meanings of multiplication and division; Develops fluency in adding, subtracting, multiplying, and dividing whole numbers; Understands numbers, ways of representing numbers, relationships among numbers, and number systems
2	**Multiplication**	
3		
4	**Division or Number Sense**	
5	**Place Value or Fractions, Decimals, and Money**	Understands numbers, ways of representing numbers, relationships among numbers, and number systems; Computes fluently and makes reasonable estimates
6	**Algebra and Algebraic Thinking**	Understands patterns, relations, and functions; Represents and analyzes mathematical situations and structures using algebraic symbols
7	**Measurement**	Understands measurable attributes of objects and the units, systems, and processes of measurement; Applies appropriate techniques and formulas to determine measurements
8		
9	**Geometry or Data Analysis**	Analyzes characteristics and properties of two-dimensional and three-dimensional geometric shapes and develops mathematical arguments about geometric relationships; Formulates questions that can be addressed with data and collects, organizes, and displays relevant data to answer them
10	**Word Problem/Logic Problem or Mathematical Reasoning**	Builds new mathematical knowledge through problem solving; Applies and adapts a variety of appropriate strategies to solve problems

Standards are listed with the permission of the National Council of Teachers of Mathematics (NCTM). NCTM does not endorse the content or validity of these alignments.

HOW TO USE THIS BOOK *(cont.)*

Using the Practice Pages

As outlined on page 4, every question is aligned to a mathematics concept and standard.

Practice pages provide instruction and assessment opportunities for each day of the school year.

Each question ties student practice to a specific mathematics concept.

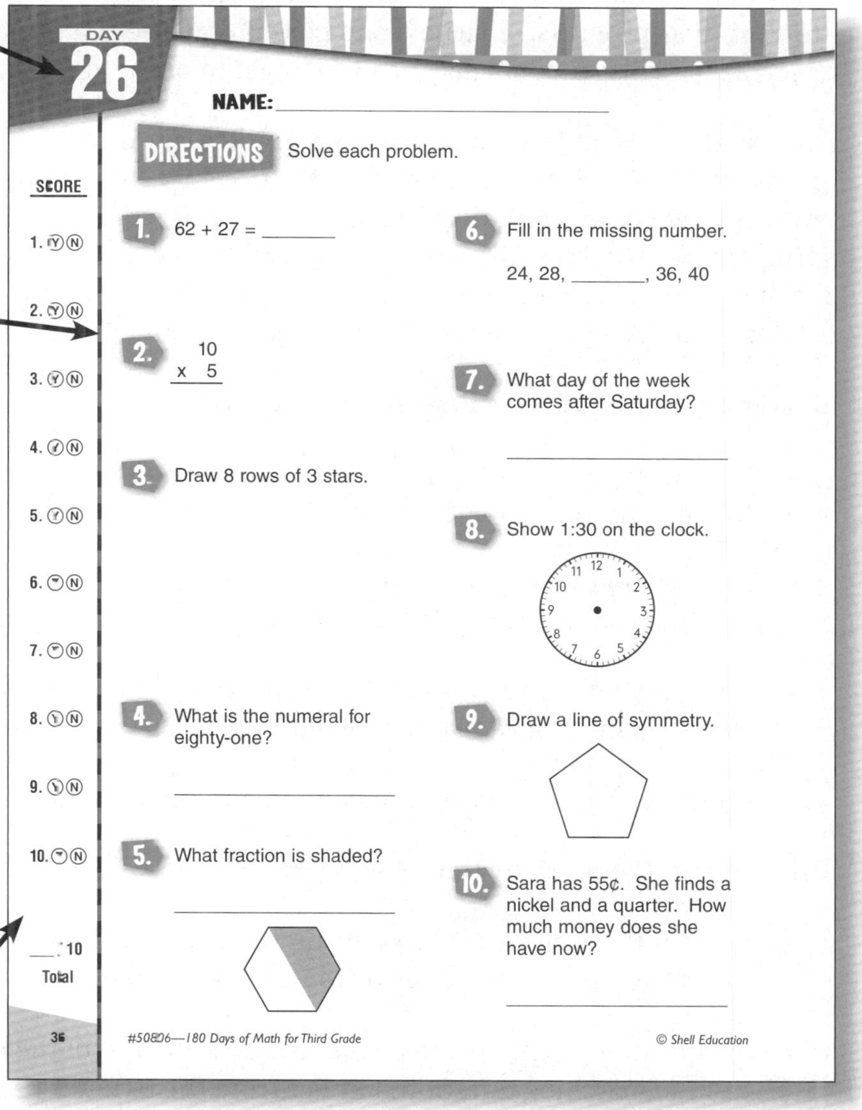

DAY 26

NAME: ______________________

DIRECTIONS Solve each problem.

SCORE

1. Y N
2. Y N
3. Y N
4. Y N
5. Y N
6. Y N
7. Y N
8. Y N
9. Y N
10. Y N

___ / 10 Total

1. 62 + 27 = ______

2. 10 x 5

3. Draw 8 rows of 3 stars.

4. What is the numeral for eighty-one?

5. What fraction is shaded?

6. Fill in the missing number.
24, 28, ______, 36, 40

7. What day of the week comes after Saturday?

8. Show 1:30 on the clock.

9. Draw a line of symmetry.

10. Sara has 55¢. She finds a nickel and a quarter. How much money does she have now?

36 #50806—180 Days of Math for Third Grade © Shell Education

Using the Scoring Guide

Use the scoring guide along the side of each practice page to check answers and see at a glance which skills may need more reinforcement.

Fill in the appropriate circle for each problem to indicate correct (Y) or incorrect (N) responses. You might wish to indicate only incorrect responses to focus on those skills. (For example, if students consistently miss numbers 2 and 6, they may need additional help with those concepts as outlined in the table on page 4.) Use the answer key at the back of the book to score the problems, or you may call out answers to have students self-score or peer-score their work.

HOW TO USE THIS BOOK *(cont.)*

Diagnostic Assessment

Teachers can use the practice pages as diagnostic assessments. The data analysis tools included with the book enable teachers or parents to quickly score students' work and monitor their progress. Teachers and parents can see at a glance which mathematics concepts or skills students may need to target in order to develop proficiency.

After students complete a practice page, grade each page using the answer key (pages 191–207). Then, complete the *Practice Page Item Analysis* (page 7) for the whole class, or the *Student Item Analysis* (page 8) for individual students. These charts are also provided in the digital resources (filenames: G3_practicepage_analysis.pdf, G3_student_analysis.pdf). Teachers can input data into the electronic files directly on the computer, or they can print the pages and analyze students' work using paper and pencil.

To complete the Practice Page Item Analysis:

- Write or type students' names in the far-left column. Depending on the number of students, more than one copy of the form may be needed or you may need to add rows.
- The question numbers are included across the top of the chart. Each item correlates with the matching question number from the practice page.
- For each student, record an *X* in the column if the student has the item incorrect. If the item is correct, leave the item blank.
- Count the *X*s in each row and column and fill in the correct boxes.

To complete the Student Item Analysis:

- Write or type the student's name on the top row. This form tracks the ongoing progress of each student, so one copy per student is necessary.
- The question numbers are included across the top of the chart. Each item correlates with the matching question number from the practice page.
- For each day, record an *X* in the column if the student has the item incorrect. If the item is correct, leave the item blank.
- Count the *X*s in each row and column and fill in the correct boxes.

Practice Page Item Analysis

Directions: Record an *X* in cells to indicate where students have missed questions. Add up the totals. You can view: (1) which questions/concepts were missed per student; (2) the total correct score for each student; and (3) the total number of students who missed each question.

Day: ______	Question #	1	2	3	4	5	6	7	8	9	10	# Correct
Student Name												
Sample Student			X			X	X				X	6/10
# of Students Missing Each Question												

HOW TO USE THIS BOOK *(cont.)*

Student Item Analysis

Directions: Record an *X* in cells to indicate where the student has missed questions. Add up the totals. You can view: (1) which questions/concepts the student missed; (2) the total correct score per day; and (3) the total number of times each question/concept was missed.

Student Name: Sample Student											
Question	**1**	**2**	**3**	**4**	**5**	**6**	**7**	**8**	**9**	**10**	**# Correct**
Day											
1		X			X						8/10
Total											

HOW TO USE THIS BOOK *(cont.)*

Using the Results to Differentiate Instruction

Once results are gathered and analyzed, teachers can use the results to inform the way they differentiate instruction. The data can help determine which concepts are the most difficult for students and which need additional instructional support and continued practice. Depending on how often the practice pages are scored, results can be considered for instructional support on a daily or weekly basis.

Whole-Class Support

The results of the diagnostic analysis may show that the entire class is struggling with a particular concept or group of concepts. If these concepts have been taught in the past, this indicates that further instruction or reteaching is necessary. If these concepts have not been taught in the past, this data is a great pre-assessment and demonstrates that students do not have a working knowledge of the concepts. Thus, careful planning for the length of the unit(s) or lesson(s) must be considered, and extra frontloading may be required.

Small-Group or Individual Support

The results of the diagnostic analysis may show that an individual or small group of students is struggling with a particular concept or group of concepts. If these concepts have been taught in the past, this indicates that further instruction or reteaching is necessary. Consider pulling aside these students while others are working independently to instruct further on the concept(s). Teachers can also use the results to help identify individuals or groups of proficient students who are ready for enrichment or above-grade level instruction. These students may benefit from independent learning contracts or more challenging activities. Students may also benefit from extra practice using games or computer-based resources.

Digital Resources

Reference page 208 for information about accessing the digital resources and an overview of the contents.

HOW TO USE THIS BOOK *(cont.)*

NCTM Standards

The lessons in this book are aligned to the National Council of Teachers of Mathematics (NCTM) standards. The standards listed on page 4 support the concepts and skills that are consistently presented on each of the practice pages.

Standards Correlations

Shell Education is committed to producing educational materials that are research and standards based. In this effort, we have correlated all of our products to the academic standards of all 50 states, the District of Columbia, and the Department of Defense Dependent Schools, as well as to the college and career readiness standards.

How to Find Standards Correlations

To print a customized correlation report of this product for your state, visit our website at **www.tcmpub.com/shell-education** and follow the on-screen directions. If you require assistance in printing correlation reports, please contact Customer Service at 1-877-777-3450.

Purpose and Intent of Standards

The No Child Left Behind legislation mandates that all states adopt academic standards that identify the skills students will learn in kindergarten through grade twelve. While many states had already adopted academic standards prior to NCLB, the legislation set requirements to ensure the standards were detailed and comprehensive.

Standards are designed to focus instruction and guide adoption of curricula. Standards are statements that describe the criteria necessary for students to meet specific academic goals. They define the knowledge, skills, and content students should acquire at each level. Standards are also used to develop standardized tests to evaluate students' academic progress.

Teachers are required to demonstrate how their lessons meet state standards. State standards are used in development of all of our products, so educators can be assured they meet the academic requirements of each state.

NAME: ______________________

DIRECTIONS Solve each problem.

1.  +  =

☐ apples

2.

$$\begin{array}{r} 5 \\ \times\ 2 \\ \hline \end{array}$$

3. Draw 3 rows of 5 circles.

4. How many rows of 2 make 14?

____

5. 5 tens + 6 ones = ________

6. Fill in the missing number.

14, 24, 34, ________, 54

7. How many days are in one week?

____

8. Circle the longer pencil.

9. What polygon has four equal sides?

____

10. There are 13 girls and 15 boys in a class. How many children are there in all?

____

SCORE

1. Ⓨ Ⓝ
2. Ⓨ Ⓝ
3. Ⓨ Ⓝ
4. Ⓨ Ⓝ
5. Ⓨ Ⓝ
6. Ⓨ Ⓝ
7. Ⓨ Ⓝ
8. Ⓨ Ⓝ
9. Ⓨ Ⓝ
10. Ⓨ Ⓝ

___ / 10
Total

DAY 2

NAME: ______________________

DIRECTIONS Solve each problem.

SCORE

1. Ⓨ Ⓝ
2. Ⓨ Ⓝ
3. Ⓨ Ⓝ
4. Ⓨ Ⓝ
5. Ⓨ Ⓝ
6. Ⓨ Ⓝ
7. Ⓨ Ⓝ
8. Ⓨ Ⓝ
9. Ⓨ Ⓝ
10. Ⓨ Ⓝ

___ / 10 Total

1.
$$\begin{array}{r} 20 \\ -\ 15 \\ \hline \end{array}$$

2. 9 x 5 = ☐

3. 4 groups of 10 is ________.

4. What is the numeral for forty-two?

____

5. What fraction of this shape is shaded?

____

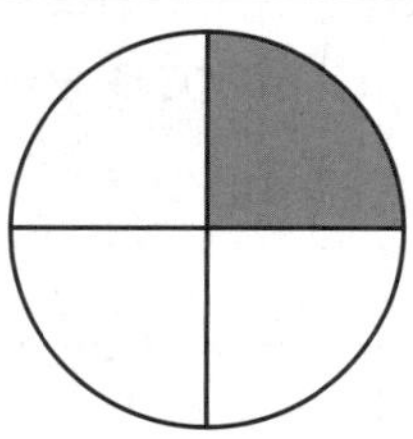

6. 4 + 5 = ☐ + 4

7. How many days are in June?

____

8. Write the time in words.

____

9. Does the drawing show a *flip, slide,* or *turn?*

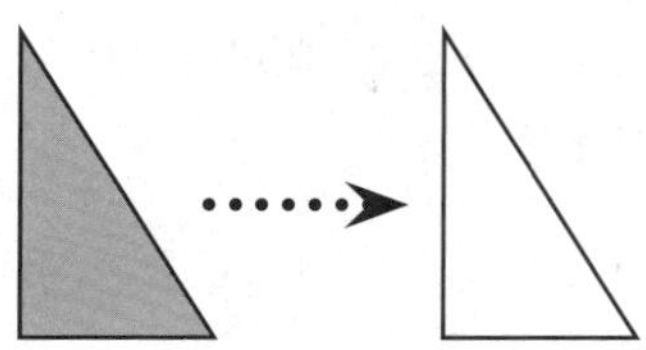

____

10. Grandma made 20 cookies. We ate 13. How many are left?

____

NAME: ______________________________

DIRECTIONS Solve each problem.

1. 16 + 3 = _______

2.

$$\begin{array}{r} 20 \\ \times \ \ 5 \\ \hline \end{array}$$

3. Draw 9 rows of 2 squares.

4. Circle half of the monkeys.

5. What is the value of the digit 1 in the number 13?

____

6. Fill in the missing number.

18, 16, ________, 12, 10

7. Name the days of the weekend.

____

8. Record the line length.

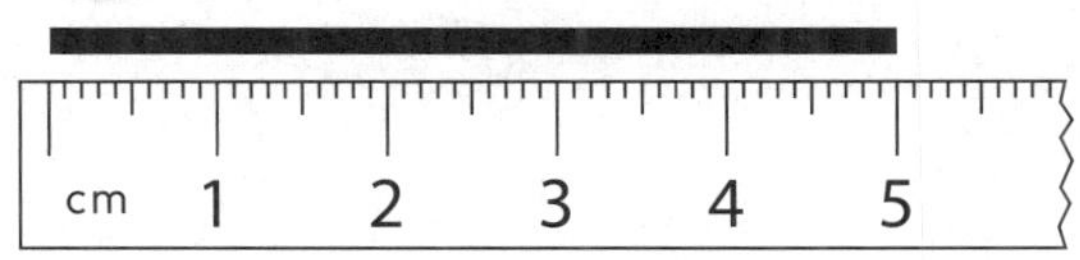

____

9. Circle the pyramids.

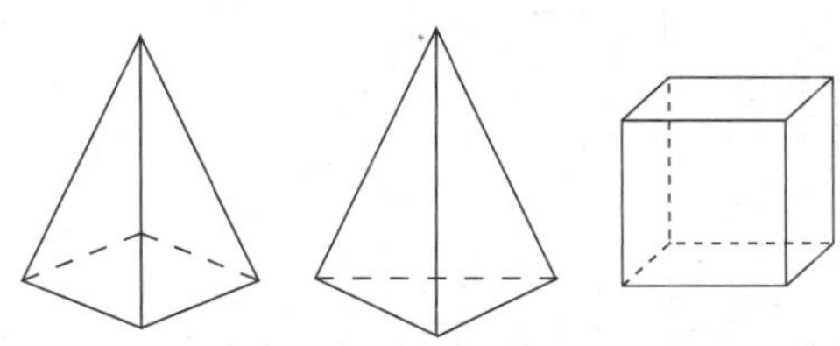

10. Tara has a red shirt, a green shirt, and blue pants. If she wears only one shirt at a time, how many different outfits can she make?

____

SCORE

1. Ⓨ Ⓝ
2. Ⓨ Ⓝ
3. Ⓨ Ⓝ
4. Ⓨ Ⓝ
5. Ⓨ Ⓝ
6. Ⓨ Ⓝ
7. Ⓨ Ⓝ
8. Ⓨ Ⓝ
9. Ⓨ Ⓝ
10. Ⓨ Ⓝ

___ / 10 Total

DAY 4

NAME: ______________________

DIRECTIONS Solve each problem.

SCORE
1. Ⓨ Ⓝ
2. Ⓨ Ⓝ
3. Ⓨ Ⓝ
4. Ⓨ Ⓝ
5. Ⓨ Ⓝ
6. Ⓨ Ⓝ
7. Ⓨ Ⓝ
8. Ⓨ Ⓝ
9. Ⓨ Ⓝ
10. Ⓨ Ⓝ
___ / 10 Total

1. $48 - 24 = \square$

2. Draw 6 rows of 5 triangles.

3.

$$\begin{array}{r} 10 \\ \times \quad 8 \\ \hline \end{array}$$

4. Write 37 in words.

____

5. What is the value of the digit 1 in the number 18?

____

6. $10 - \square = 6$

7. Circle the group of tables that would need the larger tablecloth.

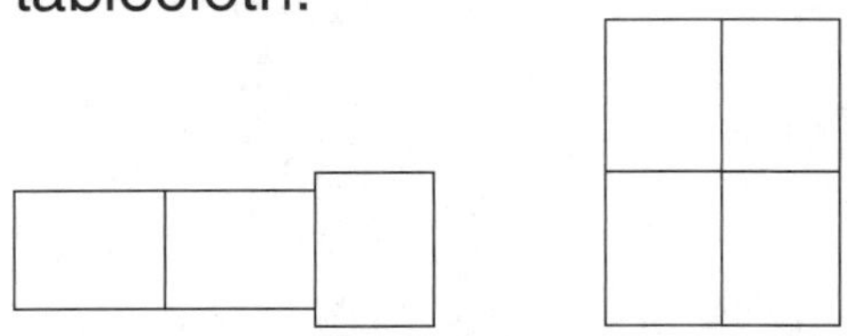

8. Write the time in words.

____

9. What is this shape?

____

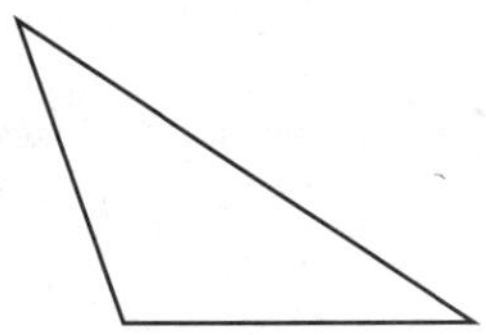

10. Double 8, then subtract 2.

____

NAME: ____________________

DIRECTIONS Solve each problem.

1.

$$\begin{array}{r} 25 \\ -\ 10 \\ \hline \end{array}$$

2. 6 x 10 = ☐

3. What are 12 groups of 2?

____

4. Is this an equal share?

Circle: yes no

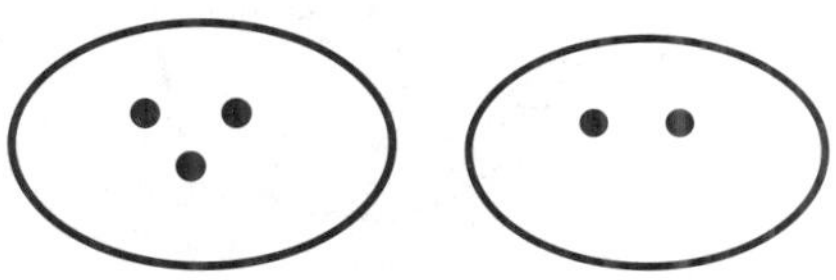

5. How many quarters are there in $4.00?

____

6. Fill in the missing number.

22, 21, ________, 19

7. What is the month before January?

____

8. Rocks were used to measure the mass of each object. Circle the object with the greatest mass.

1 rock 15 rocks 3 rocks

9. How many children like chocolate ice cream?

____

Favorite Ice Cream Flavors

Chocolate	
Vanilla	
Strawberry	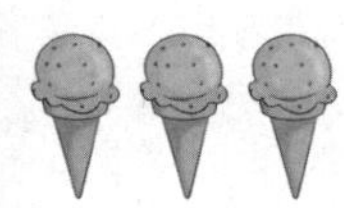

Key  = 1 child

10. I am 13 more than 52. What number am I?

____

SCORE

1. Ⓨ Ⓝ
2. Ⓨ Ⓝ
3. Ⓨ Ⓝ
4. Ⓨ Ⓝ
5. Ⓨ Ⓝ
6. Ⓨ Ⓝ
7. Ⓨ Ⓝ
8. Ⓨ Ⓝ
9. Ⓨ Ⓝ
10. Ⓨ Ⓝ

___ / 10 Total

DAY 6

NAME: ______________________________

DIRECTIONS Solve each problem.

SCORE

1. Ⓨ Ⓝ
2. Ⓨ Ⓝ
3. Ⓨ Ⓝ
4. Ⓨ Ⓝ
5. Ⓨ Ⓝ
6. Ⓨ Ⓝ
7. Ⓨ Ⓝ
8. Ⓨ Ⓝ
9. Ⓨ Ⓝ
10. Ⓨ Ⓝ

___ / 10 Total

1.  = ________

2.

$$\begin{array}{r} 3 \\ \times\ 5 \\ \hline \end{array}$$

3. Skip count by twos.

2, ______, ______, ______

4. What is the even number right before 10?

____

5. What is the total value of these coins?

____

6. 12 – ☐ = 4

7. Which covers the larger area: a ruler or a sheet of paper?

____

8. What time is shown?

____

9. Is this shape symmetrical?

Circle: yes no

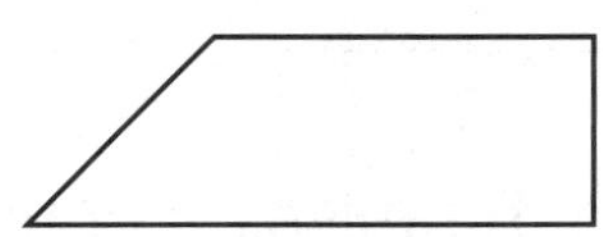

10. Write these numbers in increasing order.

345, 43, 543, 534, 34

____

NAME: ____________________

DIRECTIONS Solve each problem.

SCORE

1. 34 – 12 = ______

2. Draw 4 rows of 3 circles.

3.
$$\begin{array}{r} 5 \\ \times\ 5 \\ \hline \end{array}$$

4. How many groups of 4 are in 16?

____

5. Which is bigger: one-half or one whole?

____

6. True or false? 5 + 2 = 4 + 3

____

7. How many days are there in May?

____

8. Cubes were used to measure the volume of each box. Circle the container with the greatest volume.

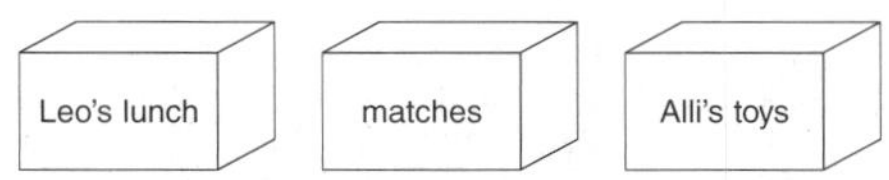

720 cubes | 80 cubes | 4,000 cubes

9. Name the solid shape.

____

10. I have 62 stickers. How many will I have if I get 17 more?

____

1. Ⓨ Ⓝ
2. Ⓨ Ⓝ
3. Ⓨ Ⓝ
4. Ⓨ Ⓝ
5. Ⓨ Ⓝ
6. Ⓨ Ⓝ
7. Ⓨ Ⓝ
8. Ⓨ Ⓝ
9. Ⓨ Ⓝ
10. Ⓨ Ⓝ

___ / 10 Total

DAY
8

NAME: ______________________________

DIRECTIONS Solve each problem.

SCORE

1. Ⓨ Ⓝ
2. Ⓨ Ⓝ
3. Ⓨ Ⓝ
4. Ⓨ Ⓝ
5. Ⓨ Ⓝ
6. Ⓨ Ⓝ
7. Ⓨ Ⓝ
8. Ⓨ Ⓝ
9. Ⓨ Ⓝ
10. Ⓨ Ⓝ

___ / 10 Total

1.
$$\begin{array}{r} 54 \\ +\ 25 \\ \hline \end{array}$$

2. 7 x 4 = ☐

3. Draw 4 rows of 2 girls.

4. What number follows 79?

____

5. In the number 274, which digit is in the tens place?

____

6. 3 ☐ 6 = 9

7. What day of the week comes after Tuesday?

____

8. Use these words to label the prism: *height*, *width*, and *length*.

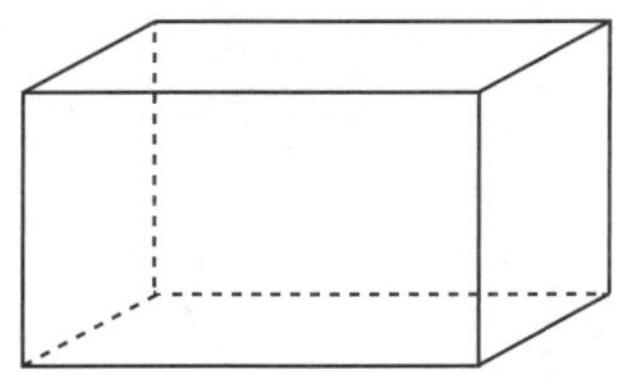

9. Draw the top view of this figure

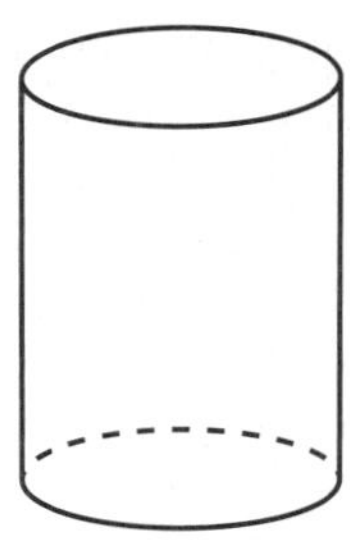

10. Write the time 12:00 in words.

____

DAY 9

NAME: ____________________

DIRECTIONS Solve each problem.

1. 50 – 36 = ☐

2.

$$\begin{array}{r} 9 \\ \times\ 3 \\ \hline \end{array}$$

3. Draw 2 rows of 8 circles.

4. How many lines of 5 make 20?

____

5. How many dimes are there in 60¢?

____

6. Fill in the missing number.

12, 18, 24, ________, 36

7. Write the time in words.

____

8. Which is shorter: a giraffe or a mouse?

____

9. Flip the triangle and draw its new position.

10. There are rocks inside the boxes. I have 7 rocks. Circle the two boxes that I have.

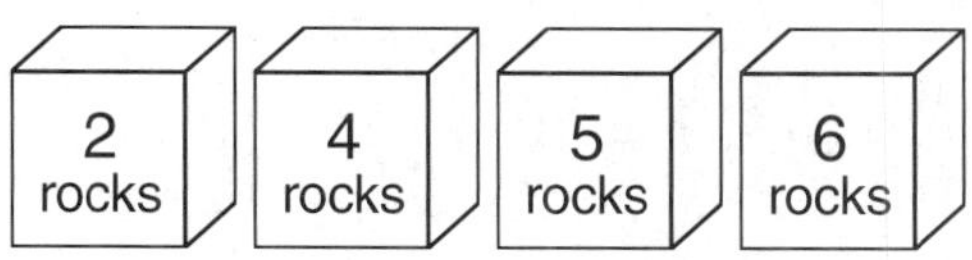

SCORE

1. Ⓨ Ⓝ
2. Ⓨ Ⓝ
3. Ⓨ Ⓝ
4. Ⓨ Ⓝ
5. Ⓨ Ⓝ
6. Ⓨ Ⓝ
7. Ⓨ Ⓝ
8. Ⓨ Ⓝ
9. Ⓨ Ⓝ
10. Ⓨ Ⓝ

___ / 10 Total

DAY 10

NAME: ______________________

DIRECTIONS Solve each problem.

SCORE

1. Ⓨ Ⓝ
2. Ⓨ Ⓝ
3. Ⓨ Ⓝ
4. Ⓨ Ⓝ
5. Ⓨ Ⓝ
6. Ⓨ Ⓝ
7. Ⓨ Ⓝ
8. Ⓨ Ⓝ
9. Ⓨ Ⓝ
10. Ⓨ Ⓝ

___ / 10 Total

1. $12 + 7 = \square$

2.
$$\begin{array}{r} 8 \\ \times\ 4 \\ \hline \end{array}$$

3. Draw 9 rows of 10 dots.

4. How many digits are there in 19?

____

5. What is the value of the digit 3 in the number 13?

____

6. $6 + 9 = 10 + \square$

7. Show 8:15 on the clock.

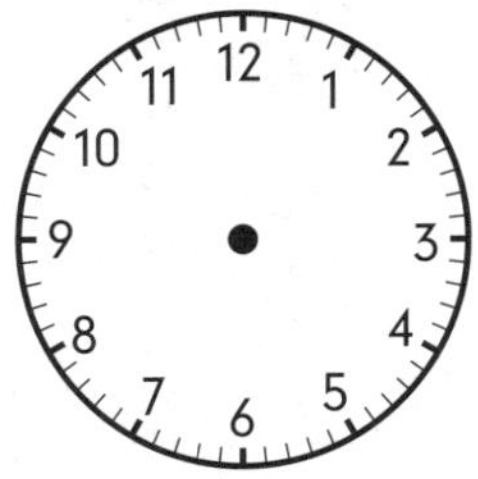

8. Which has a smaller surface area: a 12-inch ruler or this sheet of paper?

____

9. A coin is tossed 10 times. It lands with heads up 6 times. It lands with tails up 4 times. Record the data in the chart below using tally marks.

Coin Tosses

Heads	
Tails	

10. A class can have 20 students. There are 18 students in class now. How many more students can be added to the class?

____

NAME: ______________________________

DIRECTIONS Solve each problem.

1.
```
  30
-  9
----
```

2. How many legs are there on 5 dogs?

____

3. 9 x 4 = ☐

4. Use different colors to show four equal groups.

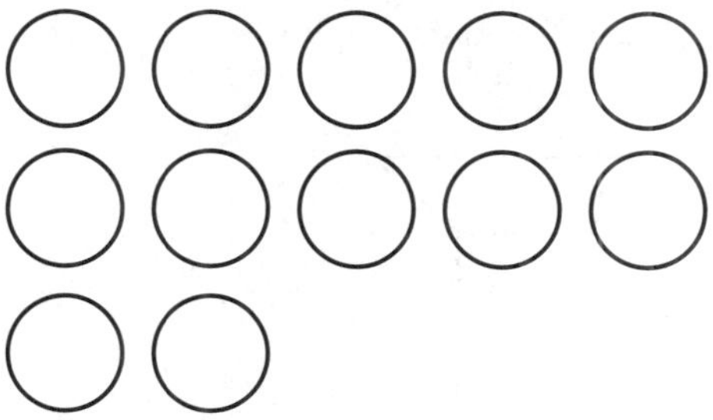

5. 3 hundreds + 2 tens + 8 ones =

____

6. Write the next 3 numbers in the pattern.

11, 22, 33, _____, _____, _____

7. Write the time in words.

____

8. Measure the height of this page in inches.

____

9. Count the solids in the objects below.

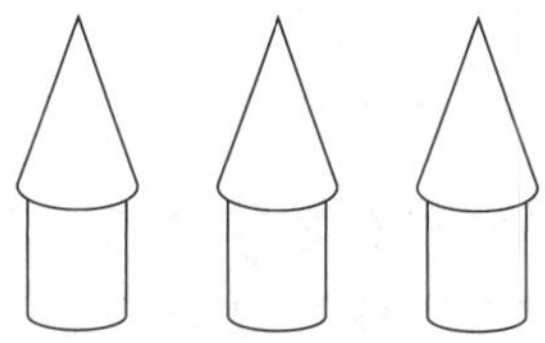

 _______

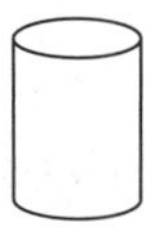 _______

10. I took a nap and woke up at 3:00. I slept for 2 hours. What time did I fall asleep?

____

SCORE

1. Ⓨ Ⓝ
2. Ⓨ Ⓝ
3. Ⓨ Ⓝ
4. Ⓨ Ⓝ
5. Ⓨ Ⓝ
6. Ⓨ Ⓝ
7. Ⓨ Ⓝ
8. Ⓨ Ⓝ
9. Ⓨ Ⓝ
10. Ⓨ Ⓝ

___ / 10
Total

DAY 12

NAME: ____________________

DIRECTIONS Solve each problem.

SCORE

1. Ⓨ Ⓝ
2. Ⓨ Ⓝ
3. Ⓨ Ⓝ
4. Ⓨ Ⓝ
5. Ⓨ Ⓝ
6. Ⓨ Ⓝ
7. Ⓨ Ⓝ
8. Ⓨ Ⓝ
9. Ⓨ Ⓝ
10. Ⓨ Ⓝ

___ / 10 Total

1. 17 + 7 = ☐

2.

$$\begin{array}{r} 10 \\ \times \quad 4 \\ \hline \end{array}$$

3. Six times one is ______.

4. What is the next even number after 6?

____

5. What fraction is shaded?

____

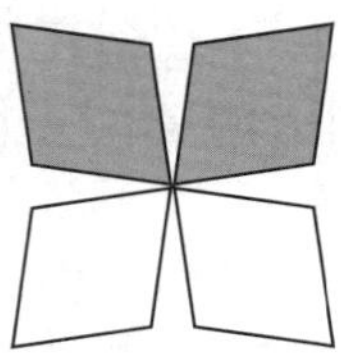

6. 8 ☐ 1 = 7

7. What is the month after April?

____

8. Circle the heavier animal.

9. Draw the top view of this shape.

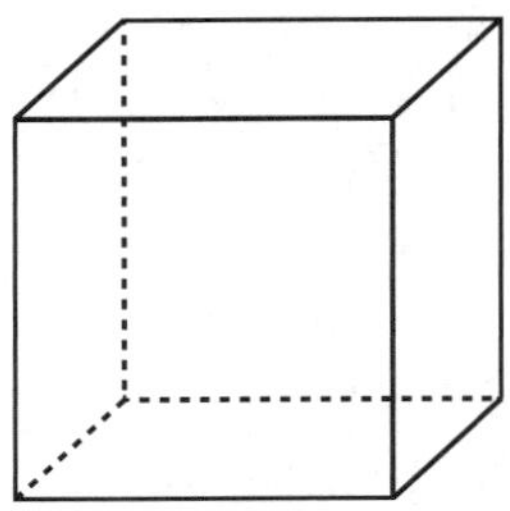

10. Circle the fifth pencil from the left.

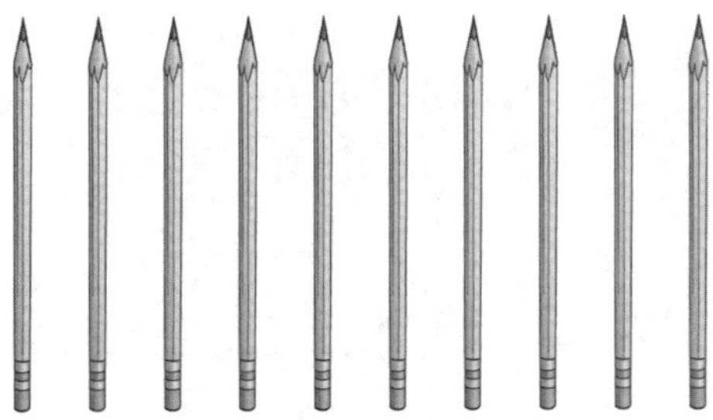

NAME: ____________________

DIRECTIONS Solve each problem.

SCORE

1. What is 12 less than 18?

   ____

2. 5 x 5 = ☐

3. Draw 4 rows of 2 sticks.

4. How many rows of 2 make 10?

   ____

5. 25¢ + 15¢ + 5¢ =

   ____

6. 5 ☐ 7 = 12

7. How many days are there in two weeks?

   ____

8. Show half past 10:00 on the clock.

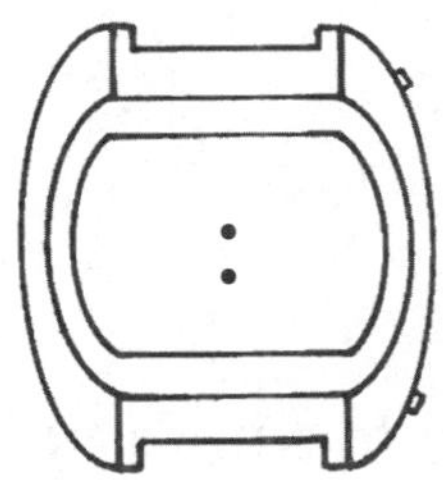

9. True or false? A cube has 6 faces.

   ____

10. Kwan has 35¢. He has 2 coins. What coins does Kwan have?

   ____

1. Ⓨ Ⓝ
2. Ⓨ Ⓝ
3. Ⓨ Ⓝ
4. Ⓨ Ⓝ
5. Ⓨ Ⓝ
6. Ⓨ Ⓝ
7. Ⓨ Ⓝ
8. Ⓨ Ⓝ
9. Ⓨ Ⓝ
10. Ⓨ Ⓝ

___ / 10

Total

DAY
14

NAME: ______________________________

DIRECTIONS Solve each problem.

SCORE

1. Ⓨ Ⓝ
2. Ⓨ Ⓝ
3. Ⓨ Ⓝ
4. Ⓨ Ⓝ
5. Ⓨ Ⓝ
6. Ⓨ Ⓝ
7. Ⓨ Ⓝ
8. Ⓨ Ⓝ
9. Ⓨ Ⓝ
10. Ⓨ Ⓝ

___ / 10
Total

1. 33 + 25 = ☐

2.

$$\begin{array}{r} 7 \\ \times\ 4 \\ \hline \end{array}$$

3. Draw 9 piles of 4 books.

4. Write the numeral for one hundred sixty.

____

5. What is the total value of these coins?

____

6. Write the next number in the pattern.

16, 20, 24, 28, ________

7. What time is shown?

____

8. Which is longer: a car or a house?

____

9. What is this shape?

____

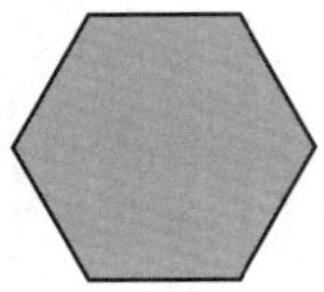

10. How many eyes are there on 20 children?

____

NAME: ______________________________

DIRECTIONS Solve each problem.

1. ● ● + ● ● ● ● = ______

2. 9 x 5 = ☐

3. Draw 3 rows of 10 oranges.

4. Circle groups of 2.

5. Write 31 in expanded notation.

____

6. 20 – ☐ = 7

7. What day of the week comes before Sunday?

____

8. Show 2:45 on the clock.

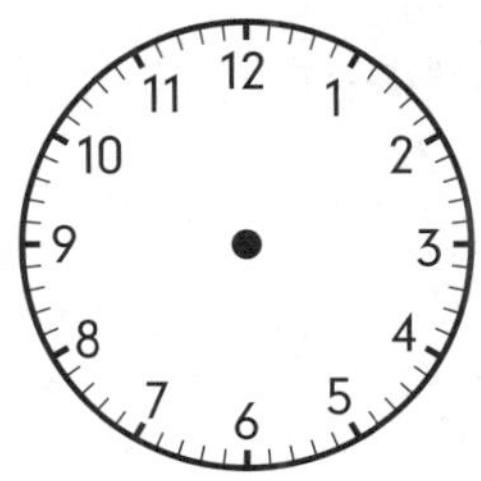

9. How many kids voted for roller skating?

____

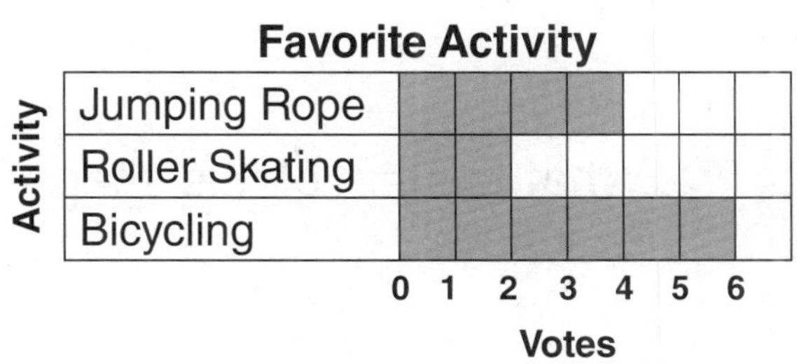

10. It is 2:00 P.M. What time will it be in 12 hours?

____

SCORE

1. Ⓨ Ⓝ
2. Ⓨ Ⓝ
3. Ⓨ Ⓝ
4. Ⓨ Ⓝ
5. Ⓨ Ⓝ
6. Ⓨ Ⓝ
7. Ⓨ Ⓝ
8. Ⓨ Ⓝ
9. Ⓨ Ⓝ
10. Ⓨ Ⓝ

___ / 10 Total

DAY
16

NAME: ______________________________

DIRECTIONS Solve each problem.

SCORE

1. Ⓨ Ⓝ
2. Ⓨ Ⓝ
3. Ⓨ Ⓝ
4. Ⓨ Ⓝ
5. Ⓨ Ⓝ
6. Ⓨ Ⓝ
7. Ⓨ Ⓝ
8. Ⓨ Ⓝ
9. Ⓨ Ⓝ
10. Ⓨ Ⓝ

___ / 10
Total

1.
$$\begin{array}{r} 47 \\ -\ 16 \\ \hline \end{array}$$

2. 8 x 5 = ☐

3. How many are in 6 groups of 10?

____

4. Draw tally marks to show the number 19.

5. What fraction of this shape is shaded?

____

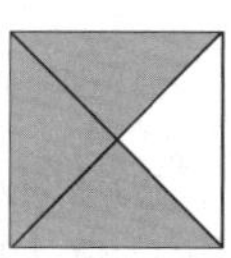

6. Fill in the missing number.

32, 36, 40, ________, 48

7. Write the time in words.

____

8. Which is shorter: a new pencil or a toothpick?

____

9. What shape has 3 sides?

____

10. A pizza is cut into 12 equal pieces. How many slices are there in half the pizza?

____

NAME: ____________________

DIRECTIONS Solve each problem.

1. 4 + 6 = ☐

2. Skip count by fives.

5, ______, ______, ______

3.

$$\begin{array}{r} 2 \\ \times\ 9 \\ \hline \end{array}$$

4. How many rows of 2 make 18?

____

5. Write the number for 15 tens.

____

6. 3 x 5 = 10 + ☐

7. What time is shown?

____

8. How many days are there in August?

____

9. Name the solid shape.

____

10. Add 3 tens and 7 ones to the number 68.

____

SCORE

1. Ⓨ Ⓝ
2. Ⓨ Ⓝ
3. Ⓨ Ⓝ
4. Ⓨ Ⓝ
5. Ⓨ Ⓝ
6. Ⓨ Ⓝ
7. Ⓨ Ⓝ
8. Ⓨ Ⓝ
9. Ⓨ Ⓝ
10. Ⓨ Ⓝ

___ / 10 Total

DAY 18

NAME: ______________________________

DIRECTIONS Solve each problem.

SCORE

1. Ⓨ Ⓝ
2. Ⓨ Ⓝ
3. Ⓨ Ⓝ
4. Ⓨ Ⓝ
5. Ⓨ Ⓝ
6. Ⓨ Ⓝ
7. Ⓨ Ⓝ
8. Ⓨ Ⓝ
9. Ⓨ Ⓝ
10. Ⓨ Ⓝ

___ / 10

Total

1. What is the difference between 18 and 8?

____

2.

$$\begin{array}{r} 6 \\ \times\ 4 \\ \hline \end{array}$$

3. Draw 7 rows of 5 books.

4. What is the odd number right before 20?

____

5. What is the value of the digit 2 in the number 28?

____

6. 15 – ☐ = 8

7. What is the month before May?

____

8. Show 12 o'clock on the clock.

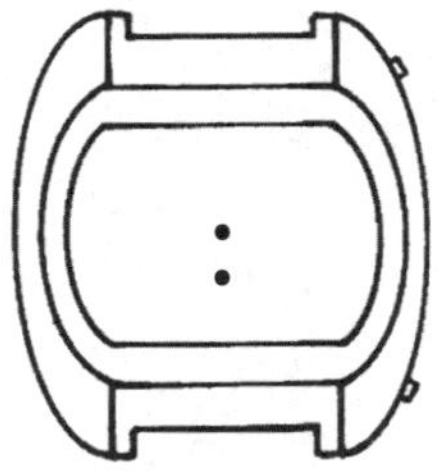

9. What shapes are used to create the large rectangle?

____

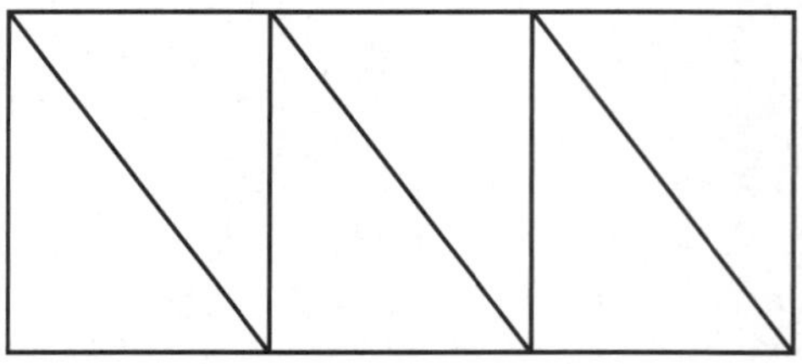

10. Mary is 140 cm tall. Thomas is 5 cm taller. How tall is Thomas?

____

NAME: ____________________

DIRECTIONS Solve each problem.

1. 7 + 5 = ☐

2. How many total fingers are there on 6 girls?

____

3.

$$\begin{array}{r} 4 \\ \times\ 2 \\ \hline \end{array}$$

4. Share 12 lollipops equally among 12 boys. How many lollipops does each boy get?

____

5. Color one-quarter of the shape.

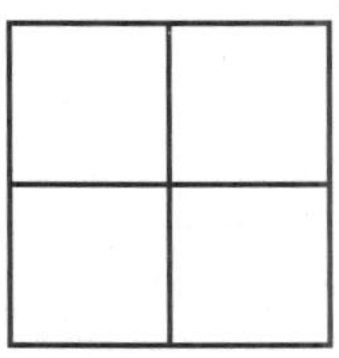

6. 20 ☐ 5 = 15

7. Write the time for midnight.

____

8. Show 10:15 on the clock.

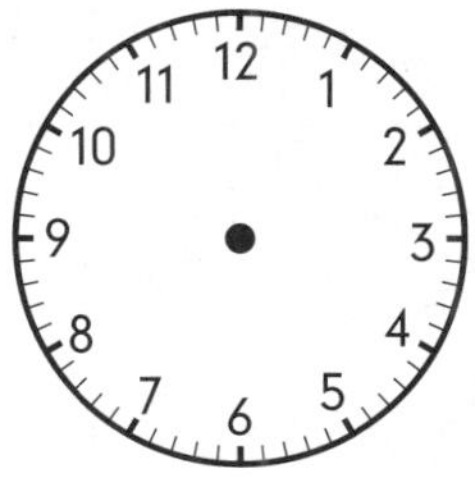

9.

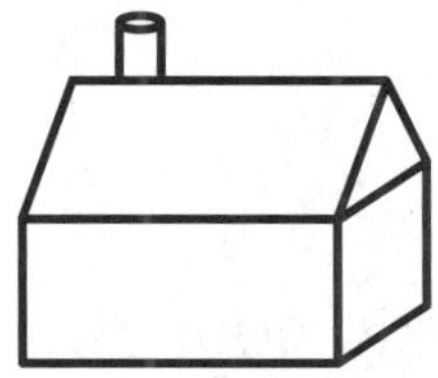

Count the solids in the drawing above.

 ____________

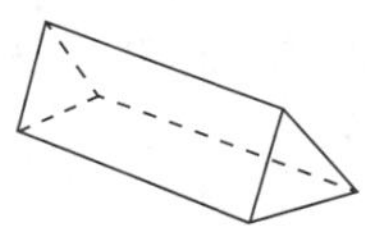 ____________

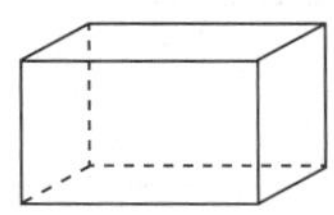 ____________

10. Matthew wants to make the largest number possible from the numeral cards below. Color the digit he should put first.

5	8	3

SCORE

1. Ⓨ Ⓝ
2. Ⓨ Ⓝ
3. Ⓨ Ⓝ
4. Ⓨ Ⓝ
5. Ⓨ Ⓝ
6. Ⓨ Ⓝ
7. Ⓨ Ⓝ
8. Ⓨ Ⓝ
9. Ⓨ Ⓝ
10. Ⓨ Ⓝ

___ / 10 Total

DAY
20

NAME: ____________________

DIRECTIONS Solve each problem.

SCORE

1. Ⓨ Ⓝ
2. Ⓨ Ⓝ
3. Ⓨ Ⓝ
4. Ⓨ Ⓝ
5. Ⓨ Ⓝ
6. Ⓨ Ⓝ
7. Ⓨ Ⓝ
8. Ⓨ Ⓝ
9. Ⓨ Ⓝ
10. Ⓨ Ⓝ

___ / 10
Total

1. What is 40 more than 16?

____

2.

$$\begin{array}{r} 6 \\ \times\ 2 \\ \hline \end{array}$$

3. Skip count by fours.

4, ______, ______, ______

4. Write 456 in words.

____

____

5. Which digit is in the ones place in the number 164?

____

6. 8 + 4 = 3 x ☐

7. Write the time in words.

____

8. What day of the week comes before Friday?

____

9.

Favorite Foods

Spaghetti	5
Tacos	3
Pizza	8
Macaroni and Cheese	4

Which food do children like the most?

____

10. Jo put some balls into rings like this:

What number sentence did she make?

A. 5 + 4 = 9

B. 20 – 5 = 15

C. 4 x 5 = 20

NAME: ______________________

DIRECTIONS Solve each problem.

1. What is 16 more than 14?

____

2.

$$\begin{array}{r} 8 \\ \times\ 4 \\ \hline \end{array}$$

3. What are 8 groups of 5?

____

4. Circle groups of 2.

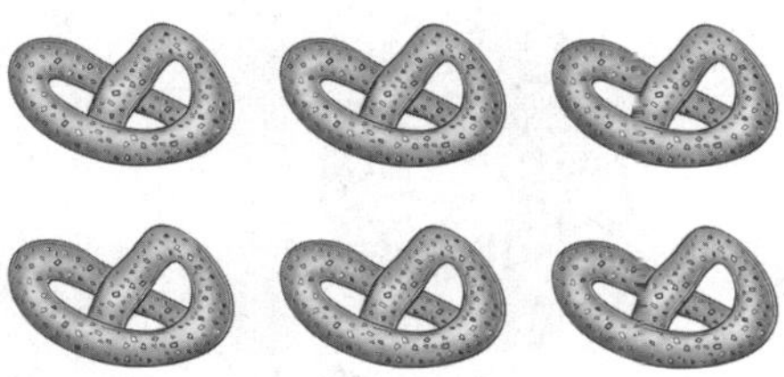

5. Write the number for 10 tens.

____

6. 10 ☐ 0 = 10

7. What time is shown?

____

8. What is the surface area of the rectangle?

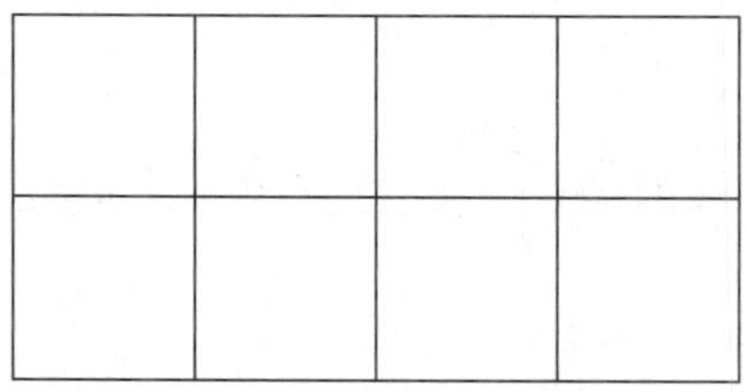

__________ squares

9. How many angles are there in a square?

____

10. Triple 9, and then add 14.

____

SCORE

1. Ⓨ Ⓝ
2. Ⓨ Ⓝ
3. Ⓨ Ⓝ
4. Ⓨ Ⓝ
5. Ⓨ Ⓝ
6. Ⓨ Ⓝ
7. Ⓨ Ⓝ
8. Ⓨ Ⓝ
9. Ⓨ Ⓝ
10. Ⓨ Ⓝ

___ / 10
Total

DAY 22

NAME: ____________________

DIRECTIONS Solve each problem.

SCORE

1. Ⓨ Ⓝ
2. Ⓨ Ⓝ
3. Ⓨ Ⓝ
4. Ⓨ Ⓝ
5. Ⓨ Ⓝ
6. Ⓨ Ⓝ
7. Ⓨ Ⓝ
8. Ⓨ Ⓝ
9. Ⓨ Ⓝ
10. Ⓨ Ⓝ

___ / 10 Total

1. $$\begin{array}{r} 36 \\ +\ 23 \\ \hline \end{array}$$

2. What are 7 groups of 10?

____

3. 2 x 4 = ☐

4. What number follows 79?

____

5. Color $\frac{1}{2}$.

6. 31 – ☐ = 6

7. What is the month after March?

____

8. Circle the heavier object.

9. Name the solid shape.

____

10. I am a solid with six faces that are squares. What solid am I?

____

NAME: ______________________________

DIRECTIONS Solve each problem.

1.
$$\begin{array}{r} 48 \\ -\ 27 \\ \hline \end{array}$$

2. 6 x 2 = ☐

3. How many are in 8 groups of 4?

____

4. How many rows of 10 make 50?

____

5. How many nickels are there in 50¢?

____

6. Fill in the missing number.

24, 32, ________, 48, 56

7. Write the time in words.

____

8. Which is shorter: a car or a bus?

____

9. Does the drawing show a *flip, slide,* or *turn*?

____

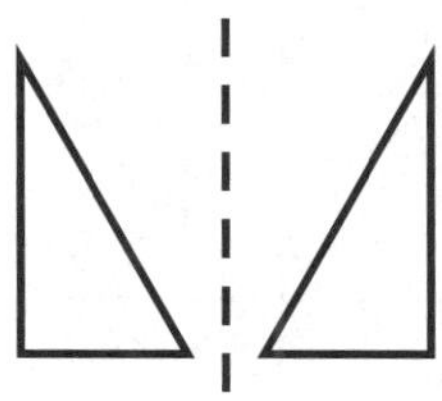

10. Erasers are sold in bags of 6. Manuel wants 9 erasers. How many bags will he need to buy?

____

SCORE

1. Ⓨ Ⓝ
2. Ⓨ Ⓝ
3. Ⓨ Ⓝ
4. Ⓨ Ⓝ
5. Ⓨ Ⓝ
6. Ⓨ Ⓝ
7. Ⓨ Ⓝ
8. Ⓨ Ⓝ
9. Ⓨ Ⓝ
10. Ⓨ Ⓝ

___ / 10 Total

DAY 24

NAME: ____________________

DIRECTIONS Solve each problem.

SCORE

1. Ⓨ Ⓝ
2. Ⓨ Ⓝ
3. Ⓨ Ⓝ
4. Ⓨ Ⓝ
5. Ⓨ Ⓝ
6. Ⓨ Ⓝ
7. Ⓨ Ⓝ
8. Ⓨ Ⓝ
9. Ⓨ Ⓝ
10. Ⓨ Ⓝ

___ / 10 Total

1. 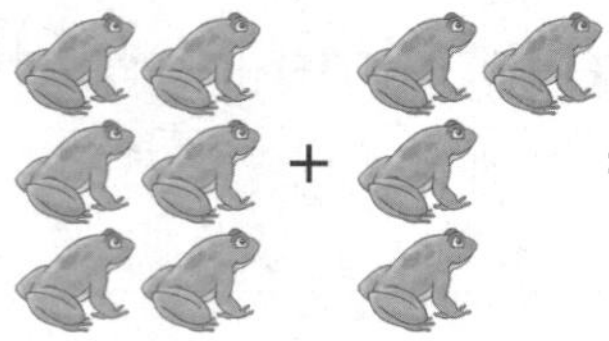

= ____

2. What is the product of 4 and 9?

____

3.

$$\begin{array}{r} 10 \\ \times \ \ 4 \\ \hline \end{array}$$

4. What is the ordinal number just before 152nd?

____

5. What is the total value of these coins?

____

6. 8 + 8 = ☐ + 4

7. How many days are there in April?

____

8. Show half past 2:00 on the clock.

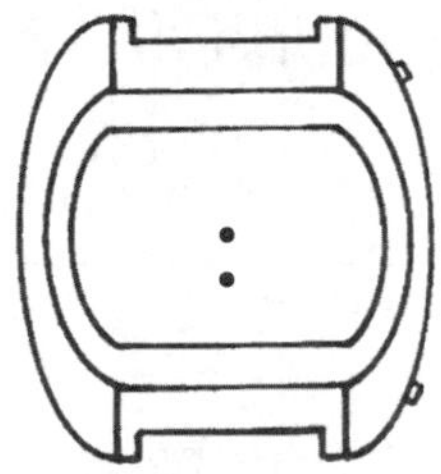

9. Draw the top view of this figure.

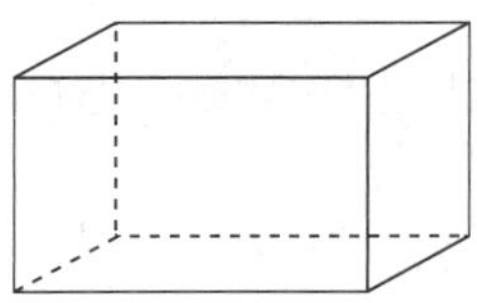

10. Bananas cost 40¢ each. Apples cost 50¢ each. If you buy 2 bananas and 3 apples, how much money will you spend?

____

DAY 25

NAME: ______________________________

DIRECTIONS Solve each problem.

1. 19 – 12 = ☐

2. 7 x 2 = ☐

3. Draw 9 rows of 5 dots.

4. If there are a total of 16 legs, how many birds are there?

____

5. $1.10 – $0.50 = __________

6. 15 – ☐ = 6

7. What day of the week comes before Thursday?

____

8. Show 9:00 on the clock.

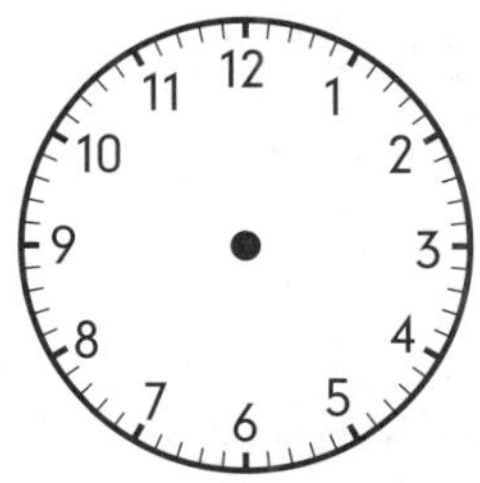

9. Fill in the bar graph based on the number of parts of the robot.

Parts of the Robot

Shapes				
Circles				
Squares				
Rectangles				
Trapezoids				
0	2	4	6	8

Number of Parts

10. What is half of 56?

____

SCORE

1. Ⓨ Ⓝ
2. Ⓨ Ⓝ
3. Ⓨ Ⓝ
4. Ⓨ Ⓝ
5. Ⓨ Ⓝ
6. Ⓨ Ⓝ
7. Ⓨ Ⓝ
8. Ⓨ Ⓝ
9. Ⓨ Ⓝ
10. Ⓨ Ⓝ

___ / 10 Total

NAME: ____________________________

DIRECTIONS Solve each problem.

SCORE

1. Ⓨ Ⓝ
2. Ⓨ Ⓝ
3. Ⓨ Ⓝ
4. Ⓨ Ⓝ
5. Ⓨ Ⓝ
6. Ⓨ Ⓝ
7. Ⓨ Ⓝ
8. Ⓨ Ⓝ
9. Ⓨ Ⓝ
10. Ⓨ Ⓝ

___ / 10
Total

1. 62 + 27 = ________

2.

$$\begin{array}{r} 10 \\ \times \ 5 \\ \hline \end{array}$$

3. Draw 8 rows of 3 stars.

4. What is the numeral for eighty-one?

____

5. What fraction is shaded?

____

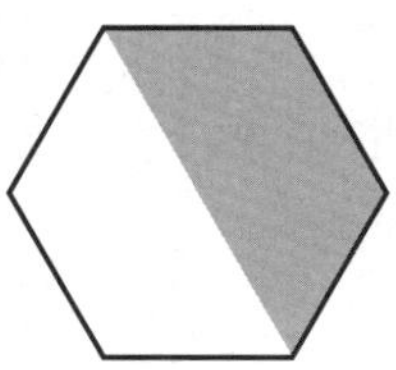

6. Fill in the missing number.

24, 28, ________, 36, 40

7. What day of the week comes after Saturday?

____

8. Show 1:30 on the clock.

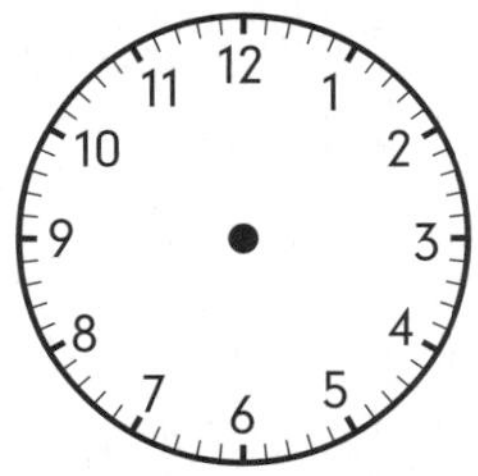

9. Draw a line of symmetry.

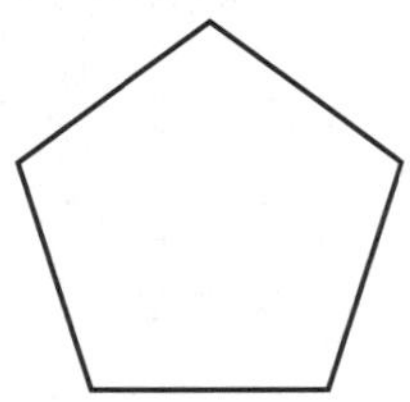

10. Sara has 55¢. She finds a nickel and a quarter. How much money does she have now?

____

NAME: ______________________

DIRECTIONS Solve each problem.

SCORE

1.

$$\begin{array}{r} 35 \\ -\ 14 \\ \hline \end{array}$$

2. What are 5 groups of 5?

____

3. 9 x 2 = ☐

4. Circle 3 groups of 3.

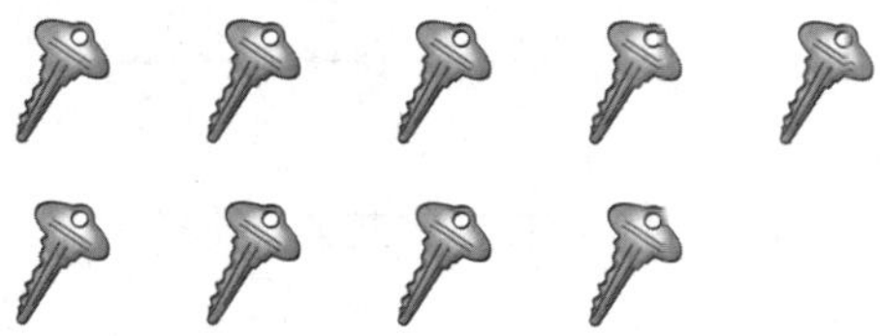

5. What is the value of the digit 6 in the number 461?

____

6. 5 + 5 + 5 + 5 = ☐ x 5

7. What time is shown?

____

8. Which would hold more: a cup or a big jug?

____

9. Draw a robot. Use 1 square, 4 rectangles, and 3 circles.

10. A math book is 3 cm thick. How thick is a stack of 7 math books?

____

1. Ⓨ Ⓝ
2. Ⓨ Ⓝ
3. Ⓨ Ⓝ
4. Ⓨ Ⓝ
5. Ⓨ Ⓝ
6. Ⓨ Ⓝ
7. Ⓨ Ⓝ
8. Ⓨ Ⓝ
9. Ⓨ Ⓝ
10. Ⓨ Ⓝ

___ / 10
Total

DAY
28

NAME: ______________________________

DIRECTIONS Solve each problem.

SCORE

1. Ⓨ Ⓝ
2. Ⓨ Ⓝ
3. Ⓨ Ⓝ
4. Ⓨ Ⓝ
5. Ⓨ Ⓝ
6. Ⓨ Ⓝ
7. Ⓨ Ⓝ
8. Ⓨ Ⓝ
9. Ⓨ Ⓝ
10. Ⓨ Ⓝ

___ / 10

Total

1. 13 + 8 = ☐

2.
```
   7
x  3
----
```

3. How many sides are there on 4 squares?

____

4. What is the next odd number after 29?

____

5. How many tens are in 79?

____

6. 15 ☐ 3 = 12

7. What is the month before August?

____

8. Show a quarter to 9 on the clock.

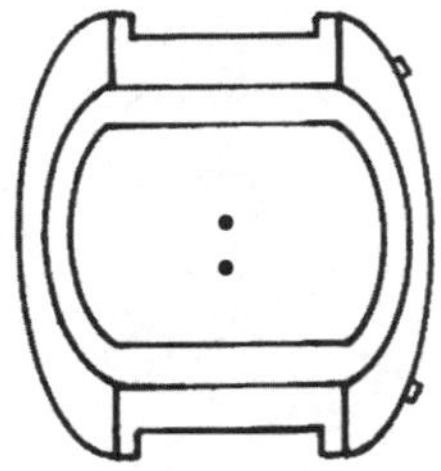

9. What shapes are used to create the large rectangle?

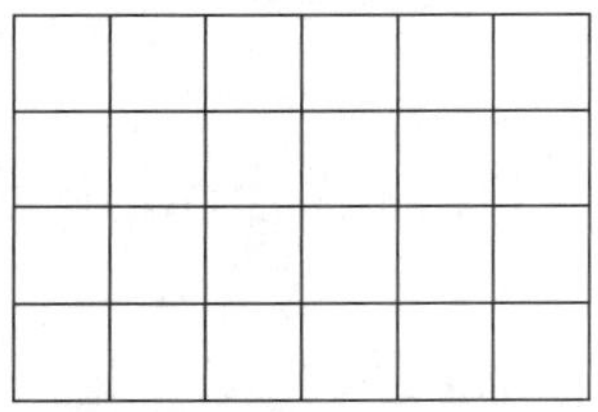

____

10. An eraser costs 11¢.
A pencil costs 15¢.
A sharpener costs 24¢.
You have 65¢. If you buy all 3 items, how much money will you have left?

____

DAY 29

NAME: ____________________

DIRECTIONS Solve each problem.

1.  − 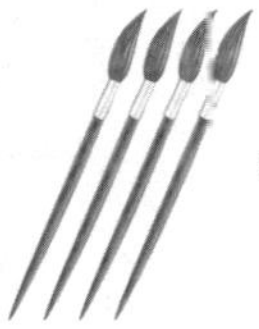 = ☐

2. What are 9 groups of 4?

____

3.
$$\begin{array}{r} 5 \\ \times\ 8 \\ \hline \end{array}$$

4. If 12 snakes are divided into two equal groups, how many are in each group?

____

5. 2 halves = ☐ whole

6. 3 x 4 = 4 + 4 + ☐

7. How many days are there in March?

____

8. Cubes were used to measure the volume of each box. Color the container with the least volume.

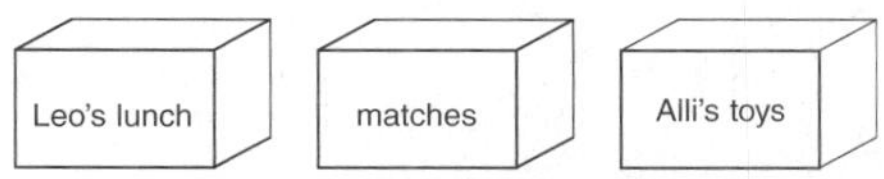

720 cubes   80 cubes   4,000 cubes

9. How many sides and angles does this hexagon have?

____

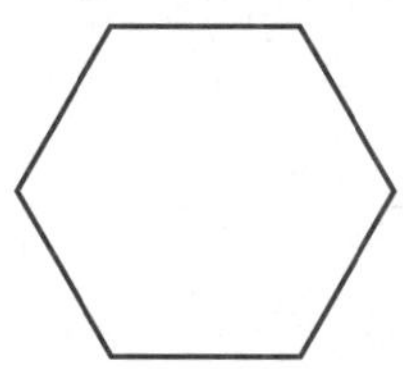

10. Four children are in line. Tom is last. Loni is second. Fred is first. What is Amy's position in line?

____

SCORE

1. Ⓨ Ⓝ
2. Ⓨ Ⓝ
3. Ⓨ Ⓝ
4. Ⓨ Ⓝ
5. Ⓨ Ⓝ
6. Ⓨ Ⓝ
7. Ⓨ Ⓝ
8. Ⓨ Ⓝ
9. Ⓨ Ⓝ
10. Ⓨ Ⓝ

___ / 10 Total

DAY 30

NAME: ____________________

DIRECTIONS Solve each problem.

SCORE

1. Ⓨ Ⓝ
2. Ⓨ Ⓝ
3. Ⓨ Ⓝ
4. Ⓨ Ⓝ
5. Ⓨ Ⓝ
6. Ⓨ Ⓝ
7. Ⓨ Ⓝ
8. Ⓨ Ⓝ
9. Ⓨ Ⓝ
10. Ⓨ Ⓝ

___ / 10 Total

1. $38 + 32 =$ ______

2. $8 \times 4 = \square$

3. Draw 5 rows of 10 cups.

4. Write 147 in words.

____

____

5. What is the value of the digit 8 in the number 48?

____

6. $14 - \square = 8$

7. Write the time in words.

____

8. Which is shorter: a path or a highway?

____

9. What smaller shapes were used to make the large rectangle?

____

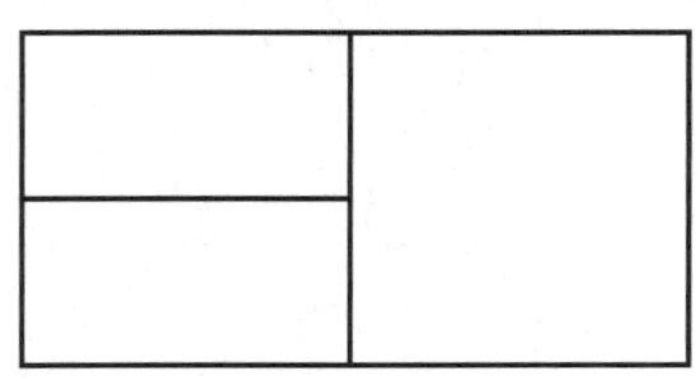

10. Some kids took off their shoes. There are 14 shoes. How many kids are there?

____

NAME: ______________________________

DIRECTIONS Solve each problem.

1.

$$\begin{array}{r} 15 \\ -\ \ 5 \\ \hline \end{array}$$

2. 7 x 4 = ☐

3. Draw 8 rows of 4 books.

4. Circle to show 4 equal groups.

5. 1 ten + 9 ones = ________

6. Write the next 3 numbers in the pattern.

250, 200, 150,

________, ________, ________

7. What is the month after June?

____

8. Show half past 3 on the clock.

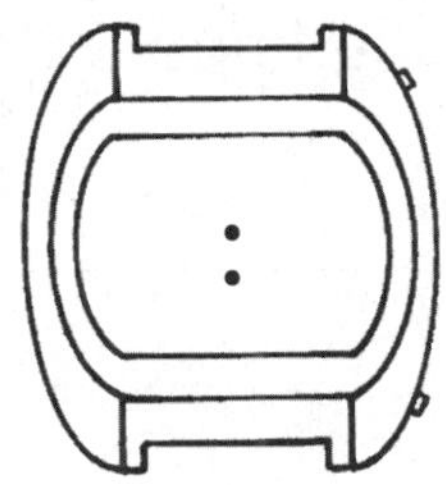

9. Name the solid shape.

____

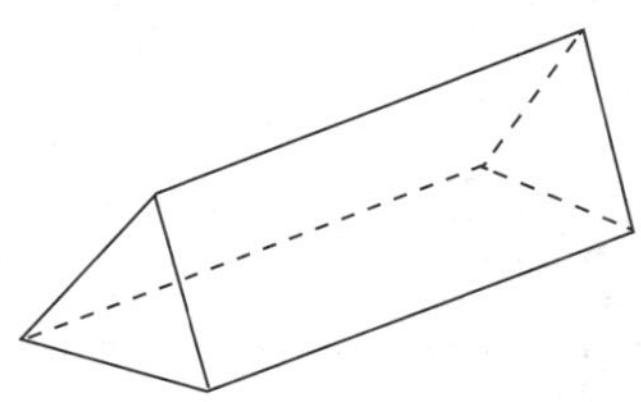

10. I am 23 less than 61. What number am I?

____

SCORE

1. Ⓨ Ⓝ
2. Ⓨ Ⓝ
3. Ⓨ Ⓝ
4. Ⓨ Ⓝ
5. Ⓨ Ⓝ
6. Ⓨ Ⓝ
7. Ⓨ Ⓝ
8. Ⓨ Ⓝ
9. Ⓨ Ⓝ
10. Ⓨ Ⓝ

___ / 10 Total

NAME: ____________________

DIRECTIONS Solve each problem.

SCORE

1. Ⓨ Ⓝ
2. Ⓨ Ⓝ
3. Ⓨ Ⓝ
4. Ⓨ Ⓝ
5. Ⓨ Ⓝ
6. Ⓨ Ⓝ
7. Ⓨ Ⓝ
8. Ⓨ Ⓝ
9. Ⓨ Ⓝ
10. Ⓨ Ⓝ

___ / 10 Total

1. 17 + 14 = ☐

2. 4 x 6 = ☐

3. 1 dog has 4 legs. How many legs do 3 dogs have?

____

4. What is the next ordinal number after 72nd?

____

5. Color $\frac{1}{8}$.

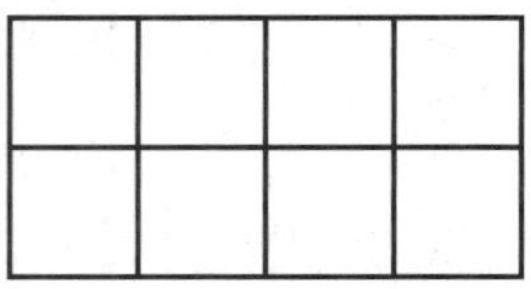

6. ☐ + 5 = 11 + 9

7. How many days are there in February?

____

8. Write the time for noon.

____

9. Draw the top view.

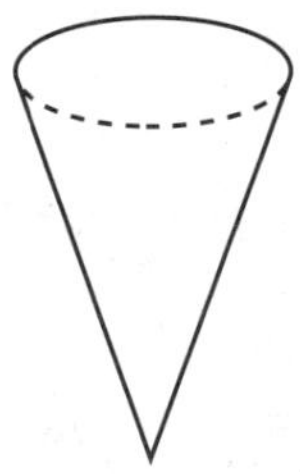

10. I am a number between 78 and 88. I have a 3 in the ones place. What number am I?

____

DAY 33

NAME: ____________________

DIRECTIONS Solve each problem.

1. 38 – 16 = ☐

2. You have 9 branches with 2 flowers on each branch. How many flowers do you have altogether?

____

3.

$$\begin{array}{r} 7 \\ \times\ 8 \\ \hline \end{array}$$

4. How many groups of 5 are there in 25?

____

5. How many dimes are there in $2.00?

____

6. $1.00 will buy how many 10¢ candies?

____

7. What time is shown?

____

8. Which is shorter: a ruler or a yardstick?

____

9. What is this solid?

____

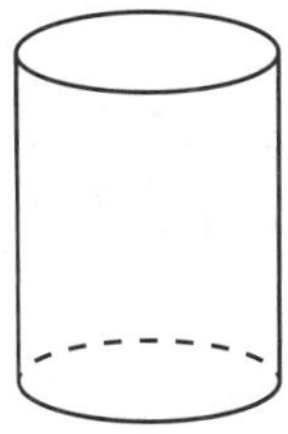

10. A new sharpener costs 65¢. How many nickels do I need to buy one?

____

SCORE

1. Ⓨ Ⓝ

2. Ⓨ Ⓝ

3. Ⓨ Ⓝ

4. Ⓨ Ⓝ

5. Ⓨ Ⓝ

6. Ⓨ Ⓝ

7. Ⓨ Ⓝ

8. Ⓨ Ⓝ

9. Ⓨ Ⓝ

10. Ⓨ Ⓝ

___ / 10

Total

NAME: ______________________

DIRECTIONS Solve each problem.

SCORE

1. Ⓨ Ⓝ
2. Ⓨ Ⓝ
3. Ⓨ Ⓝ
4. Ⓨ Ⓝ
5. Ⓨ Ⓝ
6. Ⓨ Ⓝ
7. Ⓨ Ⓝ
8. Ⓨ Ⓝ
9. Ⓨ Ⓝ
10. Ⓨ Ⓝ

___ / 10

Total

1. $\begin{array}{r} 15 \\ +\ 4 \\ \hline \end{array}$

2. 8 x 10 = ☐

3. Draw 2 groups of 4 baseballs.

4. Show tally marks for the number 20.

5. What is the total value of these coins?

____

6. 10 ☐ 2 = 20

7. What day of the week comes before Sunday?

____

8. Which would hold more: a milk jug or a mug?

____

9. What is the range of the kids' heights?

Kids' Heights

54", 50", 52", 54", 51", 52", 54"

____

10. Luis was sitting at the table. Circle the object that was on his right.

NAME: ______________________

DIRECTIONS Solve each problem.

1.  +  =

____

2. What are 10 groups of 4?

____

3.

$$\begin{array}{r} 8 \\ \times\ 3 \\ \hline \end{array}$$

4. How many faces will you have if you have a total of 10 eyes?

____

5. 50¢ + $1.00 + $1.50 =

____

6. ☐ x 6 = 2 x 12

7. Show 12:00 on the clock.

8. How many hours are there in a day?

____

9. Does the drawing show a *flip*, *slide*, or *turn*?

____

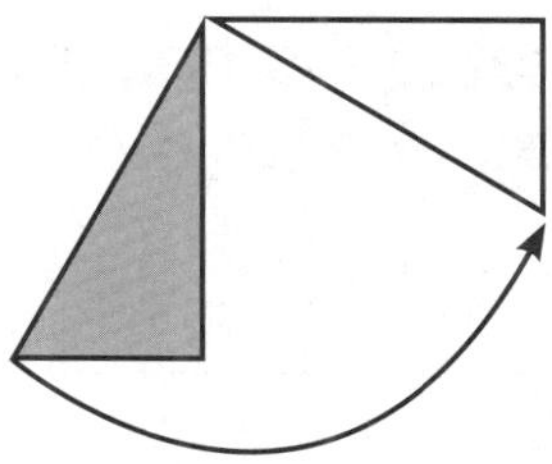

10. Carlos has 2 red cars, 3 blue cars, and 3 green cars. How many red cars and green cars does he have altogether?

____

SCORE

1. Ⓨ Ⓝ
2. Ⓨ Ⓝ
3. Ⓨ Ⓝ
4. Ⓨ Ⓝ
5. Ⓨ Ⓝ
6. Ⓨ Ⓝ
7. Ⓨ Ⓝ
8. Ⓨ Ⓝ
9. Ⓨ Ⓝ
10. Ⓨ Ⓝ

___ / 10
Total

DAY 36

NAME: ______________________________

DIRECTIONS Solve each problem.

SCORE

1. Ⓨ Ⓝ
2. Ⓨ Ⓝ
3. Ⓨ Ⓝ
4. Ⓨ Ⓝ
5. Ⓨ Ⓝ
6. Ⓨ Ⓝ
7. Ⓨ Ⓝ
8. Ⓨ Ⓝ
9. Ⓨ Ⓝ
10. Ⓨ Ⓝ

___ / 10 Total

1.
$$\begin{array}{r} 40 \\ -\ 18 \\ \hline \end{array}$$

2. True or false?
6 x 2 = 3 x 4

____

3. 8 x 9 = ☐

4. What is the next even number after 62?

____

5. $2.10 + $0.65 = ________

6. Fill in the missing number.

15, 18, ________, 24, 27

7. What time is shown?

____

8. Circle the group of tables that would need the larger tablecloth.

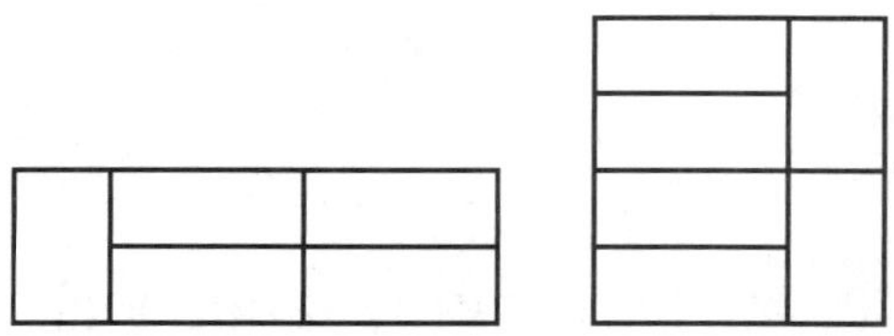

9. How many edges are there on a cube?

____

10. If you add 100 to me, you get 452. What number am I?

____

NAME: ______________________________

DIRECTIONS Solve each problem.

1. 13 + 7 = ☐

2. Draw 6 piles of 4 logs.

3. 9 x 0 = ☐

4. Circle to show 3 equal groups.

5.

$$\begin{array}{r} 0.15 \\ -\ 0.10 \\ \hline \end{array}$$

6. 10 + 10 = ☐ + 5

7. What is the month after January?

____

8. Show a quarter to 6 on the clock.

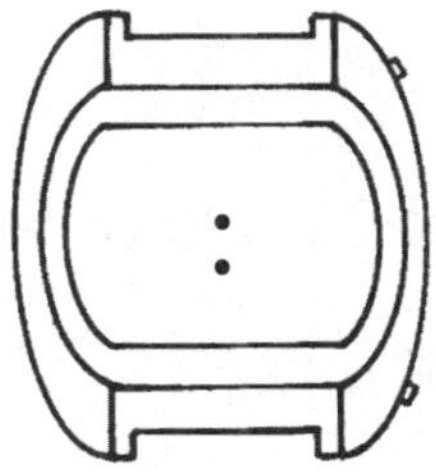

9. Does the arrow point to a *face, vertex,* or *edge*?

____

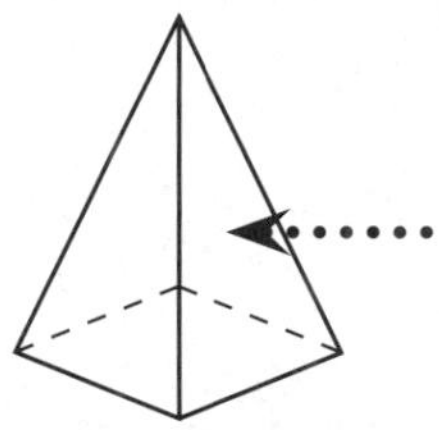

10. There are 26 pieces of popcorn and 2 children. The children want to share the popcorn equally. How many pieces of popcorn will each child get?

____

SCORE

1. Ⓨ Ⓝ
2. Ⓨ Ⓝ
3. Ⓨ Ⓝ
4. Ⓨ Ⓝ
5. Ⓨ Ⓝ
6. Ⓨ Ⓝ
7. Ⓨ Ⓝ
8. Ⓨ Ⓝ
9. Ⓨ Ⓝ
10. Ⓨ Ⓝ

___ / 10
Total

DAY
38

NAME: ____________________

DIRECTIONS Solve each problem.

SCORE

1. Ⓨ Ⓝ
2. Ⓨ Ⓝ
3. Ⓨ Ⓝ
4. Ⓨ Ⓝ
5. Ⓨ Ⓝ
6. Ⓨ Ⓝ
7. Ⓨ Ⓝ
8. Ⓨ Ⓝ
9. Ⓨ Ⓝ
10. Ⓨ Ⓝ

___ / 10
Total

1. 25 – 17 = ☐

2.

$$\begin{array}{r} 3 \\ \times\ 2 \\ \hline \end{array}$$

3. Draw 8 rows of 5 items.

4. What is the numeral for five hundred forty-three?

____

5. How many hundreds are there in 424?

____

6. 4 x ☐ = 2 x 10

7. Write the time in words.

____

8. Which covers the larger area: the classroom floor or the door?

____

9. Flip the shape and draw it.

10. Mom has 6 vases. She has 18 flowers. She wants to put an equal number of flowers in each vase. How many flowers will go in each vase?

____

NAME: ______________________________

DIRECTIONS Solve each problem.

1. 8 + 7 = ☐

2. 3 x 4 = ☐

3. Draw 4 tanks of 5 fish. How many fish are there altogether?

____

4. What is 16 shared equally among 4?

____

5. 2 quarters = ☐ dimes

6. 30 ☐ 2 = 60

7. How many days are there in September?

____

8. Which has the greater volume: a pool or a bathtub?

____

9. What is the least favorite color?

____

Favorite Color

Red	13
Blue	10
Yellow	9
Green	10

10. Mom bakes 12 cookies on Sunday. You are allowed to eat 2 cookies each day. On what day will you eat the last cookie?

____

SCORE

1. Ⓨ Ⓝ
2. Ⓨ Ⓝ
3. Ⓨ Ⓝ
4. Ⓨ Ⓝ
5. Ⓨ Ⓝ
6. Ⓨ Ⓝ
7. Ⓨ Ⓝ
8. Ⓨ Ⓝ
9. Ⓨ Ⓝ
10. Ⓨ Ⓝ

___ / 10 Total

DAY
40

NAME: ______________________________

DIRECTIONS Solve each problem.

SCORE

1. Ⓨ Ⓝ
2. Ⓨ Ⓝ
3. Ⓨ Ⓝ
4. Ⓨ Ⓝ
5. Ⓨ Ⓝ
6. Ⓨ Ⓝ
7. Ⓨ Ⓝ
8. Ⓨ Ⓝ
9. Ⓨ Ⓝ
10. Ⓨ Ⓝ

___ / 10
Total

1.

$$\begin{array}{r} 328 \\ +\ 46 \\ \hline \end{array}$$

2. What are 6 groups of 8?

____

3. 8 x 3 = ☐

4. What number follows 63?

____

5. What is the total value of these coins?

____

6. Fill in the missing number.

650, 550, 450, ________, 250

7. What day of the week comes before Thursday?

____

8. Show 6:15 on the clock.

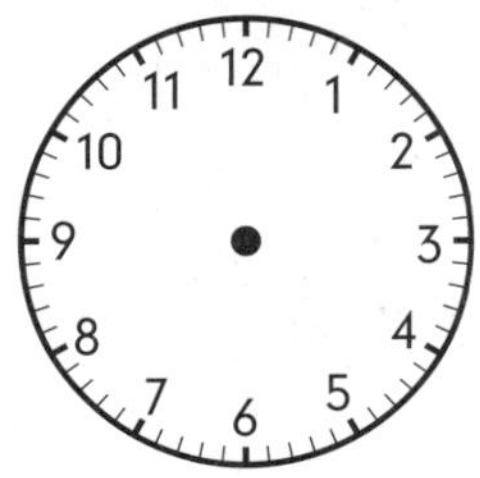

9. Which shape has 6 sides?

____

10. You see 36 wheels. How many cars are there?

____

NAME: ____________________

DIRECTIONS Solve each problem.

1.

$$\begin{array}{r} 17 \\ +\ 33 \\ \hline \end{array}$$

2. 6 x 6 = ☐

3. Draw legs on 5 cats.

4. Circle groups of 2.

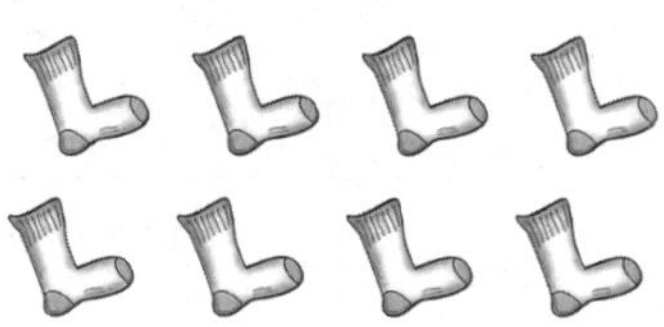

5. What is the value of the digit 5 in the number 25?

____

6. Fill in the missing number.

48, 44, ________, 36, 32

7. Write the time in words.

____

8. Which is taller: a house or a person?

____

9. True or false? A quadrilateral has 4 sides.

____

10. Sumi has $15.36 in her wallet. She spends $12.25. How much is left in her wallet?

____

SCORE

1. Ⓨ Ⓝ
2. Ⓨ Ⓝ
3. Ⓨ Ⓝ
4. Ⓨ Ⓝ
5. Ⓨ Ⓝ
6. Ⓨ Ⓝ
7. Ⓨ Ⓝ
8. Ⓨ Ⓝ
9. Ⓨ Ⓝ
10. Ⓨ Ⓝ

___ / 10

Total

DAY 42

NAME: ______________________

DIRECTIONS Solve each problem.

SCORE

1. Ⓨ Ⓝ
2. Ⓨ Ⓝ
3. Ⓨ Ⓝ
4. Ⓨ Ⓝ
5. Ⓨ Ⓝ
6. Ⓨ Ⓝ
7. Ⓨ Ⓝ
8. Ⓨ Ⓝ
9. Ⓨ Ⓝ
10. Ⓨ Ⓝ

___ / 10 Total

1. 69 – 39 = ☐

2.

$$\begin{array}{r} 9 \\ \times\ 8 \\ \hline \end{array}$$

3. Draw 6 bunches of 4 flowers.

4. Make tally marks for the number 13.

5. What is 10 more than 89?

____

6. 8 x ☐ = 4 x 4

7. How many days are there in November?

____

8. Show 5:30 on the clock.

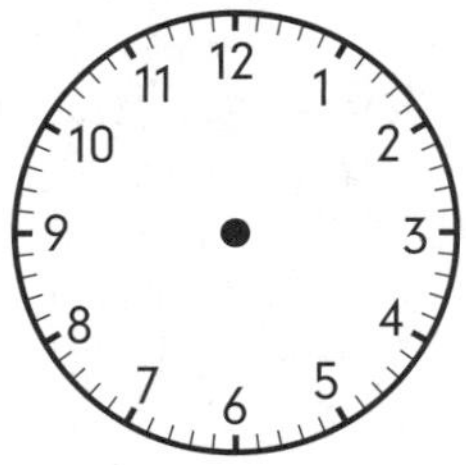

9. How many angles does a triangle have?

____

10. 6 + 6 + 6 + 6 is equal to:

A. 4 + 6
B. 6 x 6 x 6 x 6
C. 4 x 6
D. 6 ÷ 4

DAY
43

NAME: ______________________________

DIRECTIONS Solve each problem.

1. What is the difference between 56 and 26?

____

2. 3 x 6 = ☐

3. 4 x 6 = ☐

4. If you share 35 pencils equally among 5 students, how many pencils would each student get?

____

5. What is the value of the digit 1 in the number 219?

____

6. 15 ☐ 7 = 22

7. What time is shown?

____

8. Which has less volume: a mug or a bathtub?

____

9. Put the angles in order from smallest to largest.

A. 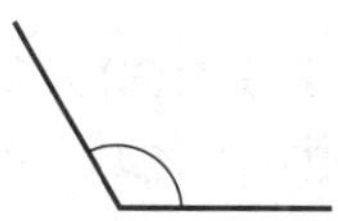 1. ________

B.  2. ________

C. 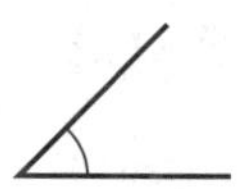 3. ________

10. Add 2 hundreds, 4 tens, and 8 ones to 437.

____

SCORE

1. Ⓨ Ⓝ
2. Ⓨ Ⓝ
3. Ⓨ Ⓝ
4. Ⓨ Ⓝ
5. Ⓨ Ⓝ
6. Ⓨ Ⓝ
7. Ⓨ Ⓝ
8. Ⓨ Ⓝ
9. Ⓨ Ⓝ
10. Ⓨ Ⓝ

___ / 10
Total

DAY 44

NAME: ____________________

DIRECTIONS Solve each problem.

SCORE

1. Ⓨ Ⓝ
2. Ⓨ Ⓝ
3. Ⓨ Ⓝ
4. Ⓨ Ⓝ
5. Ⓨ Ⓝ
6. Ⓨ Ⓝ
7. Ⓨ Ⓝ
8. Ⓨ Ⓝ
9. Ⓨ Ⓝ
10. Ⓨ Ⓝ

___ / 10

Total

1. 8 + 14 = ☐

2.

$$\begin{array}{r} 7 \\ \times\ 5 \\ \hline \end{array}$$

3. There are 5 piles of 2 books each. Calculate the product to find the total number of books.

____

4. What is the next odd number that follows 69?

____

5. Which is smaller: one half dollar or one quarter?

____

6. 6 + 8 = 7 + ☐

7. What is the month before November?

____

8. Show 7 o'clock on the clock.

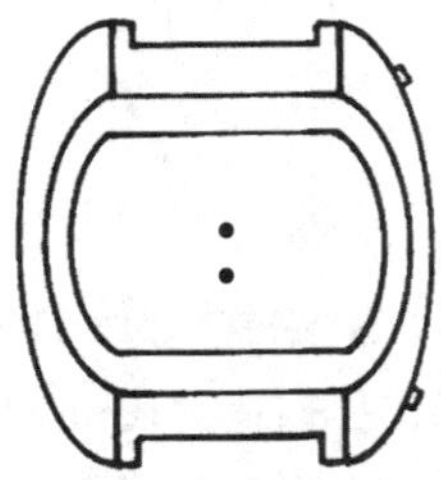

9. What is the mode?

13, 9, 2, 15, 13, 7, 12, 13, 8

____

10. Which is worth more: four nickels or one dollar?

____

NAME: ____________________

DIRECTIONS Solve each problem.

SCORE

1. 64 + 36 = ☐

2. What are 7 groups of 6?

____

3. 5 x 4 = ☐

4. There are 14 birds in 2 nests. Each nest has the same number of birds. How many birds are there in each nest?

____

5. How many quarters are there in $1.25?

____

6. 22 ☐ 7 = 15

7. What day of the week comes after Monday?

____

8. Rocks were used to measure the mass of each object. Circle the object with the least mass.

1 rock | 15 rocks | 3 rocks

9. Which shape has 5 sides?

____

10. What two numbers have a sum of 15 and a difference of 1?

____

1. Ⓨ Ⓝ
2. Ⓨ Ⓝ
3. Ⓨ Ⓝ
4. Ⓨ Ⓝ
5. Ⓨ Ⓝ
6. Ⓨ Ⓝ
7. Ⓨ Ⓝ
8. Ⓨ Ⓝ
9. Ⓨ Ⓝ
10. Ⓨ Ⓝ

___ / 10 Total

DAY 46

NAME: ____________________

DIRECTIONS Solve each problem.

SCORE

1. Ⓨ Ⓝ
2. Ⓨ Ⓝ
3. Ⓨ Ⓝ
4. Ⓨ Ⓝ
5. Ⓨ Ⓝ
6. Ⓨ Ⓝ
7. Ⓨ Ⓝ
8. Ⓨ Ⓝ
9. Ⓨ Ⓝ
10. Ⓨ Ⓝ

___ / 10
Total

1. 19 + 41 = ☐

2.

$$\begin{array}{r} 7 \\ \times\ 2 \\ \hline \end{array}$$

3. Ten times ten is ________.

4. What number follows 76?

____

5. What is the value of the digit 5 in the number 157?

____

6. 36 ÷ ☐ = 9

7. Friday is March 15th. What is the date on the next Monday?

____

8. What tool do you use to measure time?

____

9. Complete the pattern across the line of symmetry.

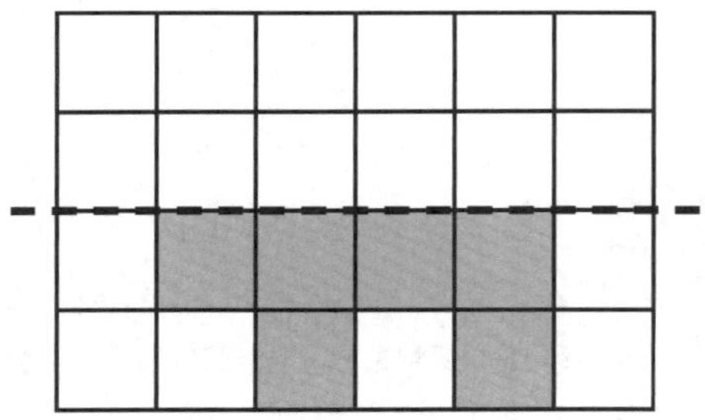

10. Pete has one nickel in his piggy bank. He doubles the amount he has in his bank each day for 4 days. How much money is in the bank after 4 days?

____

Start	Day 1	Day 2	Day 3	Day 4
5¢	10¢			

NAME: ______________________________

DIRECTIONS Solve each problem.

1.

$$\begin{array}{r} 44 \\ -\ 32 \\ \hline \end{array}$$

2. 9 x 8 = ☐

3. What are 6 groups of 0?

____

4. Circle groups of 4.

5. $1.10 – $0.50 = __________

6. ☐ x 4 = 28

7. How many days are there in October?

____

8. Which holds less: a teaspoon or a cup?

____

9. Name the angle.

____

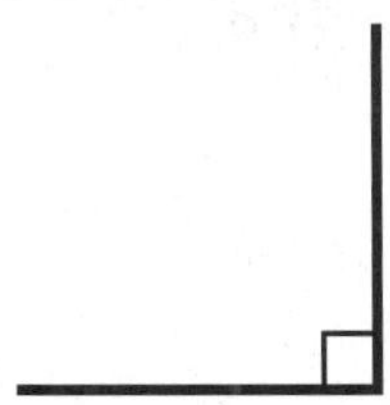

10. Make this picture symmetrical.

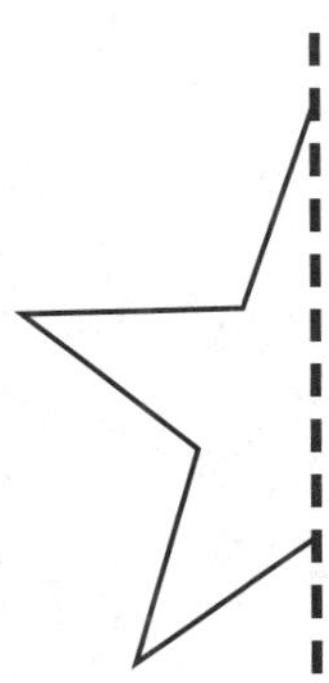

SCORE

1. Ⓨ Ⓝ
2. Ⓨ Ⓝ
3. Ⓨ Ⓝ
4. Ⓨ Ⓝ
5. Ⓨ Ⓝ
6. Ⓨ Ⓝ
7. Ⓨ Ⓝ
8. Ⓨ Ⓝ
9. Ⓨ Ⓝ
10. Ⓨ Ⓝ

___ / 10
Total

DAY 48

NAME: ____________________

DIRECTIONS Solve each problem.

SCORE

1. Ⓨ Ⓝ
2. Ⓨ Ⓝ
3. Ⓨ Ⓝ
4. Ⓨ Ⓝ
5. Ⓨ Ⓝ
6. Ⓨ Ⓝ
7. Ⓨ Ⓝ
8. Ⓨ Ⓝ
9. Ⓨ Ⓝ
10. Ⓨ Ⓝ

___ / 10 Total

1. $24 + 8 = \square$

2. Nine times nine is _______.

3.

$$\begin{array}{r} 5 \\ \times\ 0 \\ \hline \end{array}$$

4. What is the numeral for four hundred six?

____

5. What is the total value of these coins?

____

6. Fill in the missing number.

44, 48, _______, 56, 60

7. Record the area.

_______ square centimeters

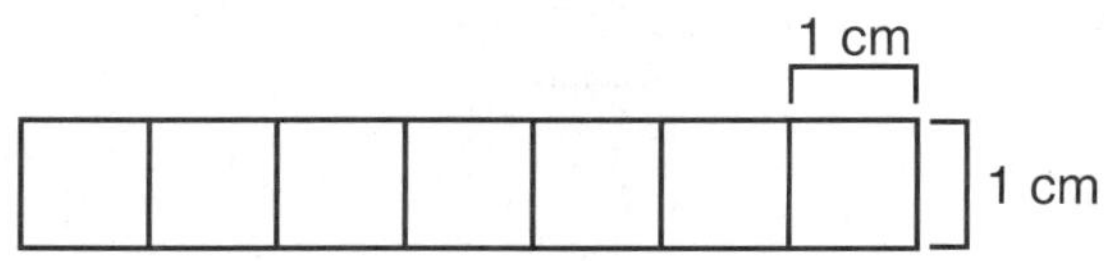

8. A 2-hour movie starts at 8:00. What time does it end?

____

9. Record the data in the chart.

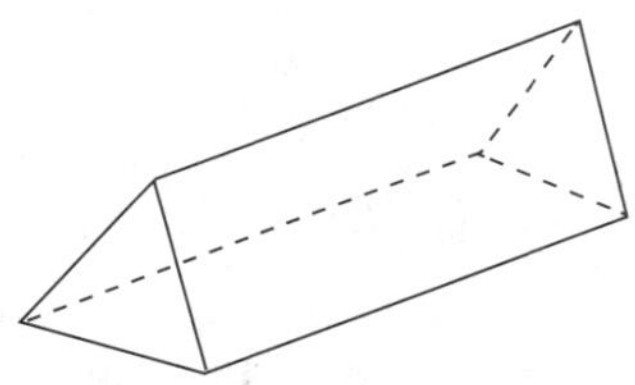

Vertices	
Edges	
Faces	

10. I have 4 faces that are triangles. I have 1 face that is a square. What solid am I?

____

NAME: ____________________

DIRECTIONS Solve each problem.

1. 98 – 93 = ☐

2.

$$\begin{array}{r} 6 \\ \times\ 6 \\ \hline \end{array}$$

3. What is the number of fingers on 2 kids?

____

4. Divide 15 into equal groups. How many are in each group?

____

5. 4 tens + 2 ones = ________

6. ☐ ÷ 4 = 7

7. How many hours are there from 9:00 A.M. to 1:00 P.M.?

____

8. 12 inches = ☐ feet

9. Circle the triangles.

A. 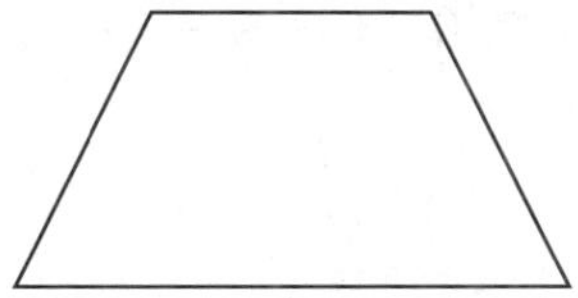

B. 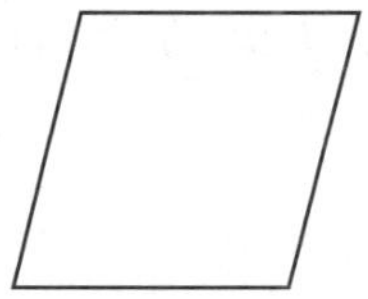

C. 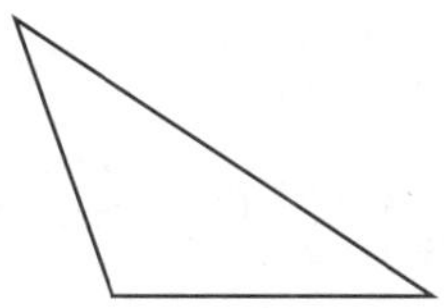

D. 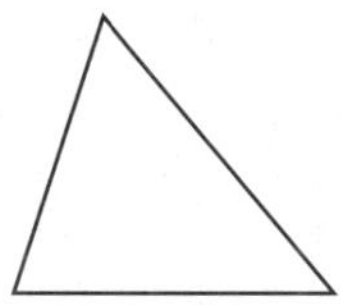

10. Mikki has an orange shirt and a red shirt. He has green shorts and blue jeans. How many different outfits can Mikki make?

____

SCORE

1. Ⓨ Ⓝ
2. Ⓨ Ⓝ
3. Ⓨ Ⓝ
4. Ⓨ Ⓝ
5. Ⓨ Ⓝ
6. Ⓨ Ⓝ
7. Ⓨ Ⓝ
8. Ⓨ Ⓝ
9. Ⓨ Ⓝ
10. Ⓨ Ⓝ

___ / 10 Total

NAME: ______________________________

DIRECTIONS Solve each problem.

SCORE

1. Ⓨ Ⓝ
2. Ⓨ Ⓝ
3. Ⓨ Ⓝ
4. Ⓨ Ⓝ
5. Ⓨ Ⓝ
6. Ⓨ Ⓝ
7. Ⓨ Ⓝ
8. Ⓨ Ⓝ
9. Ⓨ Ⓝ
10. Ⓨ Ⓝ

___ / 10
Total

1.
$$\begin{array}{r} 19 \\ +\ \ 6 \\ \hline \end{array}$$

2. 8 x 9 = ☐

3. Ten times six is ________.

4. Is 52 an even or an odd number?

____

5. What fraction is shaded?

____

6. Fill in the missing number.

30, 27, ________, 21, 18

7. How many minutes are there in an hour?

____

8. Circle the solid with the smaller volume.

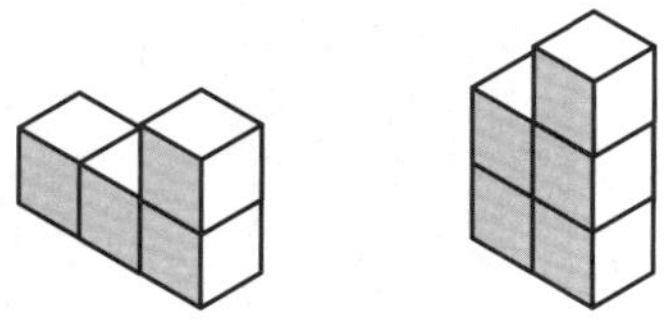

9. True or false? All faces on a prism are triangles.

____

10. There are 6 oranges. There is one less apple than there are oranges. Complete the bar graph showing this data. Remember to label the graph.

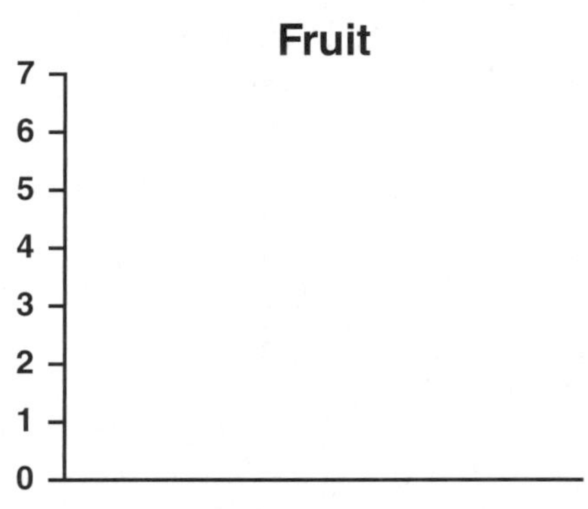

NAME: ____________________

DIRECTIONS Solve each problem.

SCORE

1. 22 – 11 = ☐

2. 4 x 8 = ☐

3. 12 x 2 = ____

4. How many chairs will you have if you have a total of 20 chair legs?

____

5. 0.20 + 0.10 + 0.20 =

____

6. Fill in the missing number.

317, 307, ________, 287, 277

7. Tuesday is June 4th. What is the date on the following Friday?

____

8. What is the perimeter?

________ cm

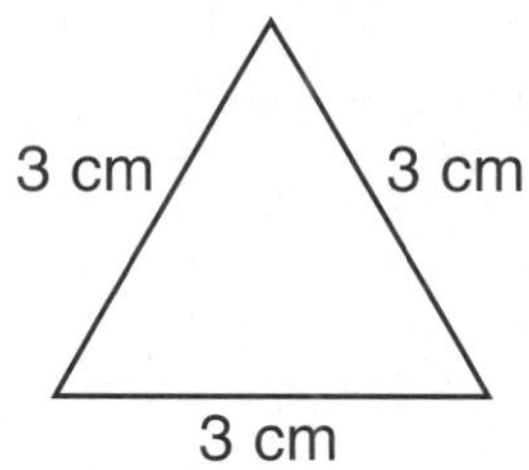

9. Label the vertex on the angle.

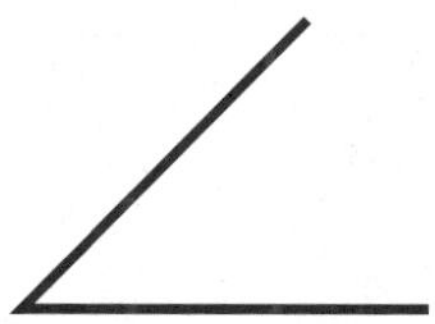

10. I am an odd number between 129 and 133. What number am I?

____

1. Ⓨ Ⓝ
2. Ⓨ Ⓝ
3. Ⓨ Ⓝ
4. Ⓨ Ⓝ
5. Ⓨ Ⓝ
6. Ⓨ Ⓝ
7. Ⓨ Ⓝ
8. Ⓨ Ⓝ
9. Ⓨ Ⓝ
10. Ⓨ Ⓝ

___ / 10 Total

DAY
52

NAME: ____________________

DIRECTIONS Solve each problem.

SCORE

1. Ⓨ Ⓝ
2. Ⓨ Ⓝ
3. Ⓨ Ⓝ
4. Ⓨ Ⓝ
5. Ⓨ Ⓝ
6. Ⓨ Ⓝ
7. Ⓨ Ⓝ
8. Ⓨ Ⓝ
9. Ⓨ Ⓝ
10. Ⓨ Ⓝ

___ / 10
Total

1. $\begin{array}{r} 37 \\ +\ 22 \\ \hline \end{array}$

2. Four times seven is

____________________.

3. 6 x 3 = ☐

4. What number follows 96?

____

5. What is the value of the digit 2 in the number 4,276?

____

6. 8 x ☐ = 80

7. List in order from heaviest to lightest: child, adult, baby.

____

8. What is the volume?

________ cubes

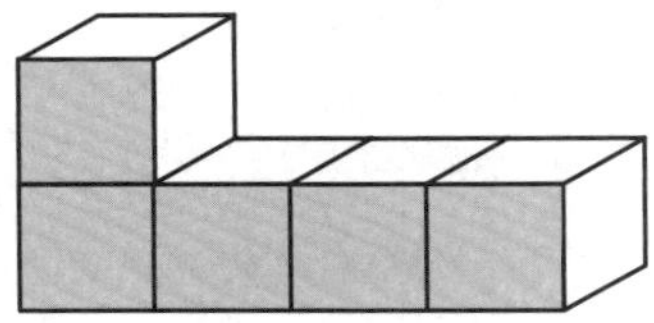

9. Circle the cylinders.

10. I woke up at 6:30 A.M. I slept for 9.5 hours. What time did I go to sleep?

____

NAME: ____________________

DIRECTIONS Solve each problem.

1. 25 + 17 = ☐

2. 6 multiplied by 8 is

____________________.

3. 8 x 8 = ________

4. Share 18 toys equally between 2 children. How many toys does each child get?

____

5. Color five-eighths.

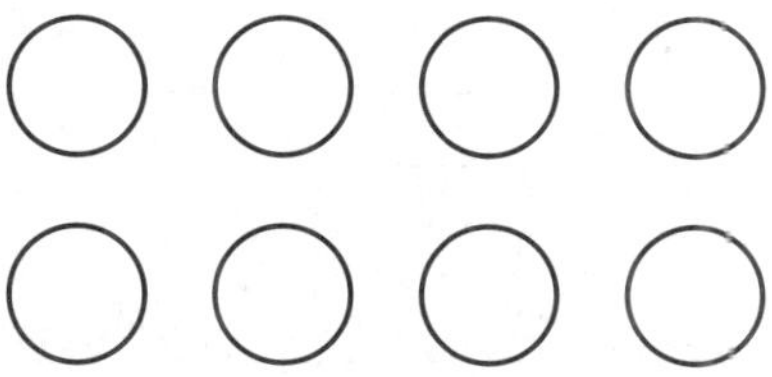

6. 15 ÷ ☐ = 3

7. Would the length of a swimming pool most likely be measured in meters or centimeters?

____________________.

8. Circle the stamp with the larger surface area.

9. What subject do most students prefer?

____

Favorite Subject in School

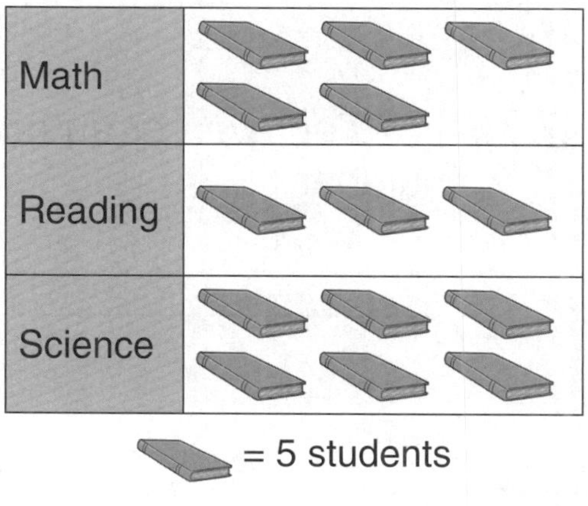

10. You buy a pack of game cards for 55¢. You pay with a dollar bill. How much change will you get?

____

SCORE

1. Ⓨ Ⓝ
2. Ⓨ Ⓝ
3. Ⓨ Ⓝ
4. Ⓨ Ⓝ
5. Ⓨ Ⓝ
6. Ⓨ Ⓝ
7. Ⓨ Ⓝ
8. Ⓨ Ⓝ
9. Ⓨ Ⓝ
10. Ⓨ Ⓝ

___ / 10
Total

DAY
54

NAME: ____________________

DIRECTIONS Solve each problem.

SCORE

1. Ⓨ Ⓝ
2. Ⓨ Ⓝ
3. Ⓨ Ⓝ
4. Ⓨ Ⓝ
5. Ⓨ Ⓝ
6. Ⓨ Ⓝ
7. Ⓨ Ⓝ
8. Ⓨ Ⓝ
9. Ⓨ Ⓝ
10. Ⓨ Ⓝ

___ / 10
Total

1. $\begin{array}{r} 45 \\ -\ \ 9 \\ \hline \end{array}$

2. 5 x 7 = ☐

3. How many are in 9 groups of 7?

____

4. Is 76 an even or an odd number?

____

5. What is the value of the digit 3 in the number 371?

____

6. 63 + ☐ = 72

7. How many hours are there from 7 P.M. to 1 A.M.?

____

8. Is a tulip taller or shorter than 1 meter?

____

9. How many edges does the solid have?

____

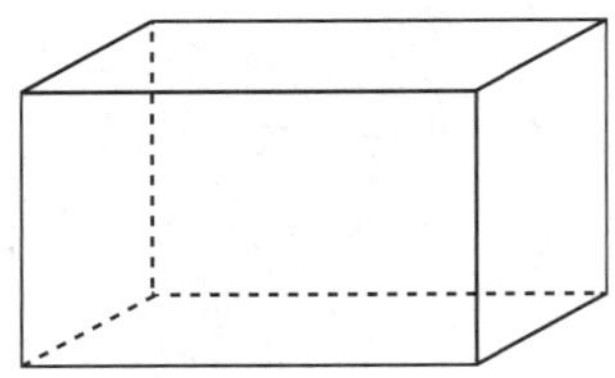

10. Sue, Eric, and Jody are standing in line. Eric is last. Jody is not first. What is the order of the children?

____

DAY 55

NAME: ____________________

DIRECTIONS Solve each problem.

1. 38 + 22 = ☐

2.
$$\begin{array}{r} 8 \\ \times\ 5 \\ \hline \end{array}$$

3. Seven times zero is

____________________.

4. How many groups of 5 are in 15?

____

5.
$$\begin{array}{r} \$1.32 \\ +\ \$2.45 \\ \hline \end{array}$$

6. How many 5-cent stickers will 50¢ buy?

____

7. Circle the container that holds the most.

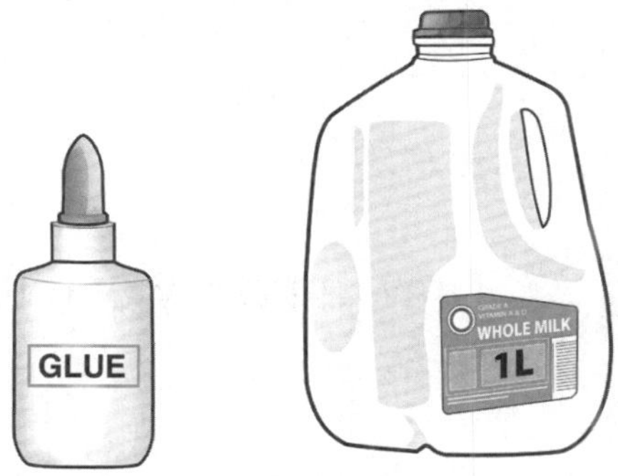

8. What is the time shown on the clock below?

____

9. True or false? Parallel lines are always the same distance apart.

____

10. A comic costs 35¢. If you buy one each week for 6 weeks, how much money will you spend on comics?

____

SCORE

1. Ⓨ Ⓝ

2. Ⓨ Ⓝ

3. Ⓨ Ⓝ

4. Ⓨ Ⓝ

5. Ⓨ Ⓝ

6. Ⓨ Ⓝ

7. Ⓨ Ⓝ

8. Ⓨ Ⓝ

9. Ⓨ Ⓝ

10. Ⓨ Ⓝ

___ / 10
Total

NAME: ____________________

DIRECTIONS Solve each problem.

SCORE

1. Ⓨ Ⓝ
2. Ⓨ Ⓝ
3. Ⓨ Ⓝ
4. Ⓨ Ⓝ
5. Ⓨ Ⓝ
6. Ⓨ Ⓝ
7. Ⓨ Ⓝ
8. Ⓨ Ⓝ
9. Ⓨ Ⓝ
10. Ⓨ Ⓝ

___ / 10 Total

1. 116 – 27 = ☐

2. Draw an array of 6 rows of 5.

3. 9 x 3 = ☐

4. What is the ordinal number before the 91st?

____

5. What is the total value of these coins?

____

6. 25 ☐ 5 = 5

7. The soccer game starts at 7:15 and ends 1 hour and 15 minutes later. What time does it end?

____

8. Which is more likely for the length of a nap: 1 hour or 1 minute?

____

9. Circle the shapes that are squares.

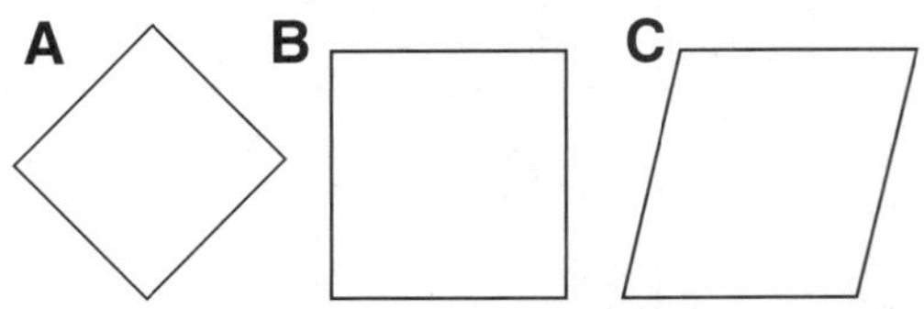

10. Together, Sammy and Trent have 14 toy cars. Half of the cars are Sammy's. How many cars belong to Trent?

____

NAME: ____________________

DIRECTIONS Solve each problem.

1. 9 + 13 = ☐

2. True or false?
4 x 2 = 2 + 2 + 2 + 2

____

3. How many are in 7 groups of 4?

____

4. There is a group of cars with a total of 16 wheels. How many cars are there?

____

5. What number is 100 more than 257?

____

6. Fill in the missing number.

85, ________, 105, 115, 125

7. What tool would you use to measure length: a ruler or a clock?

____

8. What is the perimeter?

____

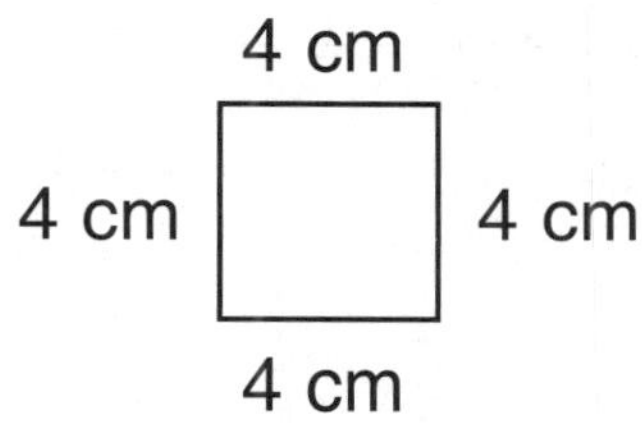

9. What kind of angle does the arrow show?

____

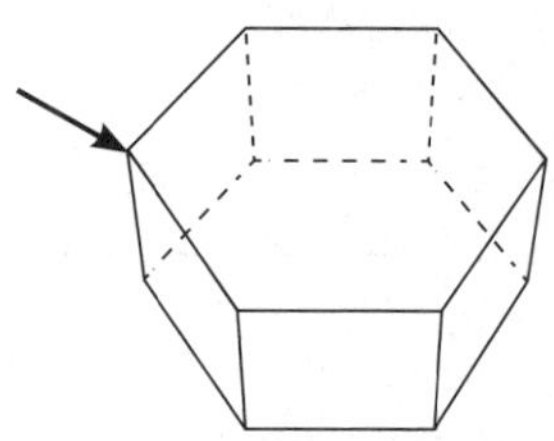

10. An insect has 6 legs. You see 48 legs. How many insects are there?

____

SCORE

1. Ⓨ Ⓝ
2. Ⓨ Ⓝ
3. Ⓨ Ⓝ
4. Ⓨ Ⓝ
5. Ⓨ Ⓝ
6. Ⓨ Ⓝ
7. Ⓨ Ⓝ
8. Ⓨ Ⓝ
9. Ⓨ Ⓝ
10. Ⓨ Ⓝ

___ / 10
Total

DAY 58

NAME: ____________________

DIRECTIONS Solve each problem.

SCORE

1. Ⓨ Ⓝ
2. Ⓨ Ⓝ
3. Ⓨ Ⓝ
4. Ⓨ Ⓝ
5. Ⓨ Ⓝ
6. Ⓨ Ⓝ
7. Ⓨ Ⓝ
8. Ⓨ Ⓝ
9. Ⓨ Ⓝ
10. Ⓨ Ⓝ

___ / 10 Total

1.

$$\begin{array}{r} 26 \\ +\ 54 \\ \hline \end{array}$$

2. Draw 4 boxes of 9 pencils. Write a multiplication equation to show the product.

____

3. 5 x 3 = ☐

4. What is the numeral for sixty-seven?

____

5. What fraction of the set is white?

____

6. 8 x ☐ = 12 x 2

7. Which is longer: a second or a minute?

____

8. Saturday is December 2nd. What is the date on the following Wednesday?

____

9. Complete the picture across the line of symmetry.

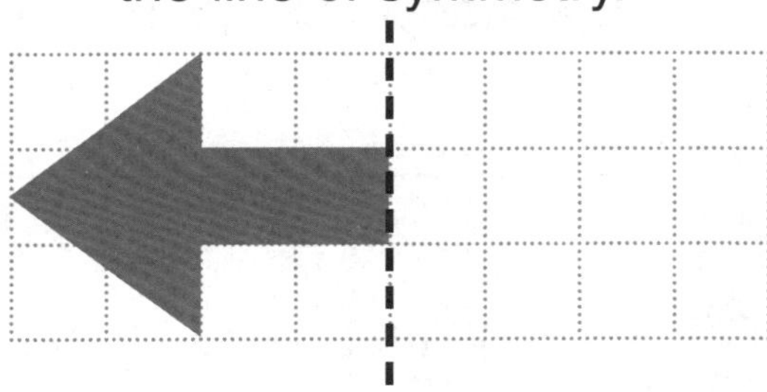

10. A licorice rope costs 27¢. A lollipop costs 15¢. A piece of chocolate costs 22¢. You have 40¢. Which two candies can you buy?

____

NAME: ______________________________

DIRECTIONS Solve each problem.

1. 35 – 19 = ☐

2. 7 x 6 = ____

3. Eight times three is ______________________.

4. 12 ÷ 4 = ☐

5. \$0.35 + \$0.25 = ________

6. 20¢ x ☐ = 80¢

7. What is the date of New Year's Day?

____

8. Which is more likely to be the weight of a child: 60 pounds or 200 pounds?

____

9. Does the arrow point to a *face, vertex,* or *edge*?

____

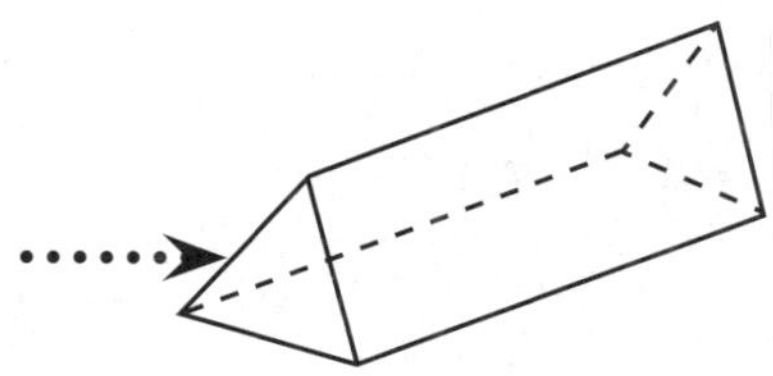

10. A pattern begins with the number 4. It increases by 3. What are the first five numbers in the pattern?

____

SCORE

1. Ⓨ Ⓝ
2. Ⓨ Ⓝ
3. Ⓨ Ⓝ
4. Ⓨ Ⓝ
5. Ⓨ Ⓝ
6. Ⓨ Ⓝ
7. Ⓨ Ⓝ
8. Ⓨ Ⓝ
9. Ⓨ Ⓝ
10. Ⓨ Ⓝ

___ / 10 Total

DAY 60

NAME: ______________________________

DIRECTIONS Solve each problem.

SCORE

1. Ⓨ Ⓝ
2. Ⓨ Ⓝ
3. Ⓨ Ⓝ
4. Ⓨ Ⓝ
5. Ⓨ Ⓝ
6. Ⓨ Ⓝ
7. Ⓨ Ⓝ
8. Ⓨ Ⓝ
9. Ⓨ Ⓝ
10. Ⓨ Ⓝ

___ / 10 Total

1.

$$\begin{array}{r} 35 \\ +\ 46 \\ \hline \end{array}$$

2. Draw seven groups of four lines. Then write an equation to show the product.

____

3. 5 x 10 = ☐

4. What number follows 73?

____

5. \$0.15 + \$0.25 + \$0.10 =

____

6. 6 x 3 = 10 + ☐

7. How many days are there in December?

____

8. Write the line length.

____

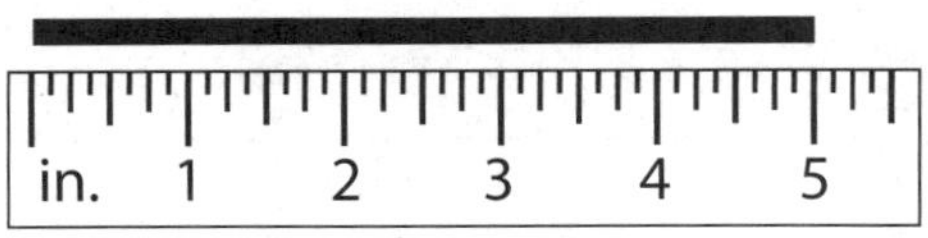

9. Draw the view of the shape from the top.

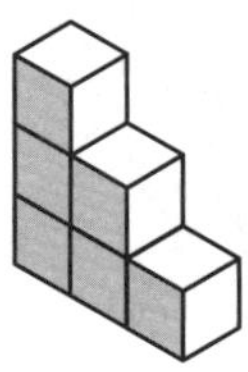

10. There are 7 quarters and 5 dimes. If you put the coins in a bag and pull one out, which kind of coin are you more likely to pull out?

____

NAME: ______________________

DIRECTIONS Solve each problem.

SCORE

1. Ⓨ Ⓝ
2. Ⓨ Ⓝ
3. Ⓨ Ⓝ
4. Ⓨ Ⓝ
5. Ⓨ Ⓝ
6. Ⓨ Ⓝ
7. Ⓨ Ⓝ
8. Ⓨ Ⓝ
9. Ⓨ Ⓝ
10. Ⓨ Ⓝ

___ / 10

Total

1.

$$\begin{array}{r} 23 \\ +\ 58 \\ \hline \end{array}$$

2. 6 x 3 = ☐

3. How many toes are there on 4 girls?

____

4. If 22 flowers are divided equally between 2 vases, how many flowers are in each vase?

____

5.

$$\begin{array}{r} \$5.45 \\ +\ \$3.25 \\ \hline \end{array}$$

6. How many 5¢ candies can you buy with 30¢?

____

7. How many hours are there from 7:00 P.M. to 11:00 P.M.?

____

8. What is the volume?

________ cubic units

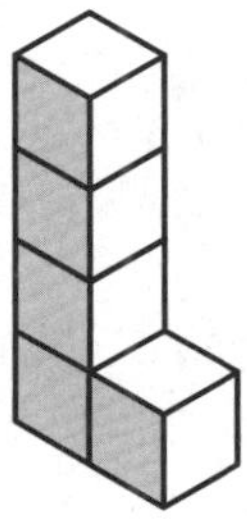

9. Create a tally chart for the following information:

Three kids like comics.
Eight kids like fairy tales.
Twelve kids like mysteries.

Favorite Book Genres

Comics	
Fairy Tales	
Mysteries	

10. Subtract 5 tens and 8 ones from 192.

____

DAY 62

NAME: ____________________

DIRECTIONS Solve each problem.

SCORE

1. Ⓨ Ⓝ
2. Ⓨ Ⓝ
3. Ⓨ Ⓝ
4. Ⓨ Ⓝ
5. Ⓨ Ⓝ
6. Ⓨ Ⓝ
7. Ⓨ Ⓝ
8. Ⓨ Ⓝ
9. Ⓨ Ⓝ
10. Ⓨ Ⓝ

___ / 10 Total

1. 46 – 31 = ☐

2. Seven times six is ______.

3.
$$\begin{array}{r} 9 \\ \times\ 4 \\ \hline \end{array}$$

4. What is the next even number after 62?

____

5. True or false?
1 half dollar = 2 quarters

____

6. 3 x 4 = 10 + ☐

7. Write the order from lightest to heaviest: horse, frog, cat.

____

8. What is the time shown below?

____

9. Turn this shape to the right 90°. Draw its new position.

10. Marcia has 3 quarters, 4 dimes, 6 nickels, and 2 pennies. How much money does she have?

____

DAY 63

NAME: ______________________________

DIRECTIONS Solve each problem.

1. 39 + 22 = ☐

2. 7 times 3 is _______.

3.

$$\begin{array}{r} 4 \\ \times\ 2 \\ \hline \end{array}$$

4. 20 ÷ 2 = ☐

5. 50 tens + 1 one = _______

6. Fill in the missing number.

121, 123, _______, 127, 129

7. How many days are there in July?

____

8. Find the perimeter.

____

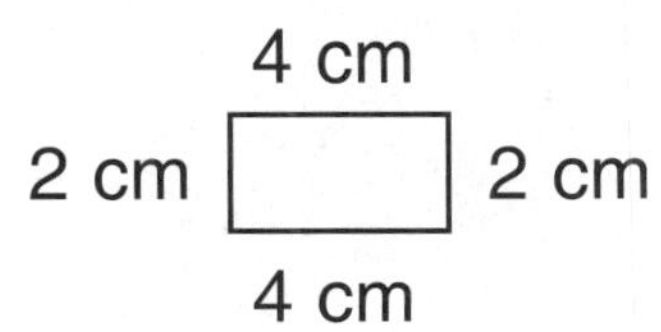

9. Flip the shape across the line of symmetry.

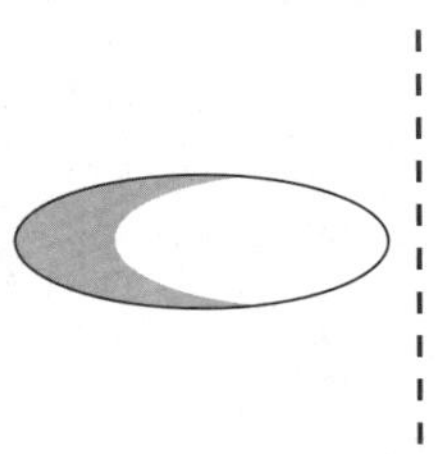

10. If a board game takes 20 minutes to finish, how many times can you play the board game in 2 hours?

____

SCORE

1. Ⓨ Ⓝ
2. Ⓨ Ⓝ
3. Ⓨ Ⓝ
4. Ⓨ Ⓝ
5. Ⓨ Ⓝ
6. Ⓨ Ⓝ
7. Ⓨ Ⓝ
8. Ⓨ Ⓝ
9. Ⓨ Ⓝ
10. Ⓨ Ⓝ

___ / 10 Total

DAY
64

NAME: ______________________________

DIRECTIONS Solve each problem.

SCORE
1. Ⓨ Ⓝ
2. Ⓨ Ⓝ
3. Ⓨ Ⓝ
4. Ⓨ Ⓝ
5. Ⓨ Ⓝ
6. Ⓨ Ⓝ
7. Ⓨ Ⓝ
8. Ⓨ Ⓝ
9. Ⓨ Ⓝ
10. Ⓨ Ⓝ
___ / 10 Total

1. $\begin{array}{r} 64 \\ -\ 19 \\ \hline \end{array}$

2. 5 x 5 = ☐

3. Ten times five is ________.

4. Divide 252 by 6.

____

5. How many nickels are there in $1.20?

____

6. 30 ☐ 3 = 90

7. What is the date two weeks from Saturday, February 13?

____

8. A baby napped from 2:30 P.M. until 4:00 P.M. How long was the nap?

____

9. True or false? A square is a quadrilateral.

____

10. If you divide me by 5, you get 8. What number am I?

____

DAY 65

NAME: ____________________

DIRECTIONS Solve each problem.

1. 19 + 42 = [ ]

2. 9 x 3 = [ ]

3. How many are in six groups of zero?

____

4. How many pairs can you make from 10 socks?

____

5. What is the value of the digit 4 in the number 564?

____

6. 6 x [ ] = 9 x 2

7. Which holds less: an ice cream bucket or a mug?

____

8. How many days are there in 3 weeks?

____

9. Name the solid.

____

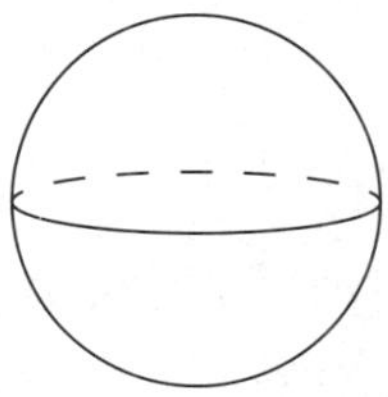

10. Kim bought a single scoop of ice cream for her mom and a double scoop for herself. How much money did she spend?

____

70¢  $1.20 

SCORE

1. Ⓨ Ⓝ
2. Ⓨ Ⓝ
3. Ⓨ Ⓝ
4. Ⓨ Ⓝ
5. Ⓨ Ⓝ
6. Ⓨ Ⓝ
7. Ⓨ Ⓝ
8. Ⓨ Ⓝ
9. Ⓨ Ⓝ
10. Ⓨ Ⓝ

___ / 10 Total

DAY
66

NAME: ____________________

DIRECTIONS Solve each problem.

SCORE

1. Ⓨ Ⓝ
2. Ⓨ Ⓝ
3. Ⓨ Ⓝ
4. Ⓨ Ⓝ
5. Ⓨ Ⓝ
6. Ⓨ Ⓝ
7. Ⓨ Ⓝ
8. Ⓨ Ⓝ
9. Ⓨ Ⓝ
10. Ⓨ Ⓝ

___ / 10
Total

1. 9 + 4 = ☐

2. 2 x 10 = ☐

3. 2 x 100 = ☐

4. What is the even number before 76?

____

5. Color one-quarter of these circles.

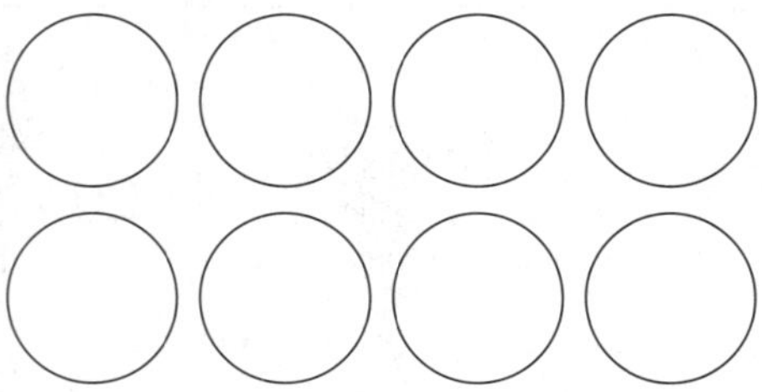

6. Fill in the missing number.

800, 700, 600, ________, 400

7. Which is shorter: a day or a month?

____

8. How many hours are there from 3:00 A.M. to 6:00 P.M.?

____

9. Which of these shapes is a pentagon?

____

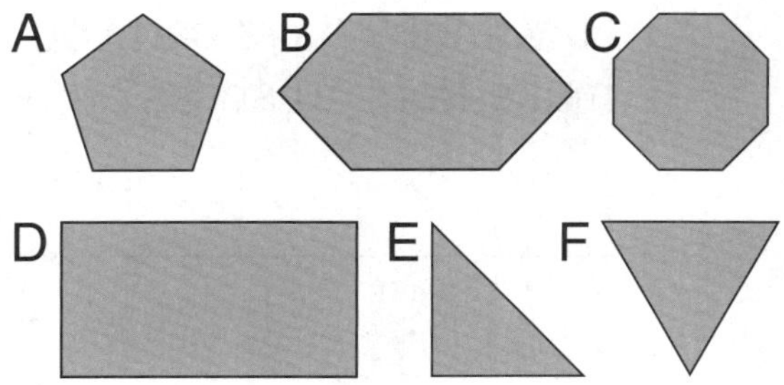

10. In 10 years, a painting will be 100 years old. How old is the painting now?

____

NAME: ______________________________

DIRECTIONS Solve each problem.

1. 70 – 50 = ☐

2. Calculate the product of 3 and 30.

____

3.
```
   7
x  6
----
```

4. If you divide 15 apples equally among 3 boxes, how many apples will be in each box?

____

5. Add one hundred to 367.

____

6. 6 x 3 = ☐ x 2

7. How many days are there in a year?

____

8. Is a flag pole taller or shorter than 1 meter?

____

9. How much older is Grandpa than Mom?

____

Person	Age
Grandpa	59
Grandma	57
Mom	32
Dad	33

10. You have $1.26. Your grandma gives you 3 quarters, 2 dimes, and 8 nickels. How much money do you have now?

____

SCORE

1. Ⓨ Ⓝ
2. Ⓨ Ⓝ
3. Ⓨ Ⓝ
4. Ⓨ Ⓝ
5. Ⓨ Ⓝ
6. Ⓨ Ⓝ
7. Ⓨ Ⓝ
8. Ⓨ Ⓝ
9. Ⓨ Ⓝ
10. Ⓨ Ⓝ

___ / 10
Total

DAY
68

NAME: ____________________

DIRECTIONS Solve each problem.

SCORE

1. Ⓨ Ⓝ
2. Ⓨ Ⓝ
3. Ⓨ Ⓝ
4. Ⓨ Ⓝ
5. Ⓨ Ⓝ
6. Ⓨ Ⓝ
7. Ⓨ Ⓝ
8. Ⓨ Ⓝ
9. Ⓨ Ⓝ
10. Ⓨ Ⓝ

___ / 10
Total

1. 38 + 22 = ☐

2.
$$\begin{array}{r} 9 \\ \times\ 2 \\ \hline \end{array}$$

3. How many fingers are there on two babies?

____

4. Write the numeral for eight hundred thirty-five.

____

5.
$$\begin{array}{r} \$1.79 \\ +\ \$2.52 \\ \hline \end{array}$$

6. How many 50¢ apples can you buy with $3.50?

____

7. What tool would you use to measure weight: a ruler or a scale?

____

8. What is the time shown on the clock below?

____

9. What is a shape that has 5 angles called?

____

10. It is August. Trudy's birthday is in 5 months. In what month is her birthday?

____

DAY 69

NAME: ______________________

DIRECTIONS Solve each problem.

1.
$$\begin{array}{r} 43 \\ -\ 26 \\ \hline \end{array}$$

2. 4 times 9 is _______.

3. 7 x 5 = ☐

4. If 20 pencils are shared equally among 4 children, how many pencils will each child get?

____

5. What is the total value of these coins?

____

6. 21 ☐ 3 = 7

7. Circle the container that holds more.

8. About how long does it take you to tie your shoes: 1 minute or 1 hour?

____

9. Which polygon forms the faces of a cube?

____

10. There are 16 pieces of bread in a loaf. You make a sandwich with 2 pieces of bread every day for lunch. How many days until you need to buy a new loaf of bread?

____

SCORE

1. Ⓨ Ⓝ
2. Ⓨ Ⓝ
3. Ⓨ Ⓝ
4. Ⓨ Ⓝ
5. Ⓨ Ⓝ
6. Ⓨ Ⓝ
7. Ⓨ Ⓝ
8. Ⓨ Ⓝ
9. Ⓨ Ⓝ
10. Ⓨ Ⓝ

___ / 10 Total

DAY 70

NAME: ____________________

DIRECTIONS Solve each problem.

SCORE

1. Ⓨ Ⓝ
2. Ⓨ Ⓝ
3. Ⓨ Ⓝ
4. Ⓨ Ⓝ
5. Ⓨ Ⓝ
6. Ⓨ Ⓝ
7. Ⓨ Ⓝ
8. Ⓨ Ⓝ
9. Ⓨ Ⓝ
10. Ⓨ Ⓝ

___ / 10 Total

1. 32 less than 55 is

____________________.

2.

$$\begin{array}{r} 10 \\ \times\ 8 \\ \hline \end{array}$$

3.

$$\begin{array}{r} 20 \\ \times\ 8 \\ \hline \end{array}$$

4. What number follows 243?

____

5. $5.35 + $4.79 =

____

6. 10 x ☐ = 100

7. What is the perimeter?

____

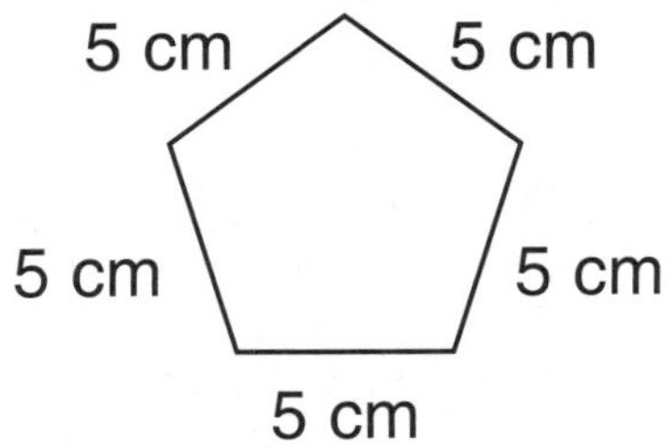

8. Which has the larger capacity: a cup of juice or a gallon of juice?

____

9. Circle the objects that are spheres.

10. Roger's favorite number is 72. Emma's favorite number has 2 fewer tens and 6 more ones. What is Emma's favorite number?

____

NAME: ____________________

DIRECTIONS Solve each problem.

1. 12 + 9 = ☐

2. 6 x 4 = ☐

3. Four times nine is ______.

4. 20 ÷ 10 = ☐

5. What is the largest number you can make using each of the digits 4, 6, and 9?

____

6. 6 x ☐ = 24

7. I was at the mall from 6:00 P.M. until 7:30 P.M. How long did I shop?

____

8. Which is longer: a month or a year?

____

9. Slide the shape and draw it.

10. Daniel earns 4 stickers a day. How many days will it take him to earn 16 stickers?

____

SCORE

1. Ⓨ Ⓝ
2. Ⓨ Ⓝ
3. Ⓨ Ⓝ
4. Ⓨ Ⓝ
5. Ⓨ Ⓝ
6. Ⓨ Ⓝ
7. Ⓨ Ⓝ
8. Ⓨ Ⓝ
9. Ⓨ Ⓝ
10. Ⓨ Ⓝ

___ / 10 Total

DAY

72

NAME: ____________________

DIRECTIONS Solve each problem.

SCORE

1. Ⓨ Ⓝ
2. Ⓨ Ⓝ
3. Ⓨ Ⓝ
4. Ⓨ Ⓝ
5. Ⓨ Ⓝ
6. Ⓨ Ⓝ
7. Ⓨ Ⓝ
8. Ⓨ Ⓝ
9. Ⓨ Ⓝ
10. Ⓨ Ⓝ

___ / 10

Total

1. 17 – 7 = ☐

2. How many sides are there on 6 triangles?

____

3. 7 x 3 = ☐

4. What number follows 34?

____

5. How many quarters are there in $5.00?

____

6. Fill in the missing number.

33, ________, 39, 42, 45

7. Thursday is June 20th. What is one week from that date?

____

8. How many hours are there from 11 P.M. to 3 A.M.?

____

9. List the angles from largest to smallest.

____

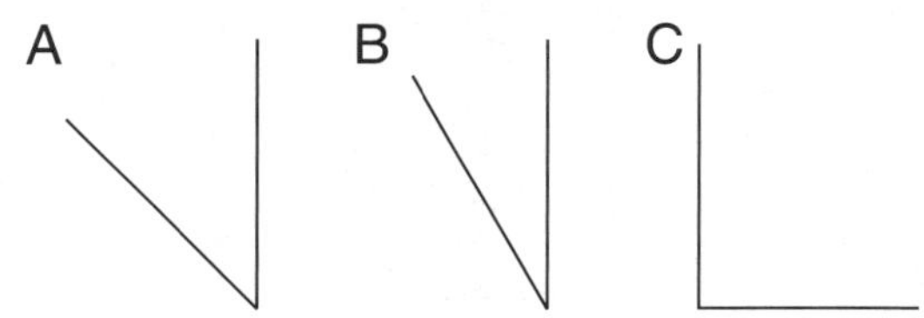

10. One-fourth of the circle is green. There is twice as much red as green. The rest is blue. Color the circle to match the data.

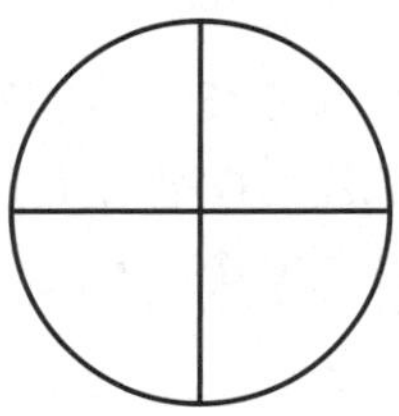

DAY
73

NAME: ______________________________

DIRECTIONS Solve each problem.

1.

$$\begin{array}{r} 23 \\ +\ 47 \\ \hline \end{array}$$

2. Draw a seven-by-two array.

3. 3 x 5 = ☐

4. How many rows of 4 make 12?

____

5. Are equal fractions shaded on the drawings below?

Circle: yes no

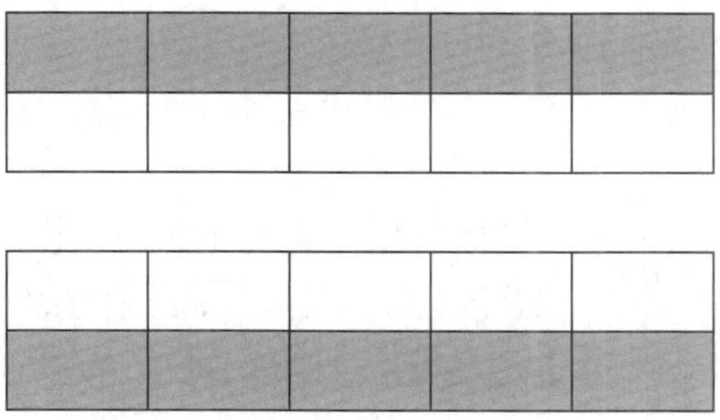

6. Fill in the missing number.

410, 400, ________, 380, 370

7. Write in order from lightest to heaviest: pencil, paper clip, book.

____

____

8. What tool would you use to measure temperature: a thermometer or a scale?

____

9. What is the mode of bedtimes?

____

Students' Bedtimes

Terri	8:30 P.M.
Juan	9:00 P.M.
Stephanie	8:00 P.M.
Param	8:30 P.M.
Damion	8:30 P.M.

10. A yo-yo costs $1.35. You pay with $1.50. The cashier gives you back two coins for change. What are the two coins?

____

SCORE

1. Ⓨ Ⓝ
2. Ⓨ Ⓝ
3. Ⓨ Ⓝ
4. Ⓨ Ⓝ
5. Ⓨ Ⓝ
6. Ⓨ Ⓝ
7. Ⓨ Ⓝ
8. Ⓨ Ⓝ
9. Ⓨ Ⓝ
10. Ⓨ Ⓝ

___ / 10
Total

DAY 74

NAME: ____________________

DIRECTIONS Solve each problem.

SCORE

1. Ⓨ Ⓝ
2. Ⓨ Ⓝ
3. Ⓨ Ⓝ
4. Ⓨ Ⓝ
5. Ⓨ Ⓝ
6. Ⓨ Ⓝ
7. Ⓨ Ⓝ
8. Ⓨ Ⓝ
9. Ⓨ Ⓝ
10. Ⓨ Ⓝ

___ / 10 Total

1.

$$\begin{array}{r} 40 \\ -\ 19 \\ \hline \end{array}$$

2. Ten times zero is _______.

3. 10 x 10 = _______

4. Is 91 an even or an odd number?

____

5. What is the value of the digit 1 in the number 541?

____

6. 6 x ☐ = 60

7. What is the month before September?

____

8. Circle the solid with the larger volume.

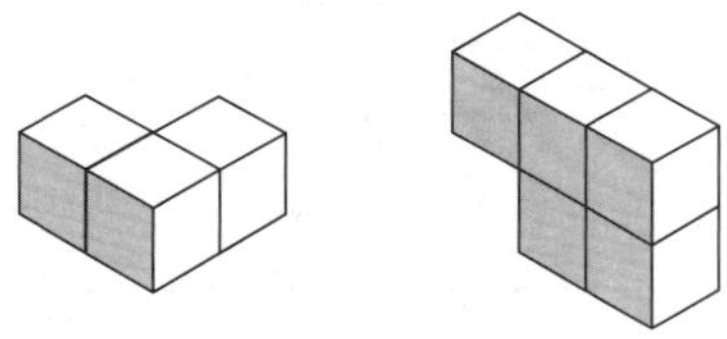

9. How many faces does a cube have?

____

10. The train left the station at 5:20 A.M. The train ride lasts 50 minutes. What time will the train arrive at its destination?

____

DAY 75

NAME: ____________________

DIRECTIONS Solve each problem.

1. 35 + 25 = ☐

2.

$$\begin{array}{r} 9 \\ \times\ 4 \\ \hline \end{array}$$

3. 2 times 10 is _______.

4. $5 \overline{)35}$

5. \$1.45 – \$0.79 = _______

6. 4 ☐ 8 = 32

7. Which holds less: a can of soda or a jug of milk?

____

8. Which is more likely to be the length of a book: 11 inches or 1 inch?

____

9. Circle the pentagon.

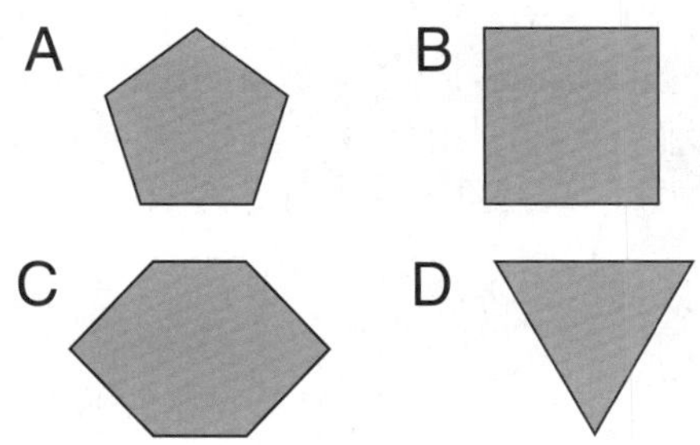

10. Nails are sold in bags of 20. Luis needs 68 nails. How many bags of nails should he buy?

____

SCORE

1. Ⓨ Ⓝ
2. Ⓨ Ⓝ
3. Ⓨ Ⓝ
4. Ⓨ Ⓝ
5. Ⓨ Ⓝ
6. Ⓨ Ⓝ
7. Ⓨ Ⓝ
8. Ⓨ Ⓝ
9. Ⓨ Ⓝ
10. Ⓨ Ⓝ

___ / 10 Total

DAY 76

NAME: ______________________

DIRECTIONS Solve each problem.

SCORE

1. Ⓨ Ⓝ
2. Ⓨ Ⓝ
3. Ⓨ Ⓝ
4. Ⓨ Ⓝ
5. Ⓨ Ⓝ
6. Ⓨ Ⓝ
7. Ⓨ Ⓝ
8. Ⓨ Ⓝ
9. Ⓨ Ⓝ
10. Ⓨ Ⓝ

___ / 10 Total

1. 19 + 43 = ________

2. How many are in six groups of eight?

____

3. 8 x 3 = ☐

4. What is the ordinal number right after 66th?

____

5. $12.49 – $5.52 = ________

6. Fill in the missing numbers.

34, 32, 30, 28 ______, ______

7. What is the month after August?

____

8. What is the volume?

______ cubic units

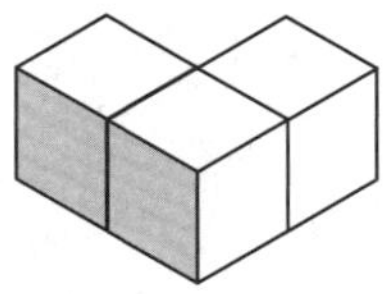

9. How many times did the coin land with heads up?

____

Coin Tosses

Heads	𝍸 𝍸 𝍸 𝍸 III
Tails	𝍸 𝍸 𝍸 𝍸 I

10. I am an even number between 457 and 462. I have a 0 in the ones place. What number am I?

____

DAY 77

NAME: ____________________

DIRECTIONS Solve each problem.

1. 13 – 9 = ☐

2. Seventeen times one is

____________________.

3.

$$\begin{array}{r} 6 \\ \times\ 5 \\ \hline \end{array}$$

4. How many rows of 2 can be made from 16?

____

5. $0.35 + $0.25 = ________

6. How many 10¢ pencils can you buy with 80¢?

____

7. Monday is July 3rd. What was the previous Sunday's date?

____

8. Which is more likely to be taller than one yard: a person or a dog?

____

9. Name the shape. ________

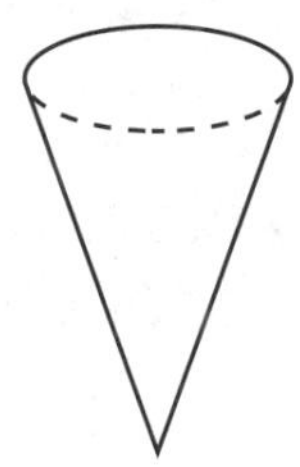

10. Eight kids are playing soccer. Two go home. What fraction of the kids are still playing?

____

SCORE

1. Ⓨ Ⓝ
2. Ⓨ Ⓝ
3. Ⓨ Ⓝ
4. Ⓨ Ⓝ
5. Ⓨ Ⓝ
6. Ⓨ Ⓝ
7. Ⓨ Ⓝ
8. Ⓨ Ⓝ
9. Ⓨ Ⓝ
10. Ⓨ Ⓝ

___ / 10 Total

DAY 78

NAME: ____________________

DIRECTIONS Solve each problem.

SCORE

1. Ⓨ Ⓝ
2. Ⓨ Ⓝ
3. Ⓨ Ⓝ
4. Ⓨ Ⓝ
5. Ⓨ Ⓝ
6. Ⓨ Ⓝ
7. Ⓨ Ⓝ
8. Ⓨ Ⓝ
9. Ⓨ Ⓝ
10. Ⓨ Ⓝ

___ / 10 Total

1.

$$\begin{array}{r} 16 \\ +\ \ 9 \\ \hline \end{array}$$

2. 7 x 8 = ☐

3. Draw 3 rows of 5 flowers. How many flowers are there?

____________________.

4. What is the next odd number after 78?

____

5. How many quarters are there in 1 whole?

____

6. 16 – ☐ = 9

7. What time is fifteen minutes after 8:45?

____

8. Circle the container that holds the lesser amount.

9. Name the angle below.

____

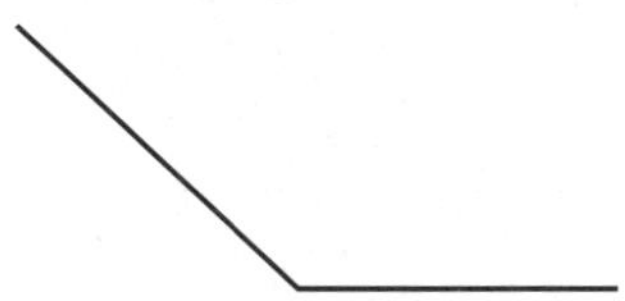

10. Phillip has $35.74 in his wallet. After paying for dinner, he has $24.31. How much did dinner cost?

____

NAME: ______________________

DIRECTIONS Solve each problem.

1. 16 – 8 = ______

2.
```
  5
x 4
```

3.
```
  6
x 4
```

4. If 20 pencils are shared equally among 4 groups, how many pencils will each group get?

____

5. Is 18 larger than 81?

Circle: yes no

6. 1,427 =

1,000 + ______ + 20 + 7

7. How many hours are there from 5 P.M. to 9 P.M.?

____

8. What is the perimeter if all sides are equal?

____

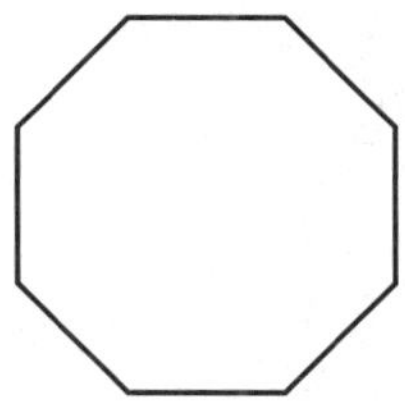

9. What is the name of a solid with 12 edges of equal length?

____

10. I am a number that equals 66 when divided by 2. What number am I?

____

SCORE

1. Ⓨ Ⓝ
2. Ⓨ Ⓝ
3. Ⓨ Ⓝ
4. Ⓨ Ⓝ
5. Ⓨ Ⓝ
6. Ⓨ Ⓝ
7. Ⓨ Ⓝ
8. Ⓨ Ⓝ
9. Ⓨ Ⓝ
10. Ⓨ Ⓝ

___ / 10 Total

DAY
80

NAME: ____________________

DIRECTIONS Solve each problem.

SCORE

1. Ⓨ Ⓝ
2. Ⓨ Ⓝ
3. Ⓨ Ⓝ
4. Ⓨ Ⓝ
5. Ⓨ Ⓝ
6. Ⓨ Ⓝ
7. Ⓨ Ⓝ
8. Ⓨ Ⓝ
9. Ⓨ Ⓝ
10. Ⓨ Ⓝ

___ / 10
Total

1. Subtract 18 from 79.

____

2. How many ears are there on 6 dogs?

____

3.
$$\begin{array}{r} 7 \\ \times\ 8 \\ \hline \end{array}$$

4. Write the numeral for two hundred fifty-three.

____

5. Add 2 tens to 68.

____

6. 5 ☐ 6 = 11

7. How many days are there in January?

____

8. Is a basketball taller or shorter than 1 meter?

____

9. Complete the picture across the line of symmetry.

10. A coach wants to organize some soccer teams. He forms 4 teams with 6 players on each team. How many total players are there on all of the teams?

____

NAME: ______________________________

DIRECTIONS Solve each problem.

1. 212 – 83 = ☐

2. 10 x 7 = ☐

3. 3 times 7 is _______.

4. 45 ÷ 5 = ☐

5. What fraction of the opossums is not shaded?

____

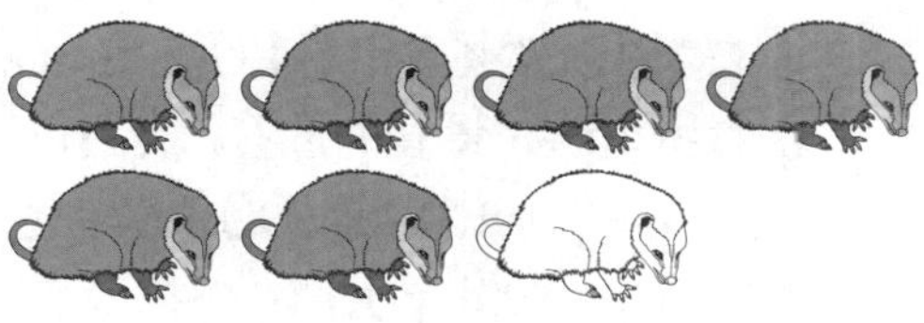

6. 30 ☐ 6 = 24

7. I ate lunch at 12:00 P.M. and a snack at 3:00 P.M. How long did I wait after lunch before having a snack?

____

8. Which measurement is more likely to be the height of a door: 7 feet or 3 feet?

____

9. How many vertices does a cylinder have?

____

10. List all the two-digit numbers that can be made using each of the digits 4, 5, and 6 once.

____

____

SCORE

1. Ⓨ Ⓝ
2. Ⓨ Ⓝ
3. Ⓨ Ⓝ
4. Ⓨ Ⓝ
5. Ⓨ Ⓝ
6. Ⓨ Ⓝ
7. Ⓨ Ⓝ
8. Ⓨ Ⓝ
9. Ⓨ Ⓝ
10. Ⓨ Ⓝ

___ / 10
Total

DAY

82

NAME: ____________________

DIRECTIONS Solve each problem.

SCORE

1. Ⓨ Ⓝ
2. Ⓨ Ⓝ
3. Ⓨ Ⓝ
4. Ⓨ Ⓝ
5. Ⓨ Ⓝ
6. Ⓨ Ⓝ
7. Ⓨ Ⓝ
8. Ⓨ Ⓝ
9. Ⓨ Ⓝ
10. Ⓨ Ⓝ

___ / 10

Total

1.

$$\begin{array}{r} 23 \\ +\ 51 \\ \hline \end{array}$$

2. 8 x 9 = ☐

3. How many are in seven groups of nine?

____

4. What number follows 156?

____

5. Do you have enough money to buy something that costs 85¢?

Circle: yes no

6. Fill in the missing number.

935, 735, ________, 335

7. Which is shorter: a centimeter or a meter?

____

8. What is the time shown on the clock below?

____

9. Record the data in the chart.

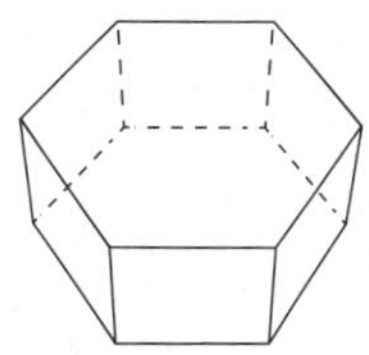

Vertices	
Edges	
Faces	

10. You buy a pencil for $0.25, a notebook for $1.00, and a backpack for $2.75. If you pay with $5.00, what change will you receive?

____

DAY
83

NAME: ______________________________

DIRECTIONS Solve each problem.

1. 50 – 25 = ☐

2.
$$\begin{array}{r} 24 \\ \times \ \ 2 \\ \hline \end{array}$$

3. 5 times 5 is _______.

4. There are a total of 35 stars in groups of 7. How many stars are in each group?

____

5.
$$\begin{array}{r} \$0.25 \\ +\ \$0.05 \\ \hline \end{array}$$

6. 6 x ☐ = 9 x 2

7. April 20th is a Tuesday. What was the date five days earlier?

____

8. Which measurement more likely describes the height of a flag pole: 20 feet or 6 feet?

____

9. Name the angle.

____

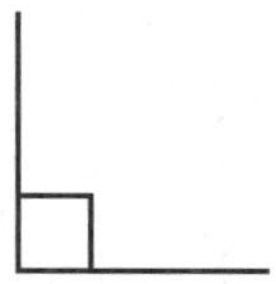

10. I am a solid figure that is round all over with no faces. What figure am I?

____

SCORE

1. Ⓨ Ⓝ
2. Ⓨ Ⓝ
3. Ⓨ Ⓝ
4. Ⓨ Ⓝ
5. Ⓨ Ⓝ
6. Ⓨ Ⓝ
7. Ⓨ Ⓝ
8. Ⓨ Ⓝ
9. Ⓨ Ⓝ
10. Ⓨ Ⓝ

___ / 10
Total

NAME: ______________________________

DIRECTIONS Solve each problem.

SCORE

1. Ⓨ Ⓝ
2. Ⓨ Ⓝ
3. Ⓨ Ⓝ
4. Ⓨ Ⓝ
5. Ⓨ Ⓝ
6. Ⓨ Ⓝ
7. Ⓨ Ⓝ
8. Ⓨ Ⓝ
9. Ⓨ Ⓝ
10. Ⓨ Ⓝ

___ / 10 Total

1. 12 + 7 = _______

2. Nineteen times zero is

_______________________.

3.

$$\begin{array}{r} 12 \\ \times \quad 4 \\ \hline \end{array}$$

4. 180 ÷ 30 = _______

5. \$0.79 – \$0.50 = _______

6. 20¢ x ☐ = \$1.20

7. What tool would you use to measure time: a calendar or a thermometer?

____

8. How many months are there in one year?

____

9. Label the vertex on the angle.

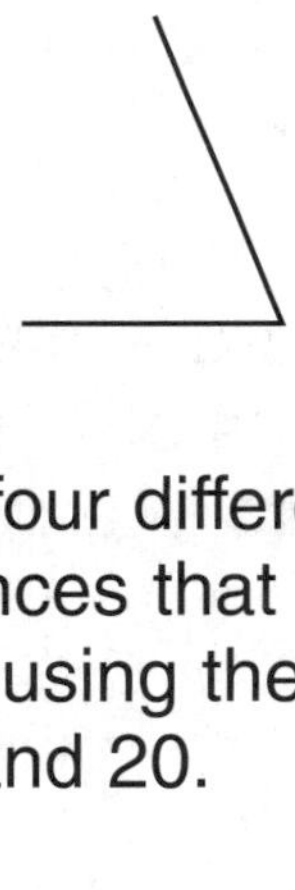

10. Write four different number sentences that can be made using the numbers 4, 5, and 20.

____

____

____

____

NAME: ______________________________

DIRECTIONS Solve each problem.

1.
$$\begin{array}{r} 64 \\ -\ 18 \\ \hline \end{array}$$

2. 3 x 7 = ☐

3. Draw 5 groups of 7 hats. How many hats are there?

____

4. $6\overline{)24}$

5. 3 tens = ________

6. ☐ x 2 = 18

7. Write in order from heaviest to lightest: chair, book, desk.

____

8. What is the volume?

____________cubic units

9. How many edges does the solid have?

____

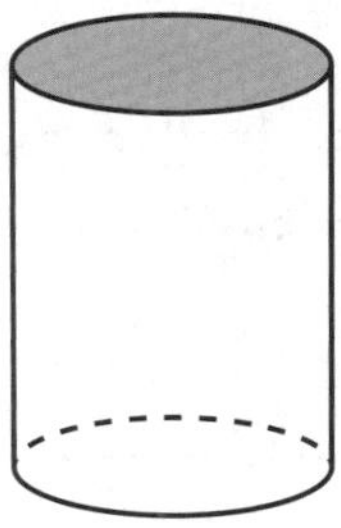

10. If you can read 20 pages in half an hour, how many pages can you read in 2 hours?

____

SCORE

1. Ⓨ Ⓝ
2. Ⓨ Ⓝ
3. Ⓨ Ⓝ
4. Ⓨ Ⓝ
5. Ⓨ Ⓝ
6. Ⓨ Ⓝ
7. Ⓨ Ⓝ
8. Ⓨ Ⓝ
9. Ⓨ Ⓝ
10. Ⓨ Ⓝ

___ / 10 Total

NAME: ______________________

DIRECTIONS Solve each problem.

SCORE

1. Ⓨ Ⓝ
2. Ⓨ Ⓝ
3. Ⓨ Ⓝ
4. Ⓨ Ⓝ
5. Ⓨ Ⓝ
6. Ⓨ Ⓝ
7. Ⓨ Ⓝ
8. Ⓨ Ⓝ
9. Ⓨ Ⓝ
10. Ⓨ Ⓝ

___ / 10 Total

1. 16 + 7 + 4 = ☐

2. How many noses are there on 4 people?

____

3.

$$\begin{array}{r} 9 \\ \times\ 5 \\ \hline \end{array}$$

4. What is the even number before 56?

____

5.

$$\begin{array}{r} \$1.25 \\ +\ \$5.36 \\ \hline \end{array}$$

6. Fill in the missing number.

35, 32, ________, 26, 23

7. How many hours are there from 7 A.M. to 7 P.M.?

____

8. Record the area.

________ rectangles

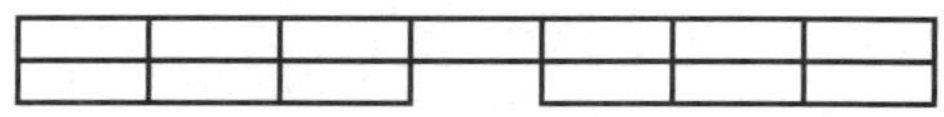

9. How many fewer people like daisies than roses?

Favorite Flower

Daisy	14
Tulip	9
Rose	15

____

10. One-half of a birthday cake is eaten at the party. One-fourth is eaten the next day. What fraction of the birthday cake is left?

____

NAME: ____________________

DIRECTIONS Solve each problem.

1. 17 – 5 = ☐

2. 4 x 8 = ☐

3. Six times four is ________.

4. If you share 18 crackers equally between 2 kids, how many crackers will each kid get?

____

5. What is the value of the digit 4 in the number 4,378?

____

6. 6 x 3 = ☐ x 2

7. What is the month after October?

____

8. Circle the container that holds the least.

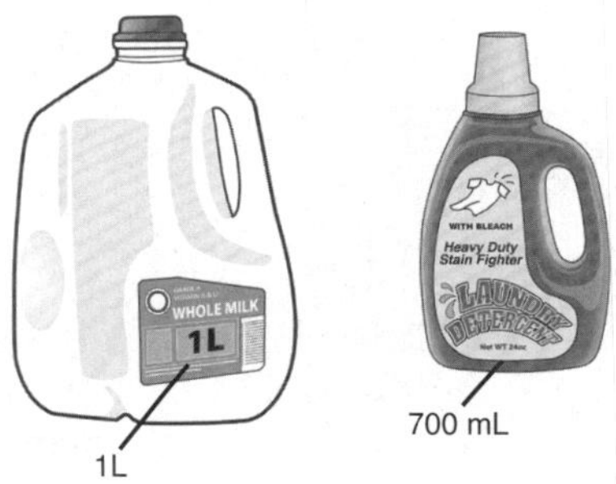

9. Are these lines perpendicular?

Circle: yes no

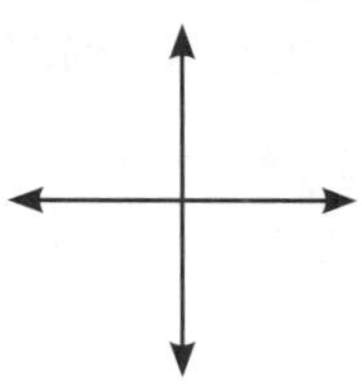

10. Tami gets $2.25 each week for allowance. How much money will she have after 4 weeks?

____

SCORE

1. Ⓨ Ⓝ
2. Ⓨ Ⓝ
3. Ⓨ Ⓝ
4. Ⓨ Ⓝ
5. Ⓨ Ⓝ
6. Ⓨ Ⓝ
7. Ⓨ Ⓝ
8. Ⓨ Ⓝ
9. Ⓨ Ⓝ
10. Ⓨ Ⓝ

___ / 10
Total

DAY
88

NAME: ____________________

DIRECTIONS Solve each problem.

SCORE

1. Ⓨ Ⓝ
2. Ⓨ Ⓝ
3. Ⓨ Ⓝ
4. Ⓨ Ⓝ
5. Ⓨ Ⓝ
6. Ⓨ Ⓝ
7. Ⓨ Ⓝ
8. Ⓨ Ⓝ
9. Ⓨ Ⓝ
10. Ⓨ Ⓝ

___ / 10
Total

1. $\begin{array}{r} 118 \\ +\ 63 \\ \hline \end{array}$

2. $\begin{array}{r} 7 \\ \times\ 2 \\ \hline \end{array}$

3. 9 times 9 is ________.

4. Make tally marks for the number 32. If you divide these tally marks into 8 equal groups, how many would be in each group?

5. Write a fraction that is equal to one.

____

6. 36 ☐ 6 = 6

7. Find the perimeter of the shape below.

____

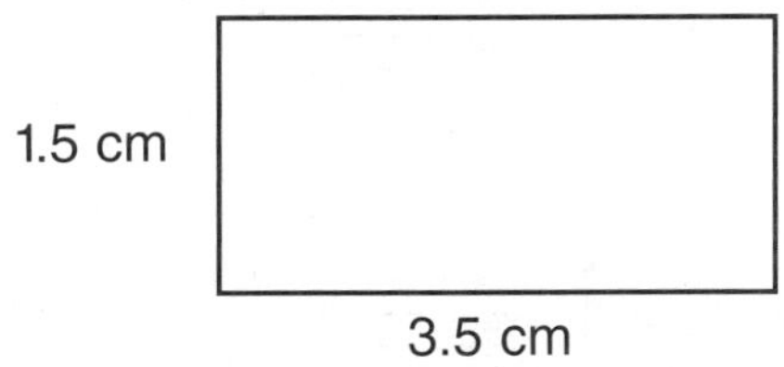

8. Write the line length.

____

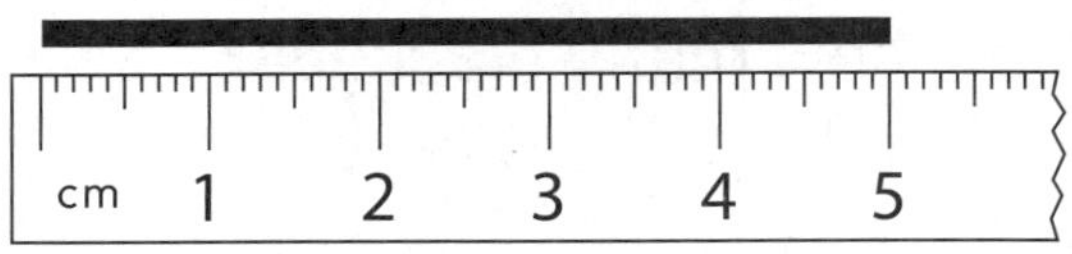

9. True or false? Some faces on a pyramid are triangles.

____

10. Lauren has 3 red marbles, 6 blue marbles, and 10 green marbles. How many red marbles and green marbles does Lauren have altogether?

____

DAY
89

NAME: ______________________________

DIRECTIONS Solve each problem.

1.

$$\begin{array}{r} 40 \\ -\ 21 \\ \hline \end{array}$$

2. 10 x 8 = ☐

3. How many ears are there on 8 people?

____

4. 15 ÷ 3 = ☐

5. How many hundreds are there in 364?

____

6. 24 ÷ ☐ = 6

7. Wednesday is May 7th. What day of the week will May 18th be?

____

8. Write in order from shortest to longest: pencil, toothpick, ruler.

____

____

9. Flip the image across the line of symmetry.

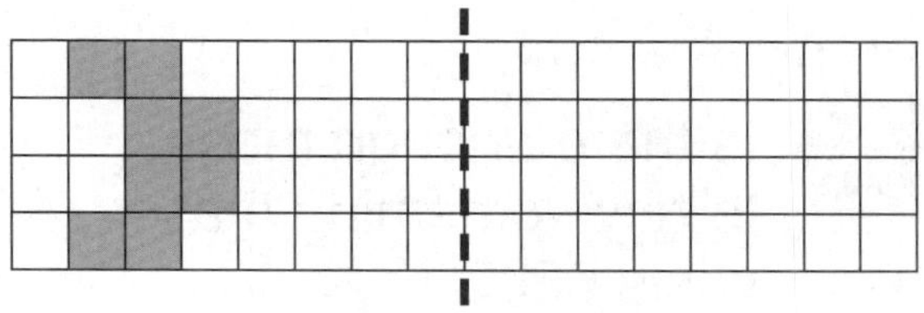

10. I am a number. The digit in my tens place is 5 less than the digit in my ones place. The digit in my ones place is 9. What number am I?

____

SCORE

1. Ⓨ Ⓝ
2. Ⓨ Ⓝ
3. Ⓨ Ⓝ
4. Ⓨ Ⓝ
5. Ⓨ Ⓝ
6. Ⓨ Ⓝ
7. Ⓨ Ⓝ
8. Ⓨ Ⓝ
9. Ⓨ Ⓝ
10. Ⓨ Ⓝ

___ / 10
Total

DAY

90

NAME: ______________________________

DIRECTIONS Solve each problem.

SCORE

1. Ⓨ Ⓝ
2. Ⓨ Ⓝ
3. Ⓨ Ⓝ
4. Ⓨ Ⓝ
5. Ⓨ Ⓝ
6. Ⓨ Ⓝ
7. Ⓨ Ⓝ
8. Ⓨ Ⓝ
9. Ⓨ Ⓝ
10. Ⓨ Ⓝ

___ / 10
Total

1. What is the difference between 50 and 29?

____

2. Ten times ten is _______.

3.

$$\begin{array}{r} 12 \\ \times\ 3 \\ \hline \end{array}$$

4. What number follows 479?

____

5. Is there enough money to buy something that costs 62¢?

Circle: yes no

6. 100 ☐ 50 = 50

7. What is the date of New Year's Eve?

____

8. A basketball game lasted 2 hours. It started at 4:30 P.M. What time did it end?

____

9. Does the arrow point to a *face, vertex,* or *edge*?

____

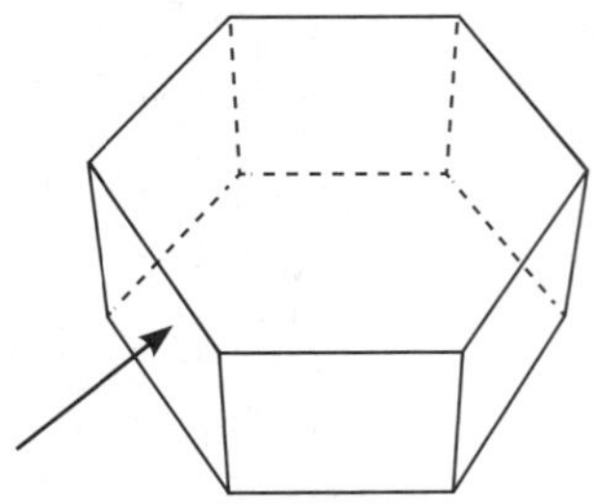

10. If you multiply me by 6, you get 36. What number am I?

____

NAME: ______________________________

DIRECTIONS Solve each problem.

1. 30 + 40 = ☐

2. Draw a 7 by 8 array.

3. 6 x 8 = ☐

4. 4 ⟌ 24

5. What fraction is shaded?

____

6. 100 – ☐ = 45

7. Circle the stamp with the smaller surface area.

8. What is the time shown on the clock below?

____

9. How many sides does a parallelogram have?

____

10. Which letter is in the square, but not in the circle or triangle?

____

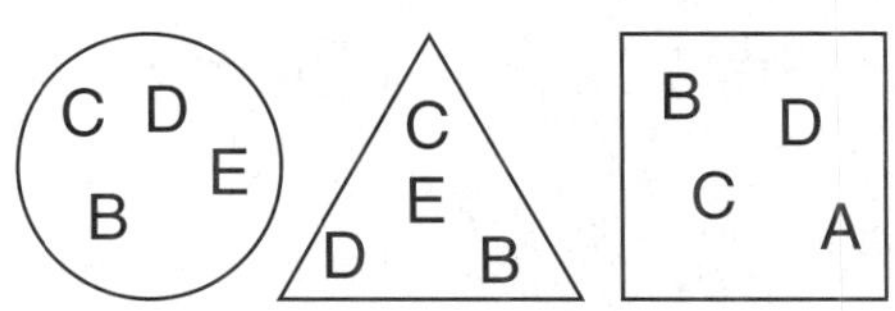

SCORE

1. Ⓨ Ⓝ
2. Ⓨ Ⓝ
3. Ⓨ Ⓝ
4. Ⓨ Ⓝ
5. Ⓨ Ⓝ
6. Ⓨ Ⓝ
7. Ⓨ Ⓝ
8. Ⓨ Ⓝ
9. Ⓨ Ⓝ
10. Ⓨ Ⓝ

___ / 10
Total

DAY 92

NAME: ____________________

DIRECTIONS Solve each problem.

SCORE

1. Ⓨ Ⓝ
2. Ⓨ Ⓝ
3. Ⓨ Ⓝ
4. Ⓨ Ⓝ
5. Ⓨ Ⓝ
6. Ⓨ Ⓝ
7. Ⓨ Ⓝ
8. Ⓨ Ⓝ
9. Ⓨ Ⓝ
10. Ⓨ Ⓝ

___ / 10 Total

1.

$$\begin{array}{r} 45 \\ -\ 23 \\ \hline \end{array}$$

2. 4 x 6 = ☐

3. 5 x 6 = ☐

4. What is the numeral for one hundred ninety-seven?

____

5. Circle the smallest number.

451, 145, 514

6. Fill in the missing number.

48, ________, 32, 24, 16

7. ________ cm = 1 m

8. What time is shown on the clock?

____

9. What is the range of the number of cousins?

Name	Number of Cousins
Anne	15
Marq	1
Jesus	3
Kelly	4
Tami	7

____

10. What is 10¢ less than 3 quarters?

____

DAY 93

NAME: ____________________________

DIRECTIONS Solve each problem.

1. 9 more than 33 is _______.

2. 6 times 8 is _______.

3.
$$\begin{array}{r} 10 \\ \times\ \ 6 \\ \hline \end{array}$$

4. $8 \div 4 = \square$

5. Subtract 3 tens from 73.

____

6. $4 \times \square = 28$

7. Show a quarter to 10:00 on the clock.

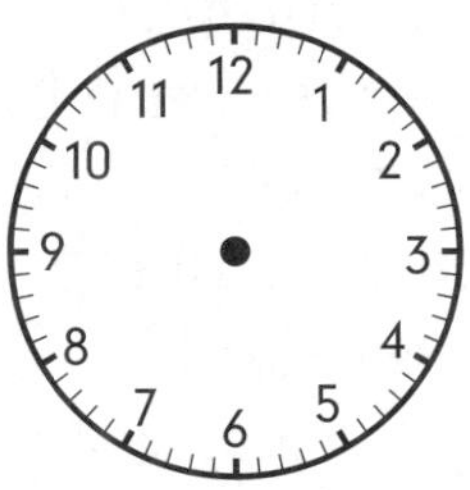

8. Circle the object that weighs less than one pound.

9. Match the solid to its top, front, and side views.

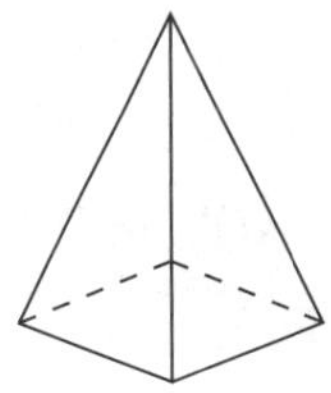

A 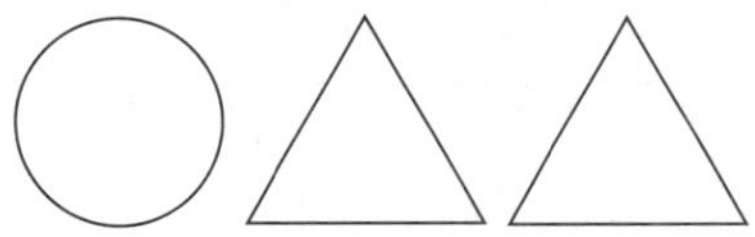

B 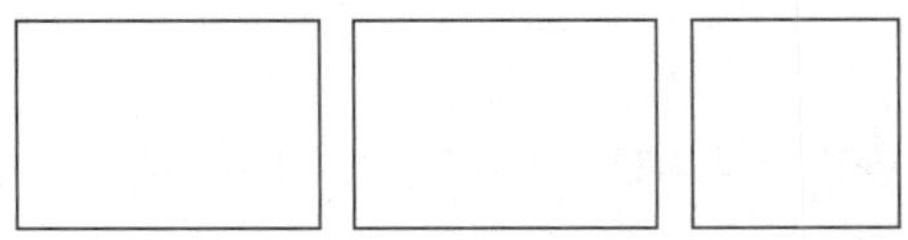

C 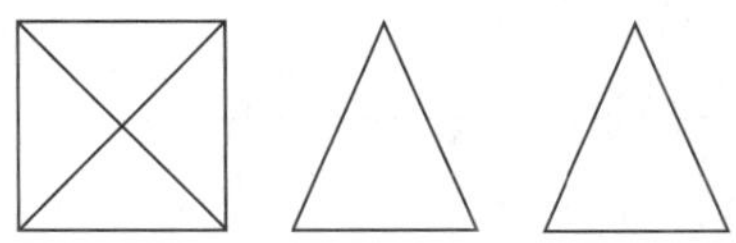

10. You have a quart of chocolate milk. How many cups of chocolate milk can you pour?

____

SCORE

1. Ⓨ Ⓝ
2. Ⓨ Ⓝ
3. Ⓨ Ⓝ
4. Ⓨ Ⓝ
5. Ⓨ Ⓝ
6. Ⓨ Ⓝ
7. Ⓨ Ⓝ
8. Ⓨ Ⓝ
9. Ⓨ Ⓝ
10. Ⓨ Ⓝ

___ / 10 Total

DAY
94

NAME: ____________________

DIRECTIONS Solve each problem.

SCORE

1. Ⓨ Ⓝ
2. Ⓨ Ⓝ
3. Ⓨ Ⓝ
4. Ⓨ Ⓝ
5. Ⓨ Ⓝ
6. Ⓨ Ⓝ
7. Ⓨ Ⓝ
8. Ⓨ Ⓝ
9. Ⓨ Ⓝ
10. Ⓨ Ⓝ

___ / 10
Total

1. 300 + 400 = ________

2.

$$\begin{array}{r} 8 \\ \times\ 8 \\ \hline \end{array}$$

3. How many legs are there on 5 cats?

____

4. What number follows 381?

____

5. How many nickels are there in 80¢?

____

6. 24 ÷ ☐ = 4

7. Record the area.

____________ $units^2$

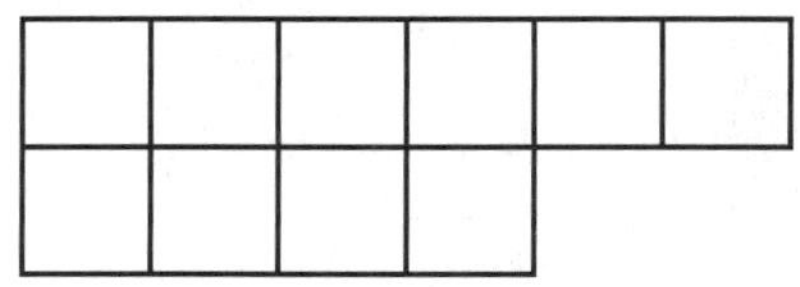

8. What would you use to measure an eraser: inches or feet?

____

9. Name the shape of the cross-section.

____

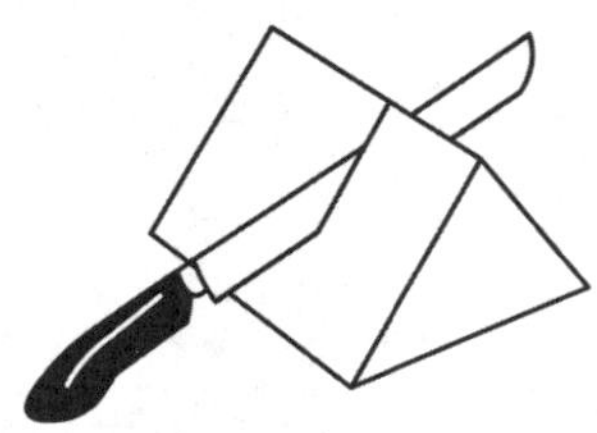

10. I am a number that ends with an 8. I am between 528 and 558. I have a 4 in the tens place. What number am I?

____

NAME: ____________________

DIRECTIONS Solve each problem.

1. 60 – 40 = ☐

2. 4 x 10 = ☐

3. Draw an array with six rows of one.

4. $5\overline{)15}$

5. 15¢ + 25¢ + 25¢ =

____

6. 56 ☐ 7 = 8

7. Circle the solid that has the greater volume.

A

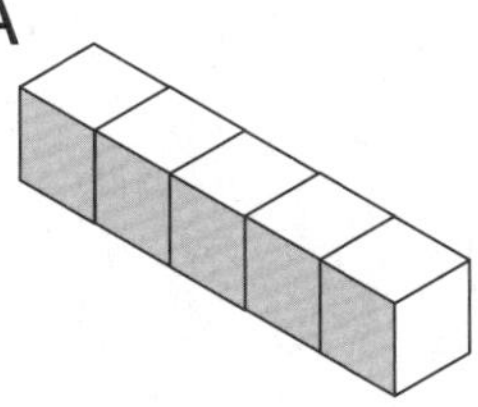

B

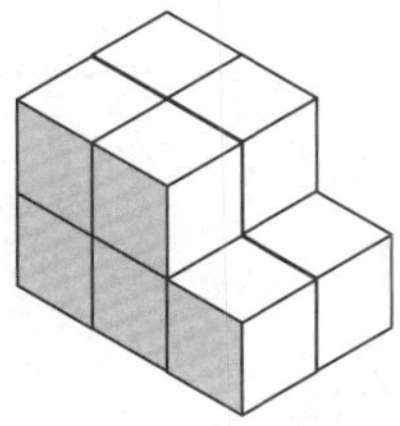

8. Is a pencil longer or shorter than one foot?

____

9. Name the solid.

____

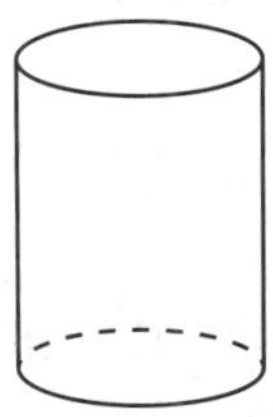

10. Two-fifths of the bar is blue. There are half as many red parts as blue parts. There are an equal number of red parts and yellow parts. The remaining parts are orange. Color the bar to match the given data.

SCORE

1. Ⓨ Ⓝ
2. Ⓨ Ⓝ
3. Ⓨ Ⓝ
4. Ⓨ Ⓝ
5. Ⓨ Ⓝ
6. Ⓨ Ⓝ
7. Ⓨ Ⓝ
8. Ⓨ Ⓝ
9. Ⓨ Ⓝ
10. Ⓨ Ⓝ

___ / 10
Total

DAY 96

NAME: ____________________

DIRECTIONS Solve each problem.

SCORE

1. Ⓨ Ⓝ
2. Ⓨ Ⓝ
3. Ⓨ Ⓝ
4. Ⓨ Ⓝ
5. Ⓨ Ⓝ
6. Ⓨ Ⓝ
7. Ⓨ Ⓝ
8. Ⓨ Ⓝ
9. Ⓨ Ⓝ
10. Ⓨ Ⓝ

___ / 10 Total

1. Subtract 70 from 140.

____

2.

$$\begin{array}{r} 11 \\ \times\ 5 \\ \hline \end{array}$$

3. How many tails are there on 8 cats?

____

4. What is the number before 382?

____

5. Is $\frac{2}{4}$ equal to $\frac{1}{2}$?

Circle: yes no

6. 75 + ☐ = 82

7. Write the time in words.

____

8. True or false? A brick has a mass of less than a ton.

____

9. Draw the view of the front (shaded area) of the shape.

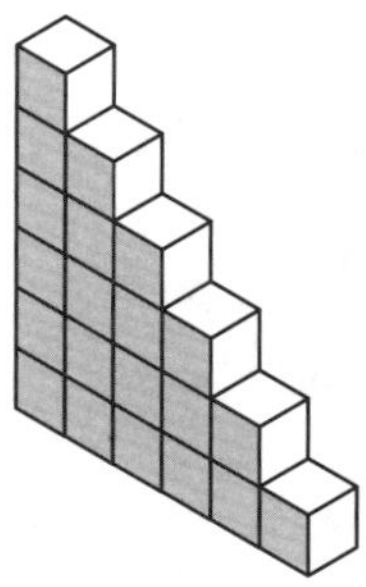

10. Which amount is less: 4 quarters and 3 dimes or 3 quarters and 4 dimes?

____

NAME: ____________________

DIRECTIONS Solve each problem.

1. 17 + 5 + 23 = ☐

2. 9 x 10 = ☐

3. 8 x 10 = ☐

4. If 16 markers are shared equally among 4 students, how many markers will each student get?

____

5. \$1.00 + 85¢ = ________

6. Fill in the missing number.

50, 46, 42, ________, 34

7. Circle the container that holds more than 1 liter.

8. Show ten minutes after seven on the clock.

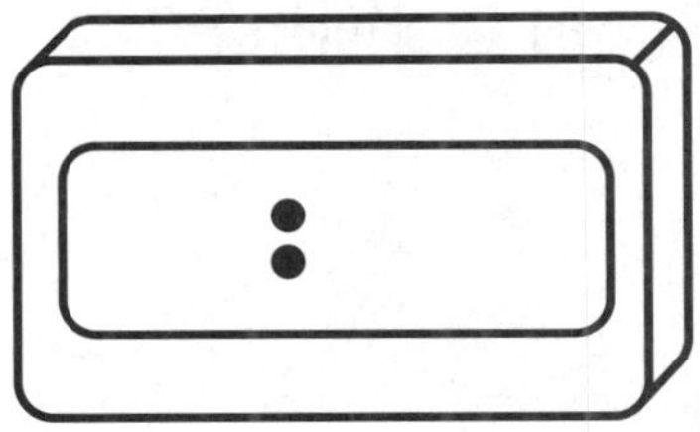

9. Use an arrow to label the right angle.

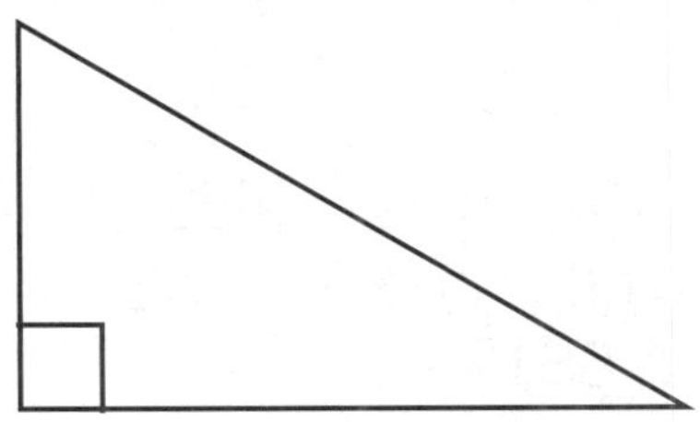

10. Emily can make a bow with 12 inches of ribbon. There are 3 yards of ribbon on a spool. How many bows can Emily make with one spool of ribbon?

____

SCORE

1. Ⓨ Ⓝ
2. Ⓨ Ⓝ
3. Ⓨ Ⓝ
4. Ⓨ Ⓝ
5. Ⓨ Ⓝ
6. Ⓨ Ⓝ
7. Ⓨ Ⓝ
8. Ⓨ Ⓝ
9. Ⓨ Ⓝ
10. Ⓨ Ⓝ

___ / 10 Total

DAY
98

NAME: ____________________

DIRECTIONS Solve each problem.

SCORE
1. Ⓨ Ⓝ
2. Ⓨ Ⓝ
3. Ⓨ Ⓝ
4. Ⓨ Ⓝ
5. Ⓨ Ⓝ
6. Ⓨ Ⓝ
7. Ⓨ Ⓝ
8. Ⓨ Ⓝ
9. Ⓨ Ⓝ
10. Ⓨ Ⓝ
___ / 10 Total

1.
$$\begin{array}{r} 75 \\ -\ 25 \\ \hline \end{array}$$

2. 10 x 5 = ☐

3. How many fingers are there on 2 children?

____

4. What is the next ordinal number after 99th?

____

5. What is the value of the digit in the tens place in 651?

____

6. 72 ☐ 12 = 6

7. These bottles are filled with cups of sand. Circle the bottle that holds the most sand.

A B C

13 cups 22 cups 24 cups

8. It is 7:10. What time will it be in half an hour?

____

9. Create a bar graph with the following information.

4 people like Halloween. 6 people like Valentine's Day. 3 people like Thanksgiving.

Favorite Holidays

Holiday	1	2	3	4	5	6
Halloween						
Valentine's Day						
Thanksgiving						

0 1 2 3 4 5 6

Votes

10. There are 8 balls. Half of the balls are blue. One-fourth of the balls are green. There are half as many red balls as green balls. How many are red?

____

NAME: ____________________

DIRECTIONS Solve each problem.

1.
$$\begin{array}{r} 43 \\ +\ 19 \\ \hline \end{array}$$

2. 4 x 10 = ☐

3. Four times seven is _____.

4. $5\overline{)30}$

5. True or false?
4 eighths = 2 fourths

____

6. 46 + ☐ = 56

7. What time is shown on the clock?

____

8. Circle the item that weighs about 10 pounds.

9. How many edges does a sphere have?

____

10. A teacher wants to give each child in her class 4 stickers. She has 32 students. How many stickers will she need?

____

SCORE

1. (Y) (N)
2. (Y) (N)
3. (Y) (N)
4. (Y) (N)
5. (Y) (N)
6. (Y) (N)
7. (Y) (N)
8. (Y) (N)
9. (Y) (N)
10. (Y) (N)

___ / 10
Total

NAME: ____________________

DIRECTIONS Solve each problem.

SCORE

1. Ⓨ Ⓝ
2. Ⓨ Ⓝ
3. Ⓨ Ⓝ
4. Ⓨ Ⓝ
5. Ⓨ Ⓝ
6. Ⓨ Ⓝ
7. Ⓨ Ⓝ
8. Ⓨ Ⓝ
9. Ⓨ Ⓝ
10. Ⓨ Ⓝ

___ / 10
Total

1. 45 less than 90 is ________.

2. 4 x 2 = ☐

3. 40 x 2 = ☐

4. What number follows 526?

____

5. What is half of 12? ________

6. ☐ x 8 = 32

7. Record the area.

____________ units^2

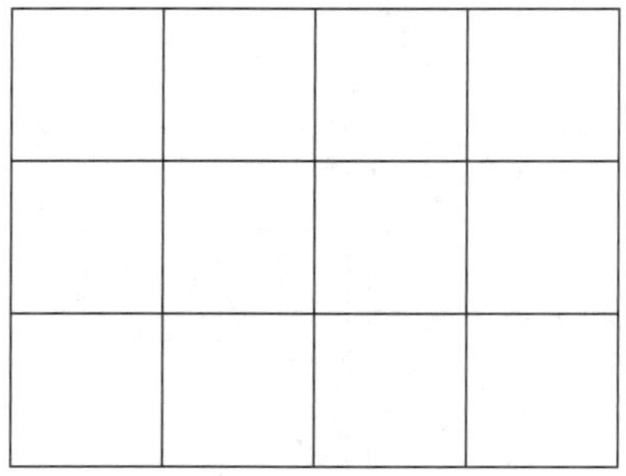

8. Show two forty-five on the clock.

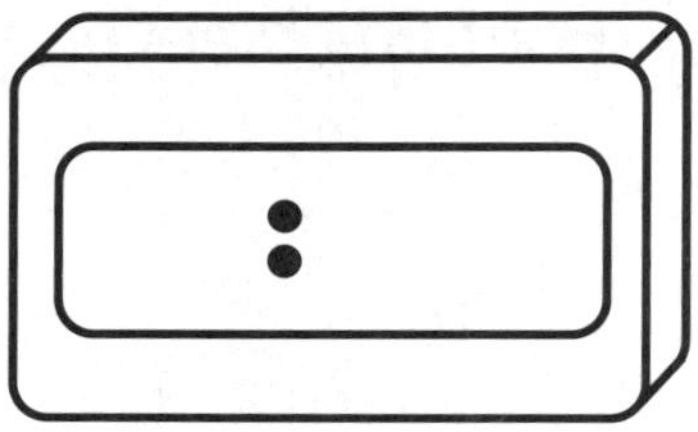

9. Are these lines parallel?

Circle: yes no

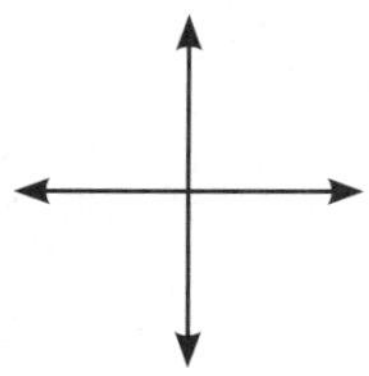

10. You see 26 wheels on the vehicles outside. One of the vehicles is an 18-wheel truck. The rest are cars. How many cars are there?

____

DAY 101

NAME: ____________________

DIRECTIONS Solve each problem.

1. 36 + 25 = ☐

2.

$$\begin{array}{r} 14 \\ \times \ 8 \\ \hline \end{array}$$

3. Draw an array with 7 rows of 10.

4. Divide 32 blocks into 4 equal piles. How many blocks are in each pile?

____

5. 5 tens + 4 ones = ________

6. 100 – ☐ = 65

7. Show a quarter to 5 on the clock face.

8. How many cubic centimeters are in the solid below?

________ cubic centimeters

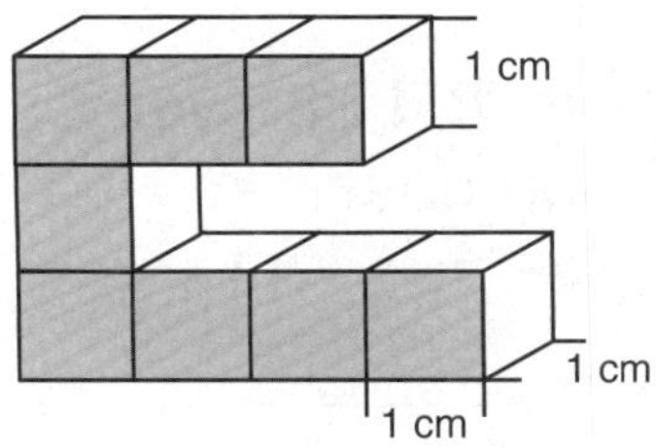

9. Name the shape of the cross-section.

____

10. Marco delivers 12 newspapers each day. How many newspapers does Marco deliver in one week?

____

SCORE

1. Ⓨ Ⓝ
2. Ⓨ Ⓝ
3. Ⓨ Ⓝ
4. Ⓨ Ⓝ
5. Ⓨ Ⓝ
6. Ⓨ Ⓝ
7. Ⓨ Ⓝ
8. Ⓨ Ⓝ
9. Ⓨ Ⓝ
10. Ⓨ Ⓝ

___ / 10 Total

NAME: ____________________

DIRECTIONS Solve each problem.

SCORE

1. Ⓨ Ⓝ
2. Ⓨ Ⓝ
3. Ⓨ Ⓝ
4. Ⓨ Ⓝ
5. Ⓨ Ⓝ
6. Ⓨ Ⓝ
7. Ⓨ Ⓝ
8. Ⓨ Ⓝ
9. Ⓨ Ⓝ
10. Ⓨ Ⓝ

___ / 10 Total

1. 132 – 85 = ☐

2. 6 x 0 = ☐

3. Nine times three is

____________________.

4. Is 104 an even or an odd number?

____

5. Color $\frac{3}{4}$ of the shape.

6. 14¢ x ☐ = 28¢

7. Write the time in words.

____

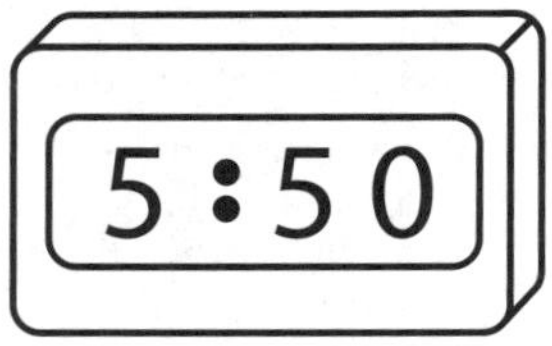

8. How many times can the bucket be filled from the liter cube?

____

9. Circle the parallel lines on the capital E.

E

10. Audrey has 4 coins that have a total value of 65¢. What coins does she have?

____

____

NAME: ____________________

DIRECTIONS Solve each problem.

1. 56 – 29 = ☐

2.

$$\begin{array}{r} 80 \\ \times \;\; 4 \\ \hline \end{array}$$

3. 9 x 6 = ☐

4. 25 ÷ 5 = ☐

5. Is there enough money shown to buy something that costs 51¢?

Circle: yes no

6. 42 ☐ 6 = 7

7. Circle the solid that has less volume.

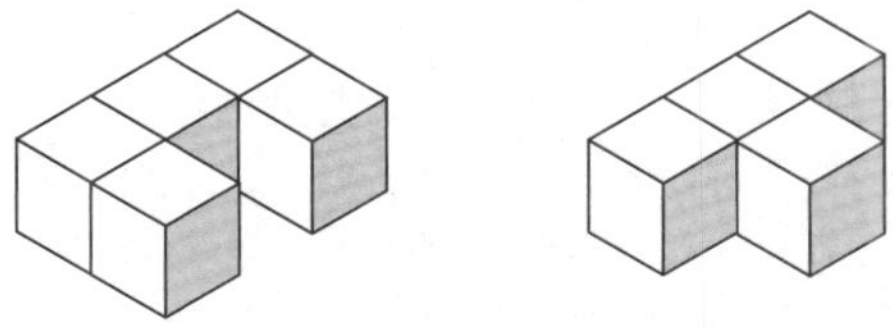

8. Is the mass of a nail more or less than one kilogram?

____

9. How many children chose the slide as their favorite?

____

Favorite Playground Equipment

Swings	☺ ☺ ☺ ☺ ☺
Slide	☺ ☺ ☺ ☺ ☺ ☺ ☺
Monkey Bars	☺ ☺ ☺

☺ = 5 children

10. What 3-digit numbers that have 7 in the hundreds place can be made using each digit 7, 4, 9, and 6 only once?

____

____

SCORE

1. Ⓨ Ⓝ
2. Ⓨ Ⓝ
3. Ⓨ Ⓝ
4. Ⓨ Ⓝ
5. Ⓨ Ⓝ
6. Ⓨ Ⓝ
7. Ⓨ Ⓝ
8. Ⓨ Ⓝ
9. Ⓨ Ⓝ
10. Ⓨ Ⓝ

___ / 10 Total

NAME: ____________________

DIRECTIONS Solve each problem.

SCORE

1. Ⓨ Ⓝ
2. Ⓨ Ⓝ
3. Ⓨ Ⓝ
4. Ⓨ Ⓝ
5. Ⓨ Ⓝ
6. Ⓨ Ⓝ
7. Ⓨ Ⓝ
8. Ⓨ Ⓝ
9. Ⓨ Ⓝ
10. Ⓨ Ⓝ

___ / 10 Total

1.

$$\begin{array}{r} 75 \\ -\ 35 \\ \hline \end{array}$$

2. 5 times 6 is _______.

3. 7 x 10 = ☐

4. What is the numeral for six hundred seventy-four?

____

5. How many dimes are there in $2.50?

____

6. 75 + ☐ = 82

7. What would you use to measure the length of a board as tall as a man: inches or pounds?

____

8. These bottles are filled with cups of sand. Circle the bottle that holds the least sand.

A B C

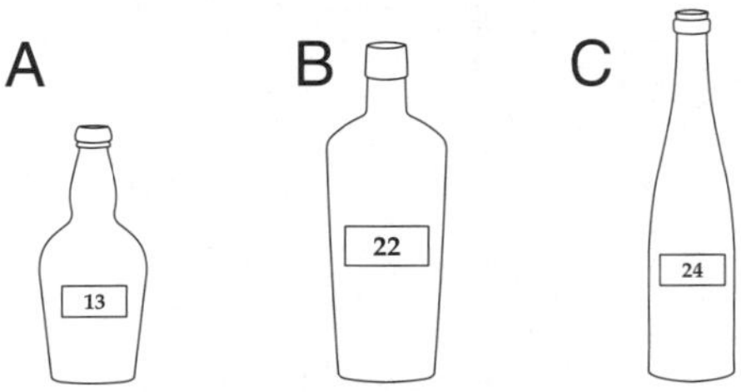

13 cups 22 cups 24 cups

9. Draw the mirror image along the line of symmetry.

10. Sasha left home at 7:40. She arrived at school 20 minutes later. She played for 10 minutes until the bell rang to start the school day. What time does school start?

____

NAME: ____________________

DIRECTIONS Solve each problem.

1. 34 + 5 + 6 = ☐

2.
$$\begin{array}{r} 9 \\ \times\ 8 \\ \hline \end{array}$$

3. Seven times zero is

____________________.

4. $4\overline{)40}$

5. What is one hundred more than 148?

____

6. Fill in the missing number.

________, 34, 32, 30, 28, 26

7. Measure the diagonal of this page to the nearest inch.

____________________ in.

8. Show the time ten minutes before 11:00 on the clock.

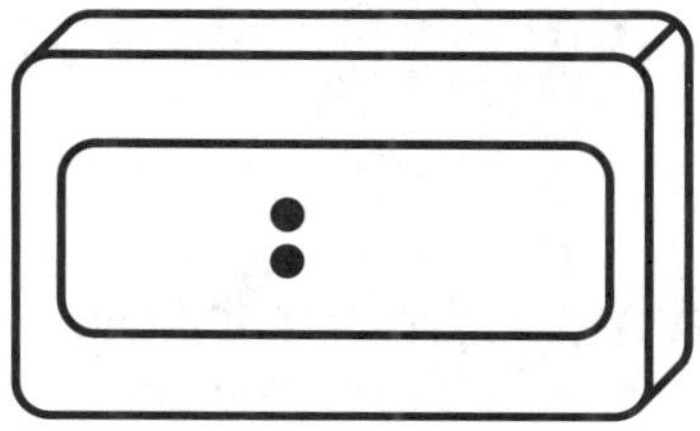

9. Name the angle.

____

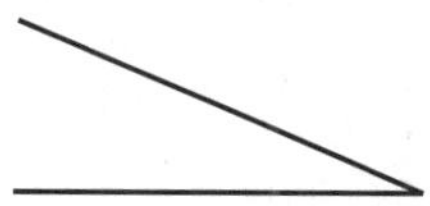

10. There are 25 students in a classroom. The teacher wants to do a project with markers. She has 50 markers to share equally among the students. How many markers will each student be able to use?

____

SCORE

1. Ⓨ Ⓝ
2. Ⓨ Ⓝ
3. Ⓨ Ⓝ
4. Ⓨ Ⓝ
5. Ⓨ Ⓝ
6. Ⓨ Ⓝ
7. Ⓨ Ⓝ
8. Ⓨ Ⓝ
9. Ⓨ Ⓝ
10. Ⓨ Ⓝ

___ / 10
Total

DAY
106

NAME: ______________________________

DIRECTIONS Solve each problem.

SCORE

1. Ⓨ Ⓝ
2. Ⓨ Ⓝ
3. Ⓨ Ⓝ
4. Ⓨ Ⓝ
5. Ⓨ Ⓝ
6. Ⓨ Ⓝ
7. Ⓨ Ⓝ
8. Ⓨ Ⓝ
9. Ⓨ Ⓝ
10. Ⓨ Ⓝ

___ / 10
Total

1. 238 + 29 = ☐

2. How many toes are there on 3 men?

____

3.
$$\begin{array}{r} 7 \\ \times\ 6 \\ \hline \end{array}$$

4. What number follows 628?

____

5. Are the shaded fractions of the bars below equal?

Circle: yes no

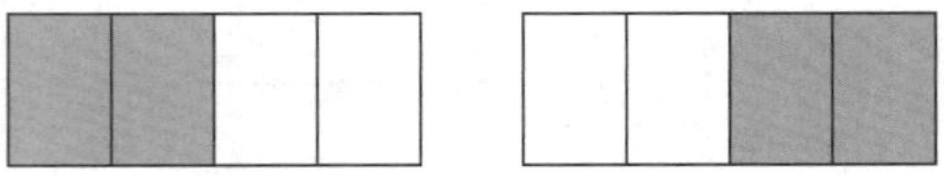

6. 65 + ☐ = 71

7. What time is shown on the clock below?

____

8. Circle the container that holds more than 1 liter.

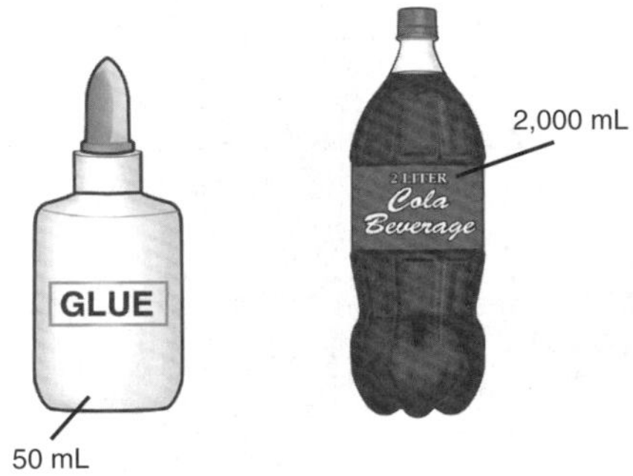

9. Create a tally chart for the following information.

Seventeen people like reading. Five more people like toys than reading. Six less people like video games than reading.

Favorite Free-Time Activities

Reading	
Video Games	
Toys	

10. An ice cream cone costs $1.35. You have 3 quarters, 4 dimes, and 2 nickels. Do you have enough money to buy an ice cream cone?

Circle: yes no

NAME: ____________________

DIRECTIONS Solve each problem.

1.

$$\begin{array}{r} 75 \\ -\ 34 \\ \hline \end{array}$$

2. 1 x 4 = ☐

3. 10 x 4 = ☐

4. If 36 crayons are shared equally among 3 children, how many crayons will each child get?

____

5. Circle the drawing with the larger shaded fraction.

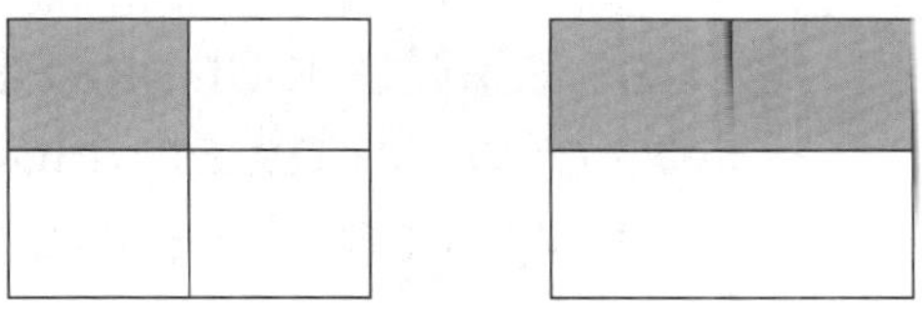

6. Fill in the missing number.

3, 9, 15, 21, ________

7. Circle the object that weighs more than one pound.

8. Is an eraser longer or shorter than a foot?

____

9. Circle the parallelogram.

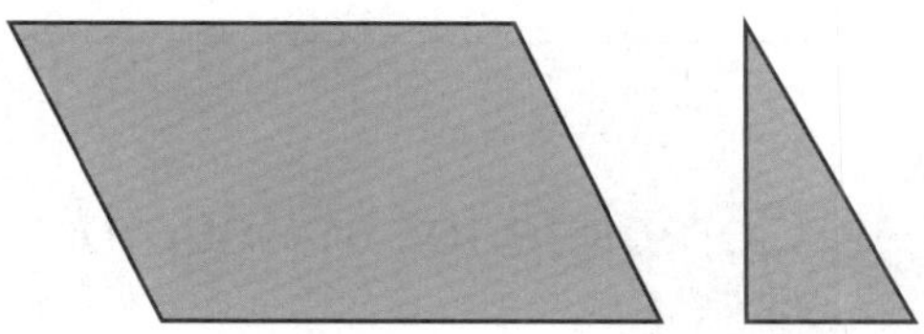

10. It is August. My birthday was 6 months ago. In what month is my birthday?

____

SCORE

1. Ⓨ Ⓝ
2. Ⓨ Ⓝ
3. Ⓨ Ⓝ
4. Ⓨ Ⓝ
5. Ⓨ Ⓝ
6. Ⓨ Ⓝ
7. Ⓨ Ⓝ
8. Ⓨ Ⓝ
9. Ⓨ Ⓝ
10. Ⓨ Ⓝ

___ / 10 Total

DAY 108

NAME: ____________________________

DIRECTIONS Solve each problem.

SCORE
1. Ⓨ Ⓝ
2. Ⓨ Ⓝ
3. Ⓨ Ⓝ
4. Ⓨ Ⓝ
5. Ⓨ Ⓝ
6. Ⓨ Ⓝ
7. Ⓨ Ⓝ
8. Ⓨ Ⓝ
9. Ⓨ Ⓝ
10. Ⓨ Ⓝ
___ / 10 Total

1. 14 + 20 + 36 = ☐

2. 10 times 0 is ________.

3.

$$\begin{array}{r} 36 \\ \times \quad 3 \\ \hline \end{array}$$

4. What is the next even number after 320?

____

5. Complete for the number 1,506:

________ thousands

________ hundreds

________ tens

________ ones

6. 24 ☐ 6 = 4

7. Circle the container that holds less than 1 liter.

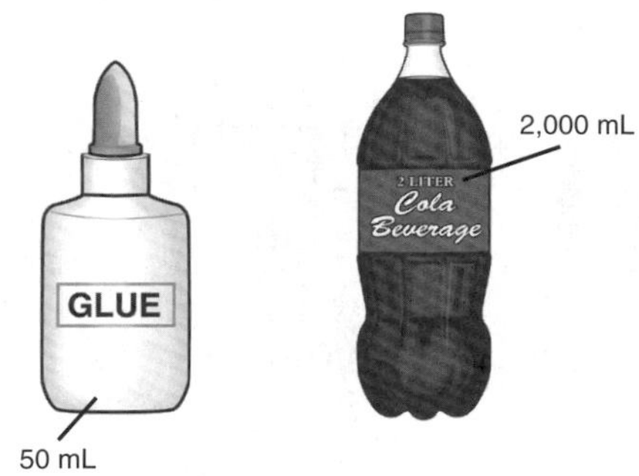

8. Show ten fifteen on the clock.

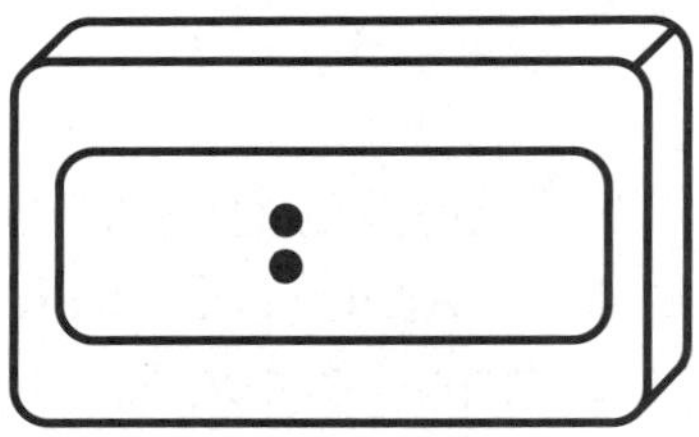

9. A __________-sided shape is called a quadrilateral.

10. Tran stacks four blocks on top of each other. How many faces are showing?

____

NAME: ______________________________

DIRECTIONS Solve each problem.

1. 600 – 400 = ☐

2. 7 x 2 = ☐

3.
$$\begin{array}{r} 7 \\ \times\ 8 \\ \hline \end{array}$$

4. 16 ÷ 4 = ☐

5. Fill in the missing values.

$\frac{1}{4}$, $\frac{2}{4}$, ________, ________

6. 42 + ☐ = 43

7. Circle the solid that has the greater volume.

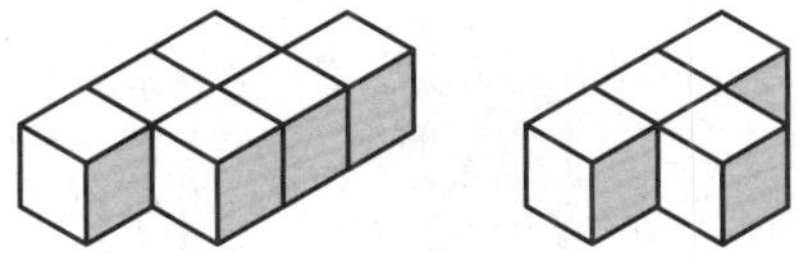

8. It is 11:45. What time will it be in half an hour?

____

9. Name the angle below.

____

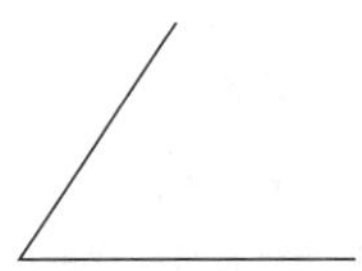

10. You and 5 friends want to order pizza. You can each eat a quarter of a pizza. How many pizzas should you order?

____

SCORE

1. Ⓨ Ⓝ
2. Ⓨ Ⓝ
3. Ⓨ Ⓝ
4. Ⓨ Ⓝ
5. Ⓨ Ⓝ
6. Ⓨ Ⓝ
7. Ⓨ Ⓝ
8. Ⓨ Ⓝ
9. Ⓨ Ⓝ
10. Ⓨ Ⓝ

___ / 10 Total

NAME: ____________________

DIRECTIONS Solve each problem.

SCORE

1. Ⓨ Ⓝ
2. Ⓨ Ⓝ
3. Ⓨ Ⓝ
4. Ⓨ Ⓝ
5. Ⓨ Ⓝ
6. Ⓨ Ⓝ
7. Ⓨ Ⓝ
8. Ⓨ Ⓝ
9. Ⓨ Ⓝ
10. Ⓨ Ⓝ

___ / 10
Total

1. 250 + 250 = ☐

2.

$$\begin{array}{r} 16 \\ \times\ \ 9 \\ \hline \end{array}$$

3. How many are in four groups of nineteen?

____

4. What is the next odd number after 452?

____

5. 20¢ + 50¢ + 5¢ = ________

6. 30 ÷ ☐ = 3

7. Show half past 2 on the clock.

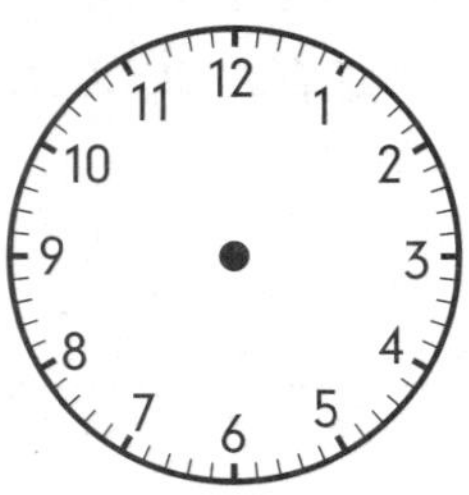

8. These bottles are filled with cups of sand. Which two bottles hold 35 cups altogether?

____

A B C

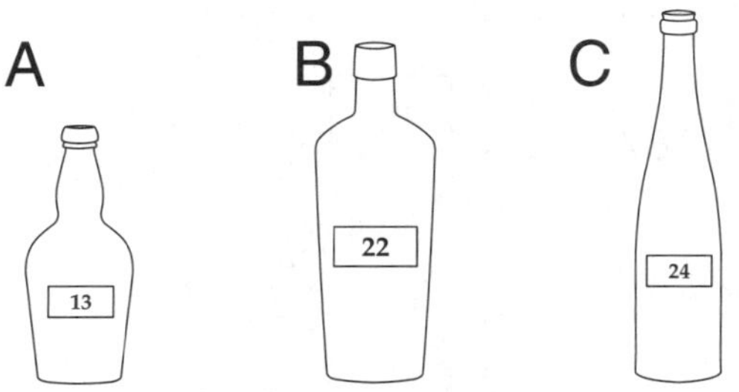

13 cups 22 cups 24 cups

9. Look at the capital X. Does it have perpendicular lines?

Circle: yes no

X

10. A koala can eat 9 leaves every hour. How many leaves can it eat in 3 hours?

____

NAME: ______________________________

DIRECTIONS Solve each problem.

1. What is the sum of 31 and 58?

____

2. 8 x 2 = ☐

3. Twenty times three is

______________________.

4. If you divide 40 apples equally among 10 groups, how many apples will each group get?

____

5. Color $\frac{3}{8}$ of the shape.

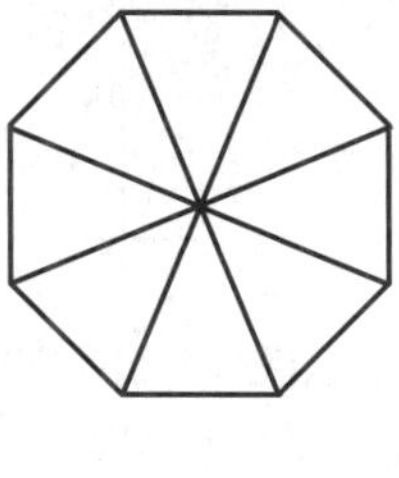

6. Fill in the missing number.

286, 291, 296, ________, 306

7. Does your teacher have a mass of more or less than a kilogram?

____

8. Show twenty minutes after eight on the clock below.

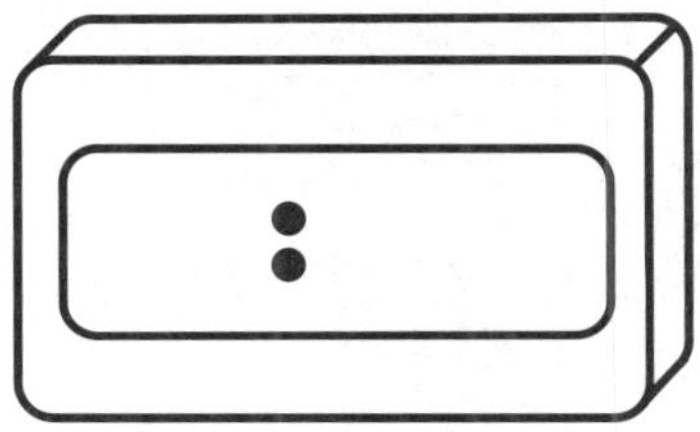

9. Draw the front and top views.

Solid	Front	Top
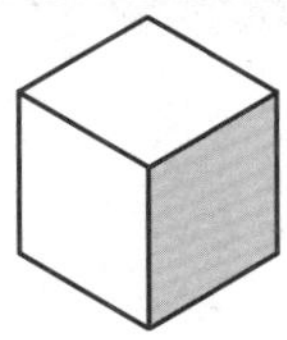		

10. Kim wants to give a Valentine's Day card to each of her 25 classmates. There are 10 cards in each box. How many boxes of cards will Kim need to buy?

____

SCORE

1. Ⓨ Ⓝ
2. Ⓨ Ⓝ
3. Ⓨ Ⓝ
4. Ⓨ Ⓝ
5. Ⓨ Ⓝ
6. Ⓨ Ⓝ
7. Ⓨ Ⓝ
8. Ⓨ Ⓝ
9. Ⓨ Ⓝ
10. Ⓨ Ⓝ

___ / 10

Total

DAY
112

NAME: ______________________

DIRECTIONS Solve each problem.

SCORE

1. Ⓨ Ⓝ
2. Ⓨ Ⓝ
3. Ⓨ Ⓝ
4. Ⓨ Ⓝ
5. Ⓨ Ⓝ
6. Ⓨ Ⓝ
7. Ⓨ Ⓝ
8. Ⓨ Ⓝ
9. Ⓨ Ⓝ
10. Ⓨ Ⓝ

___ / 10
Total

1. $20 - 11 = \square$

2. What is the product of four and ten?

____

3.
$$\begin{array}{r} 15 \\ \times \ \ 7 \\ \hline \end{array}$$

4. $7\overline{)630}$

5. Circle the largest number.

691   196   619

6. $9 \times \square = 27$

7. What time is shown below?

____

8. Circle the figure with the smaller area.

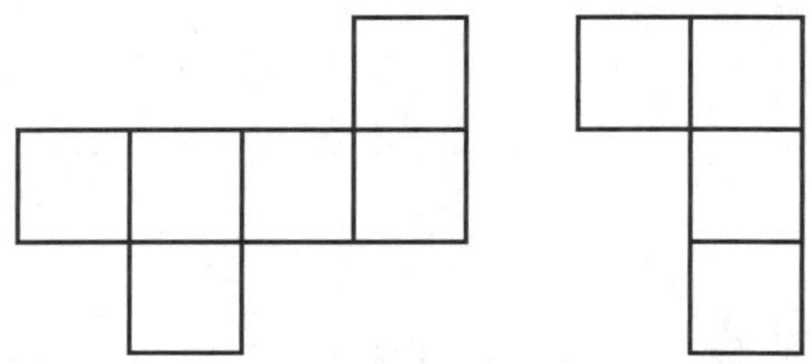

9. What is the range of pizzas sold each day?

____

Number of Pizzas Sold Each Day

Monday	Tuesday	Wednesday	Thursday	Friday	Saturday	Sunday
82	75	93	87	105	111	93

10. There are four red balls, six yellow balls, and two green balls in a box. What fraction of the balls are red?

____

NAME: ____________________

DIRECTIONS Solve each problem.

1. 4 + 4 + 4 + 4 + 4 + 4 =

____

2. 5 x 10 = ☐

3. 6 x 10 = ☐

4. 27 ÷ 3 = ☐

5. What fraction is shaded?

____

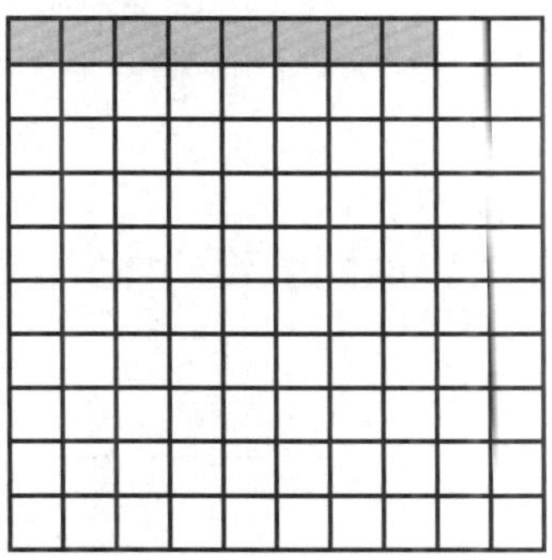

6. ☐ ÷ 5 = 17

7. Circle the solid that has less volume.

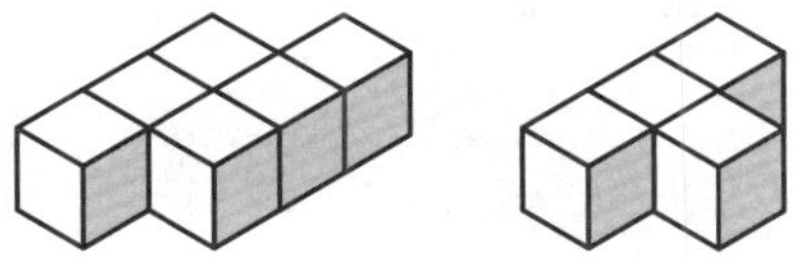

8. Measure the width of this page to the nearest centimeter.

____________________ cm

9. True or false? Parallel lines sometimes intersect.

____

10. Tony spent the same amount of time doing chores each night for a week. At the end of the week, he had spent 70 minutes doing chores. How many minutes did he spend doing chores each night?

____

SCORE

1. Ⓨ Ⓝ
2. Ⓨ Ⓝ
3. Ⓨ Ⓝ
4. Ⓨ Ⓝ
5. Ⓨ Ⓝ
6. Ⓨ Ⓝ
7. Ⓨ Ⓝ
8. Ⓨ Ⓝ
9. Ⓨ Ⓝ
10. Ⓨ Ⓝ

___ / 10 Total

DAY

114

NAME: ____________________

DIRECTIONS Solve each problem.

SCORE

1. Ⓨ Ⓝ
2. Ⓨ Ⓝ
3. Ⓨ Ⓝ
4. Ⓨ Ⓝ
5. Ⓨ Ⓝ
6. Ⓨ Ⓝ
7. Ⓨ Ⓝ
8. Ⓨ Ⓝ
9. Ⓨ Ⓝ
10. Ⓨ Ⓝ

___ / 10 Total

1. 800 – 600 = ☐

2.

$$\begin{array}{r} 11 \\ \times \ \ 3 \\ \hline \end{array}$$

3. What is the product of 2 and 14?

____

4. What is the next even number after 450?

____

5 What is the value of the digit 5 in the number 5,428?

____

6. 35 ☐ 17 = 18

7. Show a quarter to 3 on the clock.

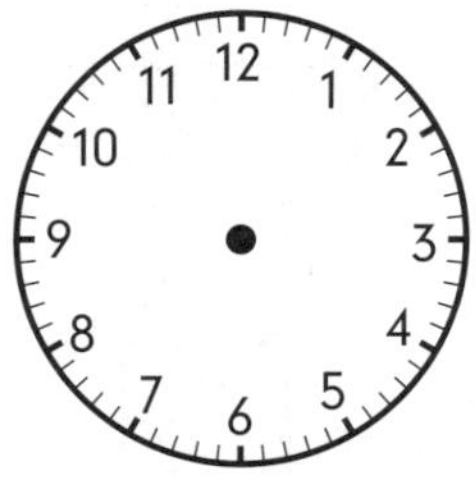

8. Record the area.

____________________ cm²

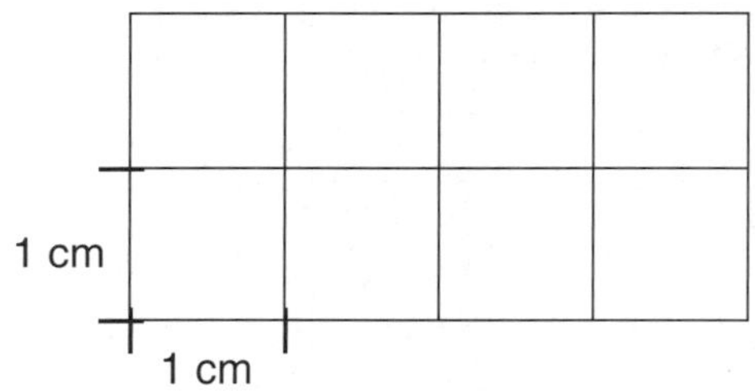

9. Name the shape of the cross-section.

____

10. What is 72 more than 87?

____

NAME: ______________________

DIRECTIONS Solve each problem.

SCORE

1. 24 + 9 = ☐

1. Ⓨ Ⓝ

2.
```
   5
x  4
----
```

2. Ⓨ Ⓝ

3.
```
  15
x  4
----
```

3. Ⓨ Ⓝ

4. Divide 36 by 4.

____

4. Ⓨ Ⓝ

5. How many quarters are there in $5.00?

____

5. Ⓨ Ⓝ

6. ☐ x 3 = 21

6. Ⓨ Ⓝ

7. Show half past 9 on the clock.

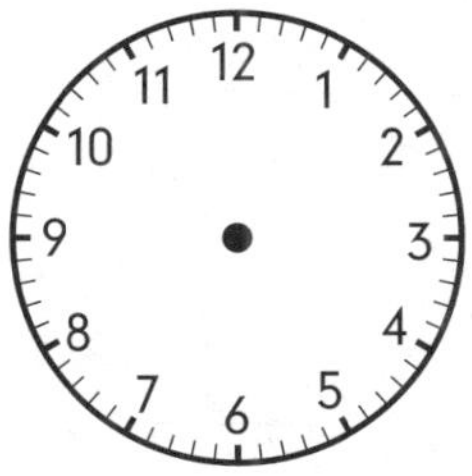

7. Ⓨ Ⓝ

8. What would you use to measure a pencil: inches or feet?

____

8. Ⓨ Ⓝ

9. How many edges does the solid below have?

____

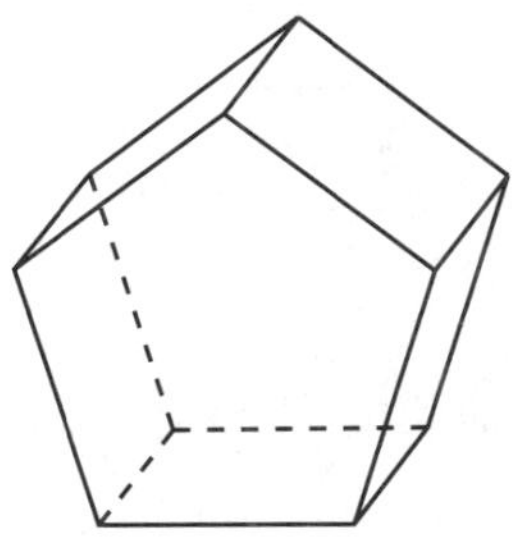

9. Ⓨ Ⓝ

10. Count by 3 beginning with 56.

56, ______, ______,

______, ______, ______

10. Ⓨ Ⓝ

___ / 10

Total

NAME: ____________________

DIRECTIONS Solve each problem.

1. $\begin{array}{r} 17 \\ +\ 43 \\ \hline \end{array}$

2. 2 x 10 = ☐

3. 2 x 11 = ☐

4. Write the numeral for eighty.

____

5. Circle the smaller fraction.

$\frac{3}{10}$ $\frac{6}{10}$

6. 67 + ☐ = 73

7. 100 cm = ________ m

8. Is a door taller or shorter than one foot?

____

9. Does the arrow point to a *face*, *vertex*, or *edge*?

____

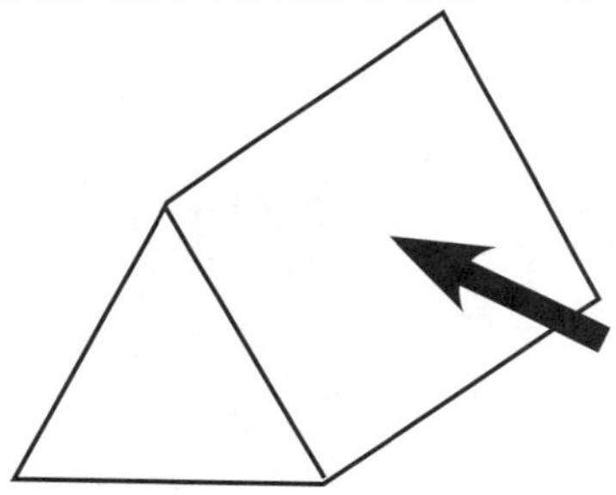

10. How much fencing is needed to enclose a yard with the dimensions shown below?

____

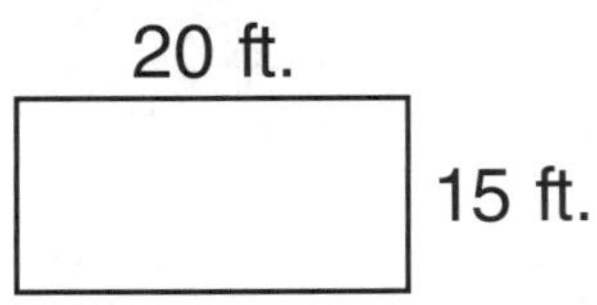

SCORE

1. Ⓨ Ⓝ
2. Ⓨ Ⓝ
3. Ⓨ Ⓝ
4. Ⓨ Ⓝ
5. Ⓨ Ⓝ
6. Ⓨ Ⓝ
7. Ⓨ Ⓝ
8. Ⓨ Ⓝ
9. Ⓨ Ⓝ
10. Ⓨ Ⓝ

___ / 10
Total

NAME: ____________________

DIRECTIONS Solve each problem.

1.
$$\begin{array}{r} 93 \\ -\ 22 \\ \hline \end{array}$$

2. How many points are there on 2 stars?

____

3.
$$\begin{array}{r} 16 \\ \times\ \ 3 \\ \hline \end{array}$$

4. $4\overline{)20}$

5. What number is 2 hundred less than 738?

____

6. 6 ☐ 2 = 3

7. Circle the object that weighs less than one pound.

8. Show twenty minutes before 3 on the clock.

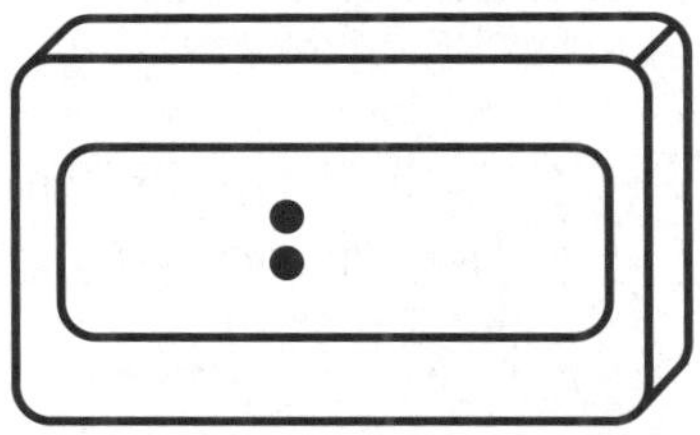

9. Name the lines below.

____

10. Can three pyramids be stacked on top of each other?

Circle: yes no

SCORE

1. Ⓨ Ⓝ
2. Ⓨ Ⓝ
3. Ⓨ Ⓝ
4. Ⓨ Ⓝ
5. Ⓨ Ⓝ
6. Ⓨ Ⓝ
7. Ⓨ Ⓝ
8. Ⓨ Ⓝ
9. Ⓨ Ⓝ
10. Ⓨ Ⓝ

___ / 10
Total

DAY
118

NAME: ______________________________

DIRECTIONS Solve each problem.

SCORE
1. Ⓨ Ⓝ
2. Ⓨ Ⓝ
3. Ⓨ Ⓝ
4. Ⓨ Ⓝ
5. Ⓨ Ⓝ
6. Ⓨ Ⓝ
7. Ⓨ Ⓝ
8. Ⓨ Ⓝ
9. Ⓨ Ⓝ
10. Ⓨ Ⓝ
___ / 10 Total

1. 4 plus 6 is ________.

2. 3 x 5 = ☐

3. How many are in seven groups of 0?

____

4. What number follows 829?

____

5. Circle the number that has a 2 in the hundreds place.

526 372 298

6. Fill in the missing number.

210, 240, ________, 300, 330

7. Write the time in words.

____

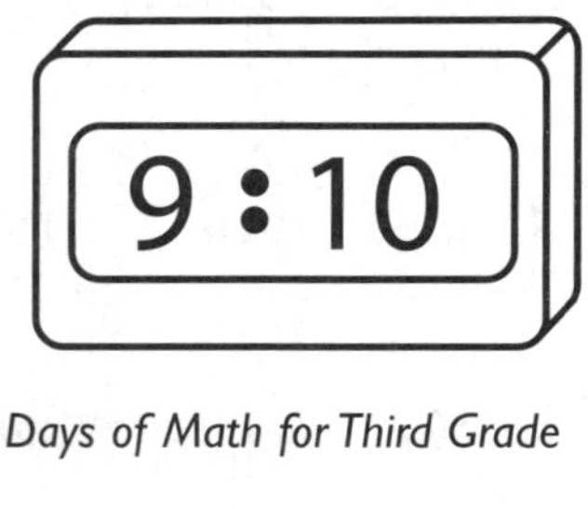

8. Circle the item that most likely weighs about 1 pound.

9. Draw the mirror image along the line of symmetry.

10. The digit in the hundreds place is 2 less than the digit in the tens place. The digit in the tens place is 1 more than the digit in the ones place. The digit in the ones place is 5. What is the number?

____

NAME: ____________________

DIRECTIONS Solve each problem.

1. The sum of 152 and 77 is

____________________.

2. 3 x 8 = ☐

3. 30 x 8 = ☐

4. Divide 25 by 5.

____

5. Add 25¢ to the coins below. What is the total value?

____

6. 42 – ☐ = 16

7. These bottles are filled with cups of sand. Which 2 bottles hold 46 cups altogether?

____

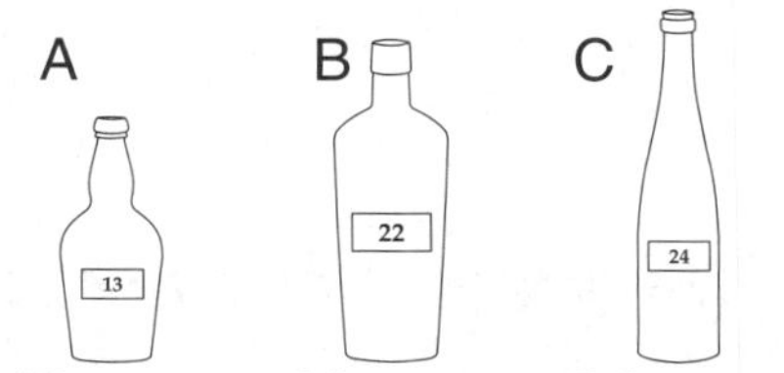

13 cups 22 cups 24 cups

8. Show two thirty on the clock.

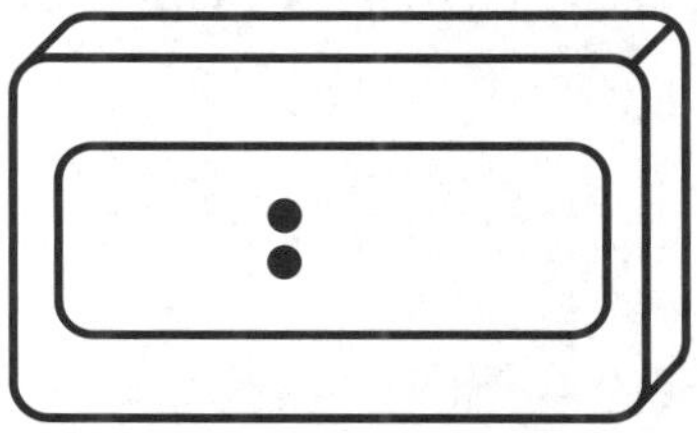

9. Match the solid to its front and side views.

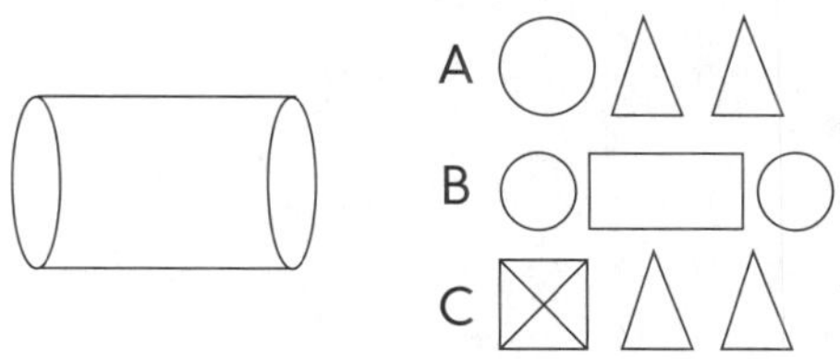

10. Larry plans to buy 20 baseball cards. The cards cost 25¢ each. How much will Larry spend on baseball cards?

____

SCORE

1. Ⓨ Ⓝ
2. Ⓨ Ⓝ
3. Ⓨ Ⓝ
4. Ⓨ Ⓝ
5. Ⓨ Ⓝ
6. Ⓨ Ⓝ
7. Ⓨ Ⓝ
8. Ⓨ Ⓝ
9. Ⓨ Ⓝ
10. Ⓨ Ⓝ

___ / 10 Total

DAY

120

NAME: ______________________________

DIRECTIONS Solve each problem.

SCORE

1. Ⓨ Ⓝ
2. Ⓨ Ⓝ
3. Ⓨ Ⓝ
4. Ⓨ Ⓝ
5. Ⓨ Ⓝ
6. Ⓨ Ⓝ
7. Ⓨ Ⓝ
8. Ⓨ Ⓝ
9. Ⓨ Ⓝ
10. Ⓨ Ⓝ

___ / 10 Total

1.

$$\begin{array}{r} 68 \\ -\ 41 \\ \hline \end{array}$$

2. 10 x 3 = ☐

3. The product of 7 and 3 is

______________________.

4. What number follows 729?

____

5. 50¢ + 50¢ + 25¢ = ________

6. 30 ÷ ☐ = 10

7. Circle the container that holds less than 1 liter.

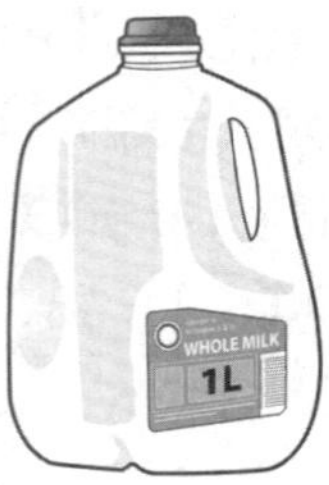

8. Measure the height of this page to the nearest centimeter.

______________ cm

9. Create a tally chart with the following information.

Thirty-two people love to go to the beach. Seventeen people love to go to the mountains. Twenty-three people love to go to the desert.

Favorite Vacation Spots

Beach	
Mountains	
Desert	

10. Kenny takes 24 steps from his kitchen to his bedroom. His dad can walk from the kitchen to Kenny's bedroom in half as many steps as Kenny. How many steps does it take Kenny's dad to walk from the kitchen to Kenny's bedroom?

____

NAME: ____________________

DIRECTIONS Solve each problem.

1. 18 + 6 = ☐

2.
$$\begin{array}{r} 24 \\ \times\ \ 5 \\ \hline \end{array}$$

3. How many paws are on 3 dogs?

____

4. There is a group of triangles with a total of 15 sides. How many triangles are there?

____

5. Which is larger: $\frac{17}{100}$ or $\frac{27}{100}$?

____

6. ☐ x 5 = 35

7. Does a sheet of paper have a mass of more or less than one kilogram?

____

8. It is 7:20. What time will it be in 20 minutes?

____

9. List the angles in order from smallest to largest.

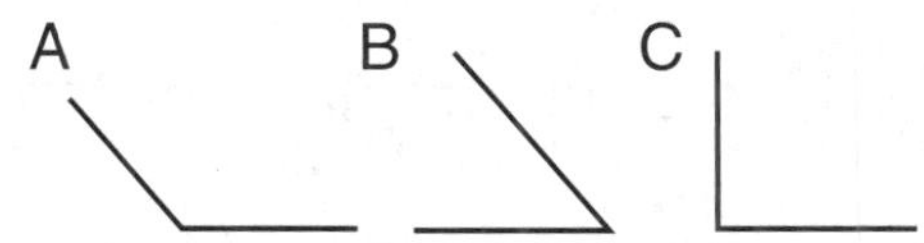

____

10. If you add 71 to me, you get 100. What number am I?

____

SCORE

1. Ⓨ Ⓝ
2. Ⓨ Ⓝ
3. Ⓨ Ⓝ
4. Ⓨ Ⓝ
5. Ⓨ Ⓝ
6. Ⓨ Ⓝ
7. Ⓨ Ⓝ
8. Ⓨ Ⓝ
9. Ⓨ Ⓝ
10. Ⓨ Ⓝ

___ / 10 Total

DAY 122

NAME: ____________________

DIRECTIONS Solve each problem.

SCORE

1. Ⓨ Ⓝ
2. Ⓨ Ⓝ
3. Ⓨ Ⓝ
4. Ⓨ Ⓝ
5. Ⓨ Ⓝ
6. Ⓨ Ⓝ
7. Ⓨ Ⓝ
8. Ⓨ Ⓝ
9. Ⓨ Ⓝ
10. Ⓨ Ⓝ

___ / 10 Total

1.

$$\begin{array}{r} 25 \\ -\ 19 \\ \hline \end{array}$$

2. Draw an array with six rows of four.

3. 5 x 4 = ☐

4. What is the ordinal number right before 237th?

____

5. Circle the smallest number.

2,417 2,147 2,471

6. 64 + ☐ = 90

7. What time is shown on the clock?

____

8. Circle the smaller area.

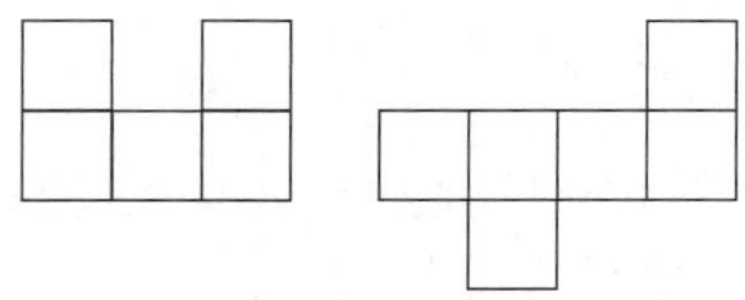

9. Name the lines.

____

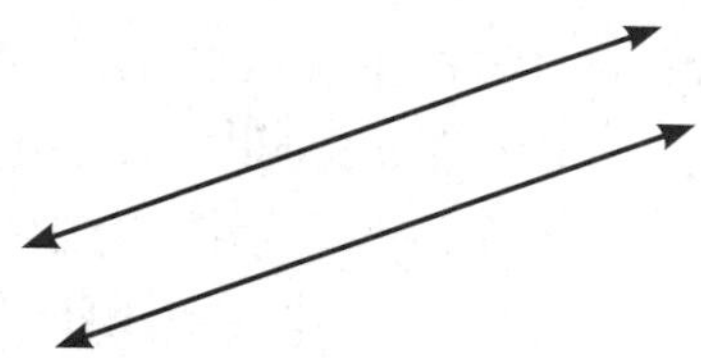

10. Sheldon has saved $82.45. He gets $15.00 for his birthday. How much money does Sheldon have now?

____

NAME: ______________________

DIRECTIONS Solve each problem.

SCORE

1. The sum of 7, 14, and 33 is

______________________.

2. Six times ten is _______.

3.

$$\begin{array}{r} 18 \\ \times \ \ 3 \\ \hline \end{array}$$

4. 15 ÷ 3 = ☐

5. What is the value of the digit 7 in the number 6,742?

____

6. Fill in the missing number.

493, 498, _______, 508, 513

7. How many cubic centimeters are in the solid?

______________ cm^3

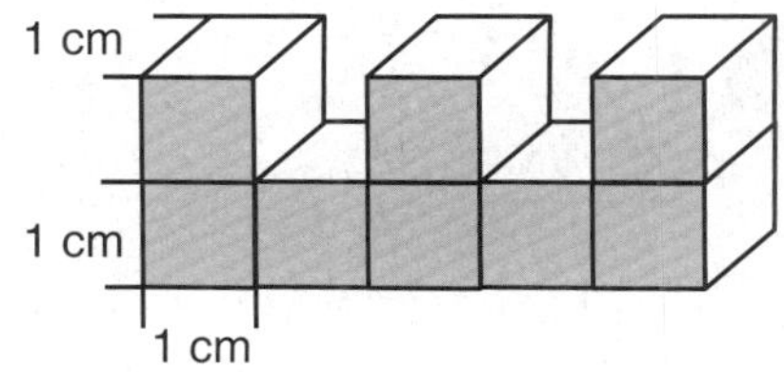

8. 12 inches = _______ foot

9. Name the shape of the cross-section.

____

10. Each row, column, and diagonal has the same sum. Complete the magic square using the numbers 1–9 only once.

		8
	5	
2		4

1. Ⓨ Ⓝ
2. Ⓨ Ⓝ
3. Ⓨ Ⓝ
4. Ⓨ Ⓝ
5. Ⓨ Ⓝ
6. Ⓨ Ⓝ
7. Ⓨ Ⓝ
8. Ⓨ Ⓝ
9. Ⓨ Ⓝ
10. Ⓨ Ⓝ

___ / 10

Total

DAY 124

NAME: ____________________

DIRECTIONS Solve each problem.

SCORE

1. Ⓨ Ⓝ
2. Ⓨ Ⓝ
3. Ⓨ Ⓝ
4. Ⓨ Ⓝ
5. Ⓨ Ⓝ
6. Ⓨ Ⓝ
7. Ⓨ Ⓝ
8. Ⓨ Ⓝ
9. Ⓨ Ⓝ
10. Ⓨ Ⓝ

___ / 10 Total

1. 18 + 44 = ______

2.

$$\begin{array}{r} 26 \\ \times \;\; 3 \\ \hline \end{array}$$

3. How many toes are there on 4 people?

____

4. If 10 dollars are shared equally among 5 people, how much money will each person get?

____

5. Add 4 tens to 478.

____

6. 6 x ☐ = 36

7. Show thirty minutes after one on the clock.

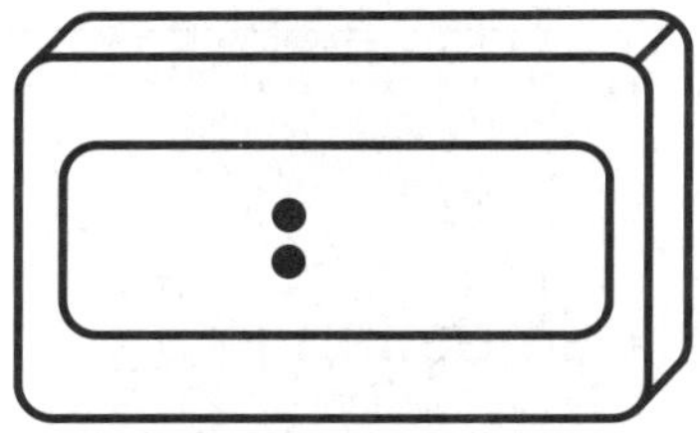

8. Show two forty-five on the clock.

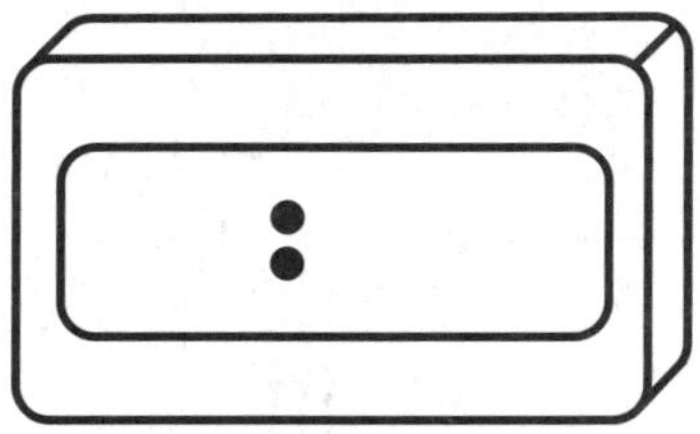

9. Draw the line of symmetry on the capital A.

A

10. Which letter is in the circle and triangle, but not in the square?

____

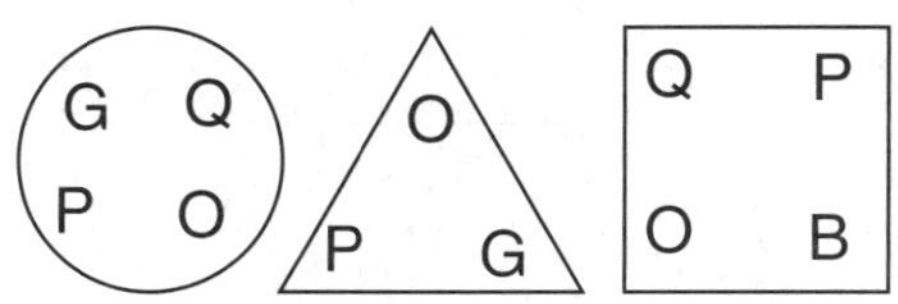

NAME: ____________________________

DIRECTIONS Solve each problem.

SCORE

1. Ⓨ Ⓝ
2. Ⓨ Ⓝ
3. Ⓨ Ⓝ
4. Ⓨ Ⓝ
5. Ⓨ Ⓝ
6. Ⓨ Ⓝ
7. Ⓨ Ⓝ
8. Ⓨ Ⓝ
9. Ⓨ Ⓝ
10. Ⓨ Ⓝ

___ / 10 Total

1.

$$\begin{array}{r} 87 \\ -\ 35 \\ \hline \end{array}$$

2. Draw an array with 7 rows of 3.

3.

$$\begin{array}{r} 14 \\ \times\ \ 7 \\ \hline \end{array}$$

4. If 27 stickers are divided equally among 3 children, how many stickers will each child get?

____

5. What is the value of the digit 3 in the number 348?

____

6. 35 ☐ 5 = 7

7. Show half past 11 on the clock.

8. How many milk jugs can be poured into the bucket?

____

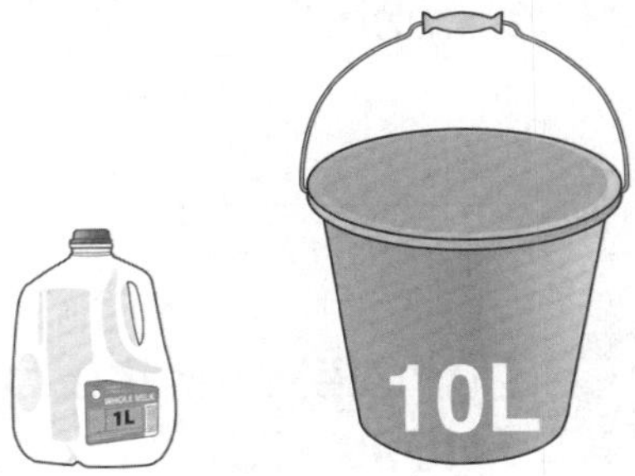

9. Name two quadrilaterals.

____

____

10. List two numbers that have a sum of 56.

____

NAME: ____________________

DIRECTIONS Solve each problem.

SCORE

1. Ⓨ Ⓝ
2. Ⓨ Ⓝ
3. Ⓨ Ⓝ
4. Ⓨ Ⓝ
5. Ⓨ Ⓝ
6. Ⓨ Ⓝ
7. Ⓨ Ⓝ
8. Ⓨ Ⓝ
9. Ⓨ Ⓝ
10. Ⓨ Ⓝ

___ / 10
Total

1. 32 – 18 = ☐

2. 5 x 6 = ☐

3. 50 x 6 = ☐

4. Is 233 an even or an odd number?

____

5. Complete for the number 1,409:

_____ thousands

_____ hundreds

_____ tens

_____ ones

6. You have a total of 24 kids to be divided equally into 6 groups. How many kids will be in each group?

____

7. Show a quarter to 7 on the clock.

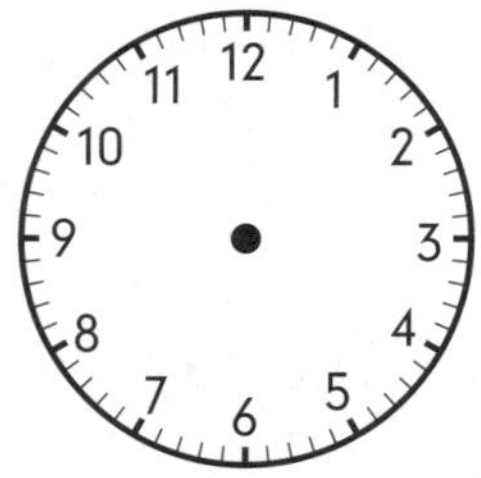

8. How many inches are there in 2 feet?

____

9. Draw the front and top views.

Solid	Front	Top
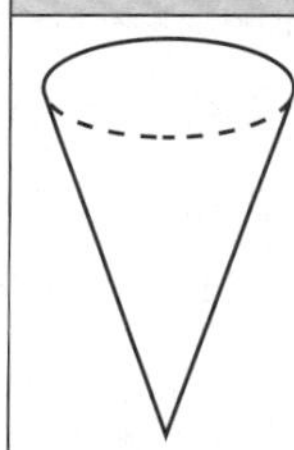		

10. Half of the candies in a jar are gumdrops. One-fourth of the candies are chocolates. There are 4 lollipops. There is an equal number of lollipops and chocolates. How many gumdrops are there?

____

DAY 127

NAME: ____________________

DIRECTIONS Solve each problem.

1.
$$\begin{array}{r} 31 \\ +\ 30 \\ \hline \end{array}$$

2. What is the product of 2 and 9?

____

3. 6 x 8 = ☐

4. $7 \overline{)35}$

5. Circle the grid that has the smaller fraction shaded.

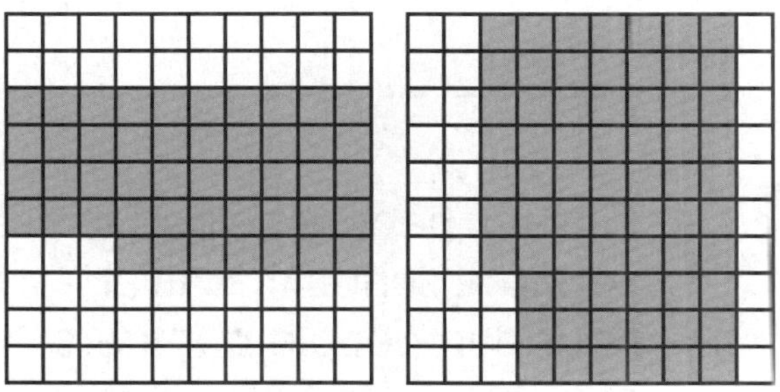

6. Fill in the missing number.

420, 480, ________, 600, 660

7. Write the time shown on the clock in words.

____

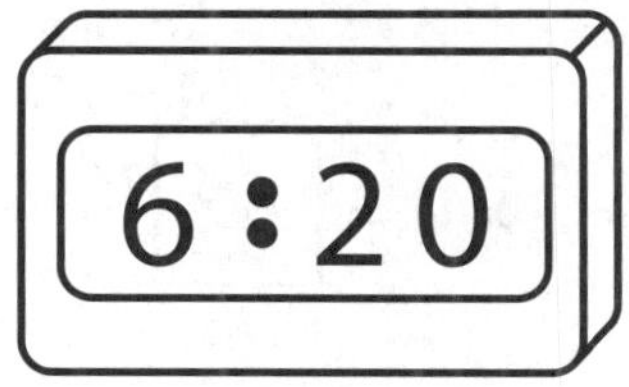

8. Circle the solid that has the greater volume.

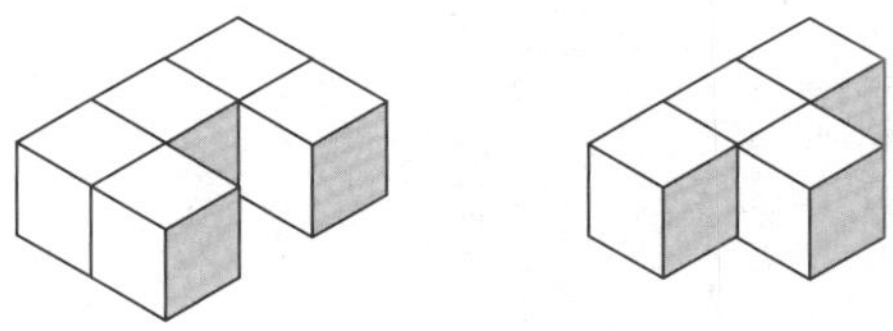

9. Circle the right angle.

10. Eighty-two third graders and 9 chaperones are going on a field trip. Each bus can hold 50 people. How many buses are needed for the field trip?

____

SCORE

1. Ⓨ Ⓝ
2. Ⓨ Ⓝ
3. Ⓨ Ⓝ
4. Ⓨ Ⓝ
5. Ⓨ Ⓝ
6. Ⓨ Ⓝ
7. Ⓨ Ⓝ
8. Ⓨ Ⓝ
9. Ⓨ Ⓝ
10. Ⓨ Ⓝ

___ / 10
Total

DAY
128

NAME: ______________________________

DIRECTIONS Solve each problem.

SCORE

1. Ⓨ Ⓝ
2. Ⓨ Ⓝ
3. Ⓨ Ⓝ
4. Ⓨ Ⓝ
5. Ⓨ Ⓝ
6. Ⓨ Ⓝ
7. Ⓨ Ⓝ
8. Ⓨ Ⓝ
9. Ⓨ Ⓝ
10. Ⓨ Ⓝ

___ / 10
Total

1. $19 - 12 = \square$

2. $7 \times 9 = \square$

3.

$$\begin{array}{r} 82 \\ \times \quad 3 \\ \hline \end{array}$$

4. What is the numeral for three hundred sixty-six?

____

5. What is my change from $2.00 if I spend $1.75?

____

6. $36 + \square = 48$

7. ________ inches = 1 foot

8. These bottles are filled with cups of sand. List the bottles in order from largest to smallest.

____

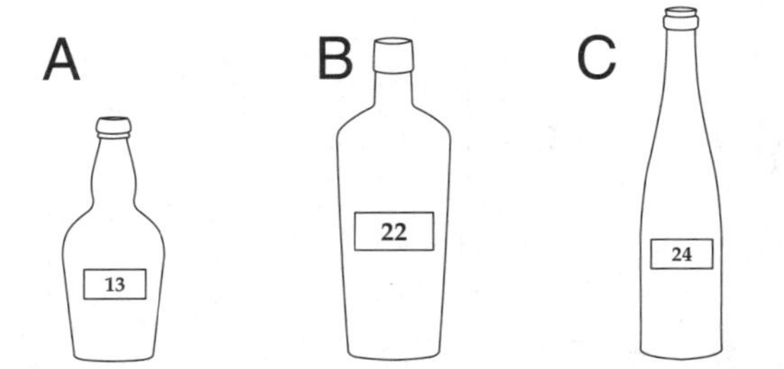

13 cups 22 cups 24 cups

9. Circle the parallelogram.

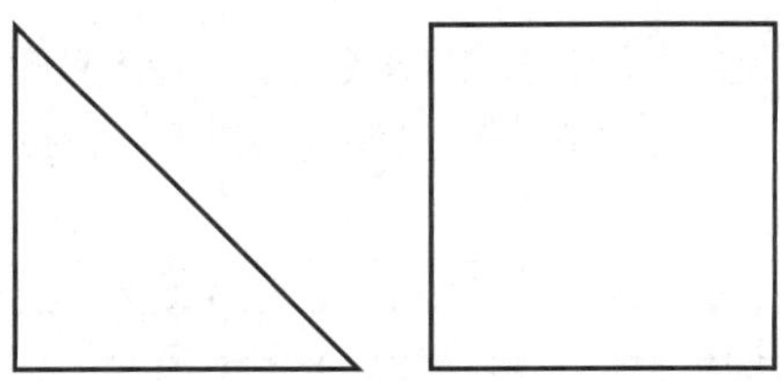

10. Fifty-six people helped to set up a school carnival. Fourteen people got there at 7:00 A.M. to help. The rest got there at 8:00 A.M. How many people got there at 8:00 A.M.?

____

DAY 129

NAME: ____________________

DIRECTIONS Solve each problem.

1. What is the sum of 26 and 54?

____

2.

$$\begin{array}{r} 10 \\ \times \ 8 \\ \hline \end{array}$$

3. There are 3 rows of 8 stars. How many stars are there?

____

4. How many groups of 3 are there in 27?

____

5. 50¢ – 35¢ = ________

6. ☐ x 6 = 54

7. It is 1:10. What time will it be in 20 minutes?

____

8. Write the line length.

____

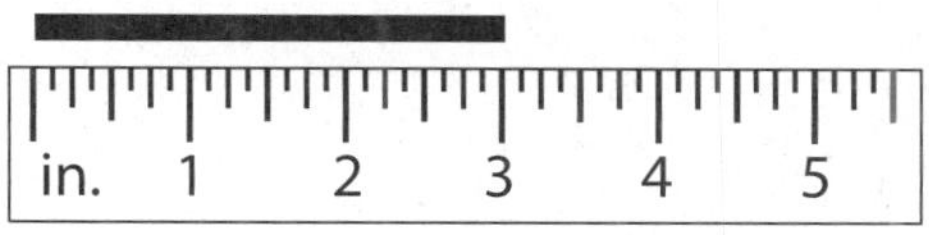

9. Create a picture graph with the following information.
Fifty people like pepperoni.
Twenty people like pineapple.
Forty people like cheese.

Favorite Pizza Toppings

Pepperoni	
Pineapple	
Cheese	

 = 10 people

10. Atherton Elementary School has four hundred forty-three students in kindergarten through third grade. One hundred six are in kindergarten. Ninety-nine are in first grade. One hundred twenty-five are in second grade. How many students are in third grade?

____

SCORE

1. Ⓨ Ⓝ
2. Ⓨ Ⓝ
3. Ⓨ Ⓝ
4. Ⓨ Ⓝ
5. Ⓨ Ⓝ
6. Ⓨ Ⓝ
7. Ⓨ Ⓝ
8. Ⓨ Ⓝ
9. Ⓨ Ⓝ
10. Ⓨ Ⓝ

___ / 10 Total

DAY 130

NAME: ______________________________

DIRECTIONS Solve each problem.

SCORE

1. Ⓨ Ⓝ
2. Ⓨ Ⓝ
3. Ⓨ Ⓝ
4. Ⓨ Ⓝ
5. Ⓨ Ⓝ
6. Ⓨ Ⓝ
7. Ⓨ Ⓝ
8. Ⓨ Ⓝ
9. Ⓨ Ⓝ
10. Ⓨ Ⓝ

___ / 10
Total

1.
$$\begin{array}{r} 93 \\ -\ 42 \\ \hline \end{array}$$

2. 6 x 8 = ☐

3. Four times two is_______.

4. What number follows 692?

____

5. 50¢ – 15¢ = _______

6. 36 + ☐ = 90

7. Circle the object that weighs more than one pound.

8. Does a pencil weigh more or less than one kilogram?

____

9. Name the lines.

____

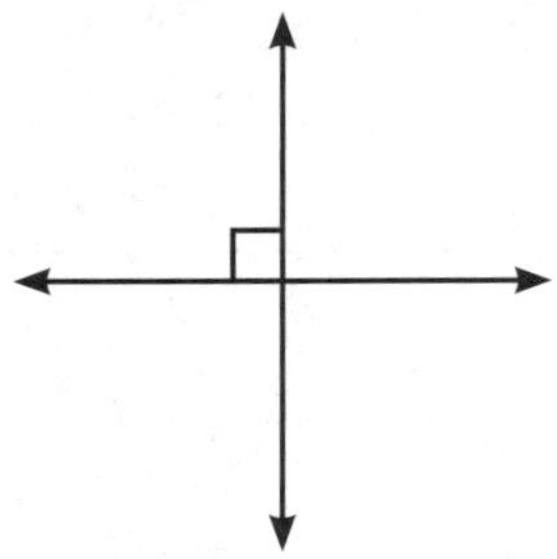

10. Daisy has 49 stickers. She wants to give an equal number of stickers to each of her 7 friends. How many stickers will each friend get?

____

DAY 131

NAME: ______________________________

DIRECTIONS Solve each problem.

1. 87 – 34 = ☐

2.

$$\begin{array}{r} 80 \\ \times\ 2 \\ \hline \end{array}$$

3. Ninety times two is

______________________.

4. 27 ÷ 3 = ☐

5. $\frac{1}{8}$ of 16 is _______.

6. 32 ☐ 2 = 16

7. Write the time shown below.

____

8. Record the area.

__________________ cm²

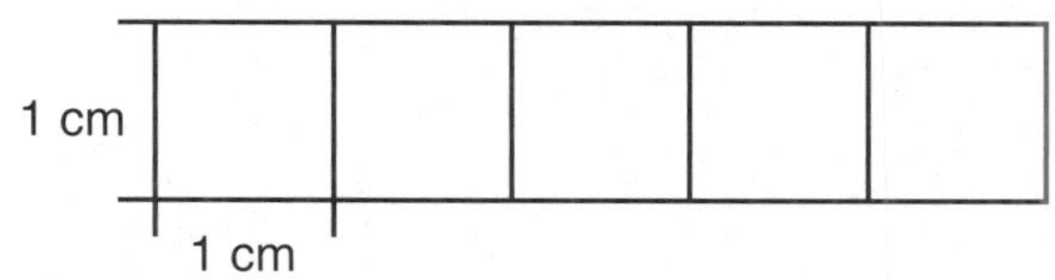

9. Name the shape of the cross-section.

____

10. What is the smallest number that can be made using the digits 3, 8, 6, and 2?

____

SCORE

1. Ⓨ Ⓝ
2. Ⓨ Ⓝ
3. Ⓨ Ⓝ
4. Ⓨ Ⓝ
5. Ⓨ Ⓝ
6. Ⓨ Ⓝ
7. Ⓨ Ⓝ
8. Ⓨ Ⓝ
9. Ⓨ Ⓝ
10. Ⓨ Ⓝ

___ / 10

Total

DAY
132

NAME: ____________________

DIRECTIONS Solve each problem.

SCORE

1. Ⓨ Ⓝ
2. Ⓨ Ⓝ
3. Ⓨ Ⓝ
4. Ⓨ Ⓝ
5. Ⓨ Ⓝ
6. Ⓨ Ⓝ
7. Ⓨ Ⓝ
8. Ⓨ Ⓝ
9. Ⓨ Ⓝ
10. Ⓨ Ⓝ

___ / 10
Total

1. 19 + 9 = ☐

2. 7 x 2 = ☐

3. 70 x 2 = ☐

4. What is the next even number after 434?

____

5. Add 2 nickels to the coins below and write the total.

____

6. Fill in the missing number.

264, 268, ________, 276, 280

7. How many minutes are there in 2 hours?

____

8. Circle the container that holds more than 1 liter.

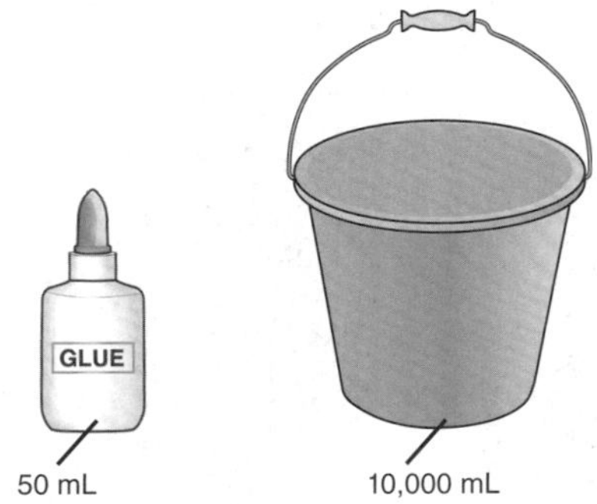

9. How many angles are there in a pentagon?

____

10. Nicole gets $12.00 in allowance each week. She saves $4.00 of it and spends the rest. How much does she spend in 4 weeks?

____

NAME: ______________________________

DIRECTIONS Solve each problem.

1.
$$\begin{array}{r} 30 \\ -\ 14 \\ \hline \end{array}$$

2. How many wheels are there on 6 bikes?

____

3. 8 x 9 = ☐

4. $6\overline{)60}$

5. 7 tens and 2 ones =

____

6. 43 – ☐ = 9

7. What would you use to measure the height of a door: inches or liters?

____

8. What is the volume of the solid?

______________________ cm³

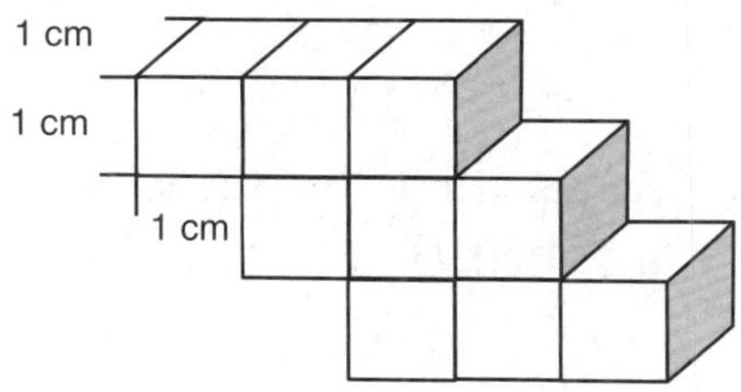

9. True or false? Parallel lines meet at a right angle.

____

10. Double eighty-four, then calculate half of that number.

____

SCORE

1. Ⓨ Ⓝ
2. Ⓨ Ⓝ
3. Ⓨ Ⓝ
4. Ⓨ Ⓝ
5. Ⓨ Ⓝ
6. Ⓨ Ⓝ
7. Ⓨ Ⓝ
8. Ⓨ Ⓝ
9. Ⓨ Ⓝ
10. Ⓨ Ⓝ

___ / 10
Total

DAY 134

NAME: ______________________________

DIRECTIONS Solve each problem.

SCORE

1. Ⓨ Ⓝ
2. Ⓨ Ⓝ
3. Ⓨ Ⓝ
4. Ⓨ Ⓝ
5. Ⓨ Ⓝ
6. Ⓨ Ⓝ
7. Ⓨ Ⓝ
8. Ⓨ Ⓝ
9. Ⓨ Ⓝ
10. Ⓨ Ⓝ

___ / 10 Total

1.

$$\begin{array}{r} 16 \\ 15 \\ +\ 14 \\ \hline \end{array}$$

2. How many fingers are on 4 hands?

____

3. $9 \times 6 = \square$

4. Make tally marks for the number 6.

5. $1.00 – 65¢ = ________

6. If 6 pieces of candy cost 24¢, how much do two pieces of candy cost?

____

7. Show fifteen minutes after 2:00 on the clock.

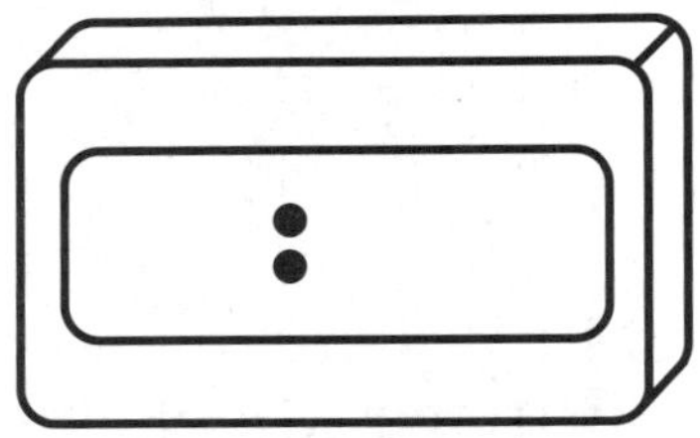

8. Does a teaspoon hold more than or less than 1 liter?

____

9. Match the solid to its top, front, and side views.

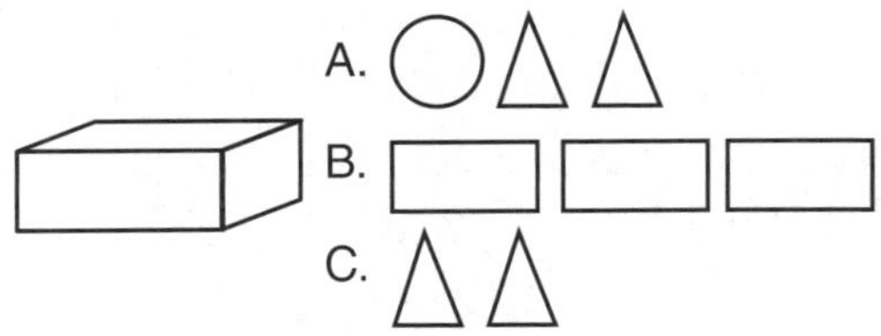

10. Juan has 26 marbles. He loses 3. Mark gives him 5. He trades 4 of his marbles for 3 of Sam's. How many marbles does Juan have now?

____

NAME: ____________________

DIRECTIONS Solve each problem.

1. What is 7 more than 12?

____

2.

$$\begin{array}{r} 15 \\ \times\ 6 \\ \hline \end{array}$$

3. Draw an array of 5 rows of 9.

4. Divide 6 into 18.

____

5. 50¢ – 25¢ = ________

6. 14 + 3 + ☐ = 27

7. True or false? A handprint has an area of more than 1 m^2.

____

8. Circle the smaller shape.

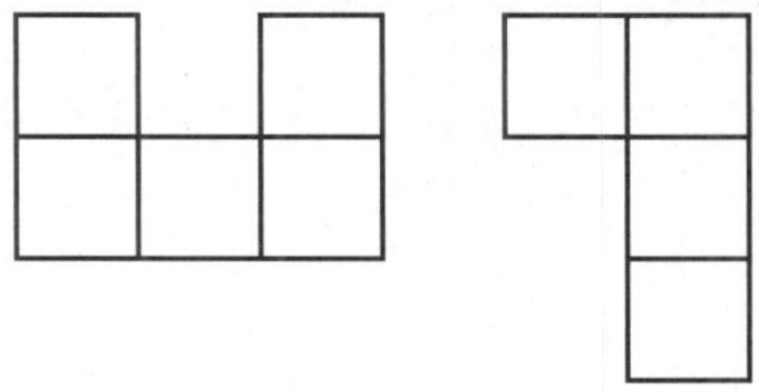

9. How many more people have been to the Grand Canyon than to Hawaii?

____

Places Visited

Grand Canyon	132
New York City	214
Hawaii	83

10. A child's step is about 12 inches long. If a child walks 3 yards, how many steps will the child take?

____

SCORE

1. Ⓨ Ⓝ
2. Ⓨ Ⓝ
3. Ⓨ Ⓝ
4. Ⓨ Ⓝ
5. Ⓨ Ⓝ
6. Ⓨ Ⓝ
7. Ⓨ Ⓝ
8. Ⓨ Ⓝ
9. Ⓨ Ⓝ
10. Ⓨ Ⓝ

___ / 10 Total

DAY
136

NAME: ____________________

DIRECTIONS Solve each problem.

SCORE

1. Ⓨ Ⓝ
2. Ⓨ Ⓝ
3. Ⓨ Ⓝ
4. Ⓨ Ⓝ
5. Ⓨ Ⓝ
6. Ⓨ Ⓝ
7. Ⓨ Ⓝ
8. Ⓨ Ⓝ
9. Ⓨ Ⓝ
10. Ⓨ Ⓝ

___ / 10
Total

1.
$$\begin{array}{r} 20 \\ -\ 17 \\ \hline \end{array}$$

2. 7 x 30 = ☐

3. What is the product of 6 and 6?

____

4. What is the odd number right before 727?

____

5. Does $\frac{1}{2}$ equal $\frac{4}{8}$?

Circle: yes no

6. 5 x ☐ = 30

7. Show half past 1:00 on the clock.

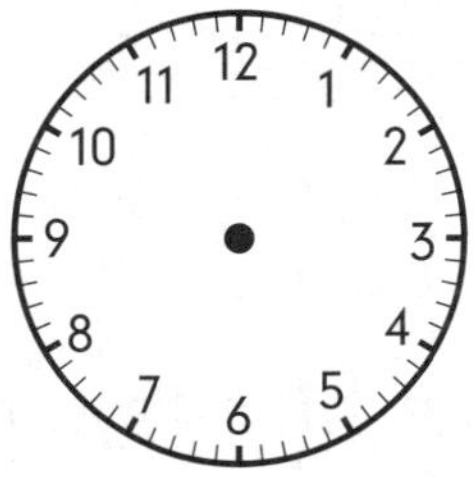

8. How many minutes are there from 10:50 A.M. to 11:10 A.M.?

____

9. Are there perpendicular lines in the capital K?

____

K

10. Twelve children are doing a tap dance act in the talent show. How many total pairs of shoes will they be wearing?

____

DAY
137

NAME: ____________________________

DIRECTIONS Solve each problem.

1. What is the sum of 5, 16, and 35?

____

2. Nine times three is

____________________.

3.

$$\begin{array}{r} 45 \\ \times \ \ 6 \\ \hline \end{array}$$

4. 54 ÷ 6 = ☐

5. What is the value of the digit 9 in the number 4,934?

____

6. 14 ☐ 8 = 22

7. 1 gallon = _______ quarts

8. What unit of time is used to measure how long it takes to complete this page?

____

9. Circle the parallelogram.

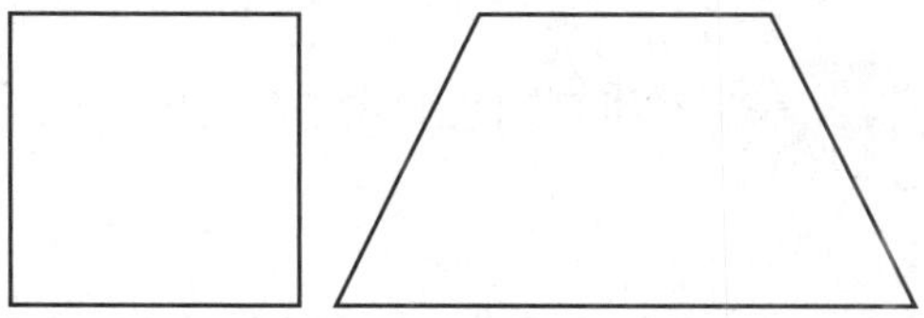

10. You have a gallon of juice. How many cups of juice can you pour?

____

SCORE

1. Ⓨ Ⓝ
2. Ⓨ Ⓝ
3. Ⓨ Ⓝ
4. Ⓨ Ⓝ
5. Ⓨ Ⓝ
6. Ⓨ Ⓝ
7. Ⓨ Ⓝ
8. Ⓨ Ⓝ
9. Ⓨ Ⓝ
10. Ⓨ Ⓝ

___ / 10
Total

DAY 138

NAME: ____________________

DIRECTIONS Solve each problem.

SCORE

1. Ⓨ Ⓝ
2. Ⓨ Ⓝ
3. Ⓨ Ⓝ
4. Ⓨ Ⓝ
5. Ⓨ Ⓝ
6. Ⓨ Ⓝ
7. Ⓨ Ⓝ
8. Ⓨ Ⓝ
9. Ⓨ Ⓝ
10. Ⓨ Ⓝ

___ / 10 Total

1. 30 – 18 = ☐

2. How many hands are there on 8 children?

____

3. 8 x 9 = ☐

4. What number follows 719?

____

5. Write 248 in expanded notation.

____

6. Fill in the missing number.

317, 312, 307, ________, 297

7. True or false? A pen has a mass greater than 1 kg.

____

8. 4 cups = ________ quart

9. Draw all the lines of symmetry.

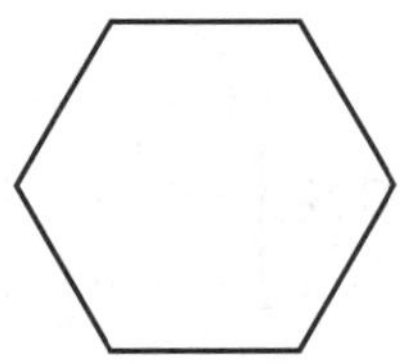

10. Jacqueline has 15 outfits in her closet. One-third of the outfits are dressy clothes for fancy occasions. How many dressy outfits does Jacqueline have?

____

NAME: ____________________

DIRECTIONS Solve each problem.

1. 43 + 17 = ☐

2. 3 x 7 = ☐

3. 30 x 7 = ☐

4. $6\overline{)36}$

5. 100 + 60 + 5 = ☐

6. 16 ÷ ☐ = 4

7. How many times can the 12-liter bucket be filled by the 1-liter cube?

____

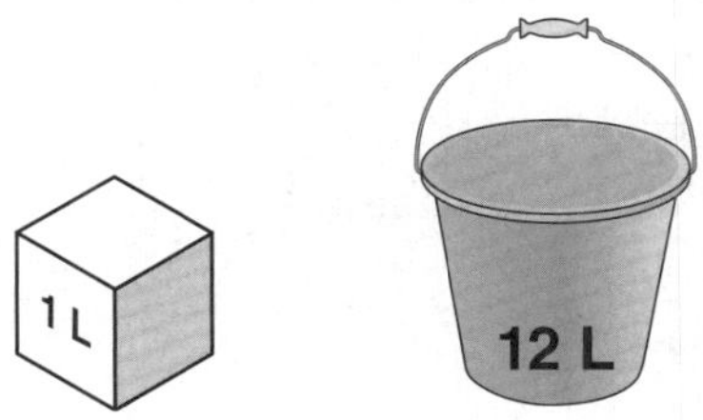

8. Measure the line length.

____

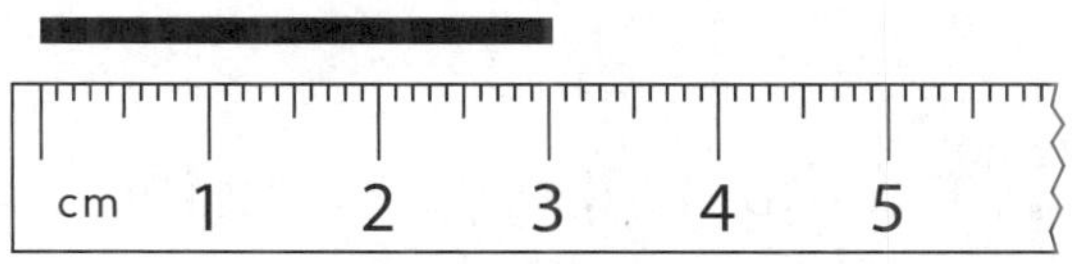

9. Draw a rectangular prism.

10. Which is larger: 545 or 554?

____

SCORE

1. Ⓨ Ⓝ
2. Ⓨ Ⓝ
3. Ⓨ Ⓝ
4. Ⓨ Ⓝ
5. Ⓨ Ⓝ
6. Ⓨ Ⓝ
7. Ⓨ Ⓝ
8. Ⓨ Ⓝ
9. Ⓨ Ⓝ
10. Ⓨ Ⓝ

___ / 10
Total

DAY
140

NAME: ____________________

DIRECTIONS Solve each problem.

SCORE

1. Ⓨ Ⓝ
2. Ⓨ Ⓝ
3. Ⓨ Ⓝ
4. Ⓨ Ⓝ
5. Ⓨ Ⓝ
6. Ⓨ Ⓝ
7. Ⓨ Ⓝ
8. Ⓨ Ⓝ
9. Ⓨ Ⓝ
10. Ⓨ Ⓝ

___ / 10
Total

1. What is ten less than twenty-six?

____

2. 8 x 7 = ☐

3.
```
  80
x  7
----
```

4. What is the numeral for ninety-seven?

____

5. What is my change from $3.00 if I spend $1.50?

____

6. ☐ + 72 = 90

7. What is the area of a square with 4-cm sides?

____

8. Which is measured in grams: a pencil or a car?

____

9. Draw all the faces of the pyramid.

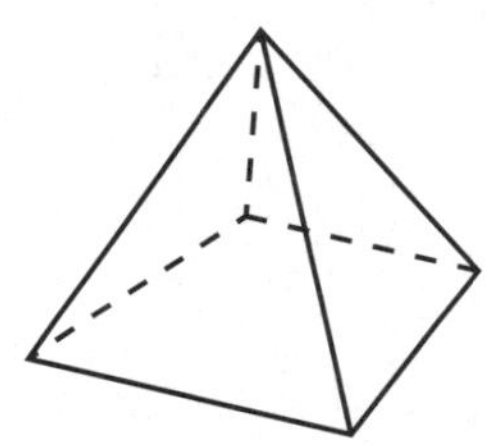

10. Collin has to read a book that has 63 pages in it. He has to have it read in one week. How many pages should he read each day to be done in time?

____

DAY 141

NAME: ____________________

DIRECTIONS Solve each problem.

1. 8 + 3 + 2 = ☐

2. What is the product of 1 and 10?

____

3. 10 x 9 = ☐

4. 24 ÷ 3 = ☐

5. $\frac{1}{4}$ of 16 is ________.

6. Fill in the missing number.

493, 488, ________, 478

7. 8 cups = ________ gallon(s)

8. Which has more mass: a bag of rocks or a bag of leaves?

____

9. What shape is the cross-section of a sphere?

____

10. Marissa has $1.35. She has 6 coins. What coins does she have?

____

SCORE

1. Ⓨ Ⓝ
2. Ⓨ Ⓝ
3. Ⓨ Ⓝ
4. Ⓨ Ⓝ
5. Ⓨ Ⓝ
6. Ⓨ Ⓝ
7. Ⓨ Ⓝ
8. Ⓨ Ⓝ
9. Ⓨ Ⓝ
10. Ⓨ Ⓝ

___ / 10 Total

DAY
142

NAME: ______________________

DIRECTIONS Solve each problem.

SCORE

1. Ⓨ Ⓝ
2. Ⓨ Ⓝ
3. Ⓨ Ⓝ
4. Ⓨ Ⓝ
5. Ⓨ Ⓝ
6. Ⓨ Ⓝ
7. Ⓨ Ⓝ
8. Ⓨ Ⓝ
9. Ⓨ Ⓝ
10. Ⓨ Ⓝ

___ / 10 Total

1. $$\begin{array}{r} 20 \\ -\ 16 \\ \hline \end{array}$$

2. Thirteen times one is

______________________.

3. $9 \times 9 = \square$

4. What number follows 736?

____

5. What number is 100 more than 98?

____

6. $42 \div 7 = 2 \times \square$

7. Jo painted these cupboards. Circle the one that needed the most paint.

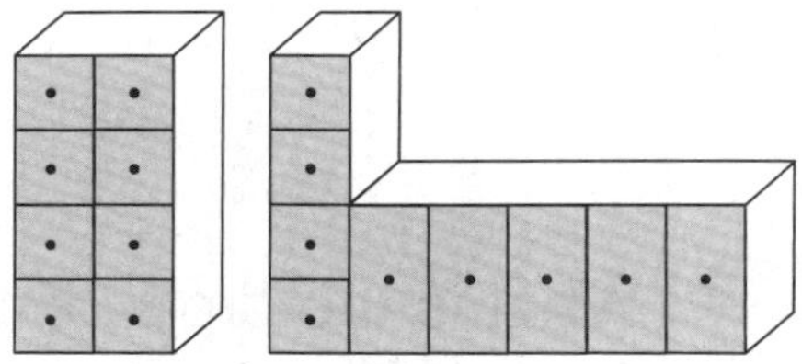

8. Is a bed longer or shorter than one meter?

____

9. How many fewer people liked skiing than snowboarding?

____

Favorite Winter Sports

Snowboarding	Sledding	Skiing	Ice Skating
324	225	278	175

10. Rachel walks to school every day. At the end of the week, she has spent 45 minutes walking to school. How long does it take Rachel to walk to school every day?

____

DAY
143

NAME: ____________________

DIRECTIONS Solve each problem.

1. 437 + 19 = ☐

2. 8 x 4 = ☐

3. How many eyes are there on 3 birds?

____

4. Divide 6 into 60.

____

5. Write $\frac{1}{4}$ in words.

____

6. 42 + ☐ = 50

7. Circle the item that has a mass less than 1 kilogram.

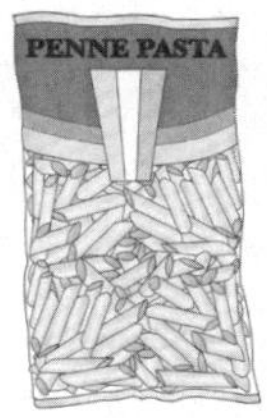

pasta

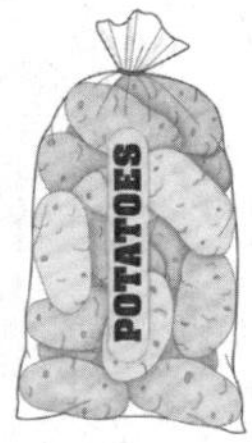

potatoes

8. How many centimeters are there in 90 millimeters?

____

9. Circle the parallel lines on the capital F.

F

10. In a pet shop, one-half of the animals are dogs. One-fourth of the animals are bunnies. Six of the animals are cats. There are an equal number of cats and bunnies. How many dogs are there in the pet shop?

____

SCORE

1. Ⓨ Ⓝ
2. Ⓨ Ⓝ
3. Ⓨ Ⓝ
4. Ⓨ Ⓝ
5. Ⓨ Ⓝ
6. Ⓨ Ⓝ
7. Ⓨ Ⓝ
8. Ⓨ Ⓝ
9. Ⓨ Ⓝ
10. Ⓨ Ⓝ

___ / 10 Total

NAME: ____________________

DIRECTIONS Solve each problem.

SCORE

1. Ⓨ Ⓝ
2. Ⓨ Ⓝ
3. Ⓨ Ⓝ
4. Ⓨ Ⓝ
5. Ⓨ Ⓝ
6. Ⓨ Ⓝ
7. Ⓨ Ⓝ
8. Ⓨ Ⓝ
9. Ⓨ Ⓝ
10. Ⓨ Ⓝ

___ / 10 Total

1. The difference between 418 and 18 is

____________________.

2. 1 x 0 = ☐

3. 10 x 0 = ☐

4. What is the next even number after 526?

____

5. Add 4 pennies to the coins below and write the total.

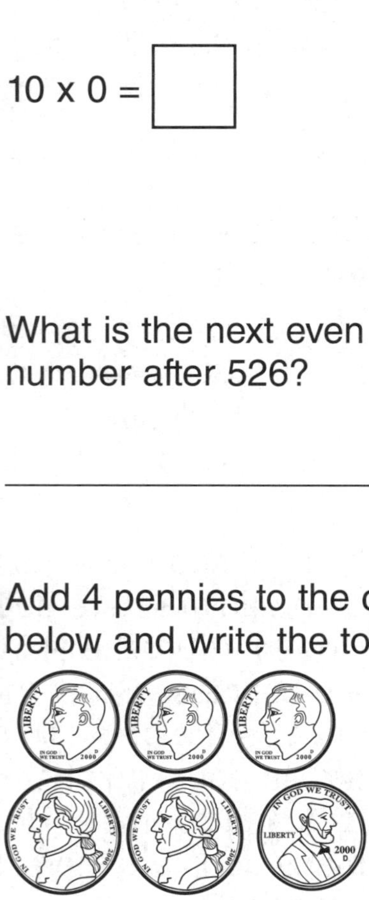

____

6. 80 ☐ 10 = 8

7. Name the last month of the year.

____

8. Could it be 30°C on a hot day?

Circle: yes no

9. Which solid has 6 square faces?

____

10. A monkey eats 6 bananas a day. How many bananas will it eat in 2 weeks?

____

NAME: ______________________________

DIRECTIONS Solve each product.

SCORE

1. Ⓨ Ⓝ
2. Ⓨ Ⓝ
3. Ⓨ Ⓝ
4. Ⓨ Ⓝ
5. Ⓨ Ⓝ
6. Ⓨ Ⓝ
7. Ⓨ Ⓝ
8. Ⓨ Ⓝ
9. Ⓨ Ⓝ
10. Ⓨ Ⓝ

___ / 10 Total

1. $\begin{array}{r} 70 \\ -\ 55 \\ \hline \end{array}$

2. Seven times seven is

______________________.

3. 40 x 3 = _______

4. 48 ÷ 6 = _______

5. $5.00 + $1.50 = _______

6. ☐ + 47 = 90

7. How many cups are there in a pint?

____

8. Would you use centimeters or meters to measure the width of a book?

____

9. Write the number of each for the solid below.

surfaces _______

edges _______

vertices _______

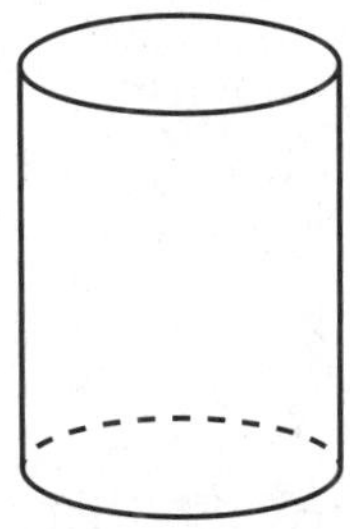

10. What is the largest odd number that can be made with 5, 6, and 7?

____

NAME: ______________________

DIRECTIONS Solve each problem.

SCORE

1. Ⓨ Ⓝ
2. Ⓨ Ⓝ
3. Ⓨ Ⓝ
4. Ⓨ Ⓝ
5. Ⓨ Ⓝ
6. Ⓨ Ⓝ
7. Ⓨ Ⓝ
8. Ⓨ Ⓝ
9. Ⓨ Ⓝ
10. Ⓨ Ⓝ

___ / 10
Total

1. 40 – 16 = ________

2. 6 x 7 = ☐

3. 13 x 1 = ☐

4. If you make 25 tally marks, how many groups of 5 will there be?

____

5. What is 3 hundred more than 1,306?

____

6. 9 x ☐ = 54

7. Circle the floor that needs more tile.

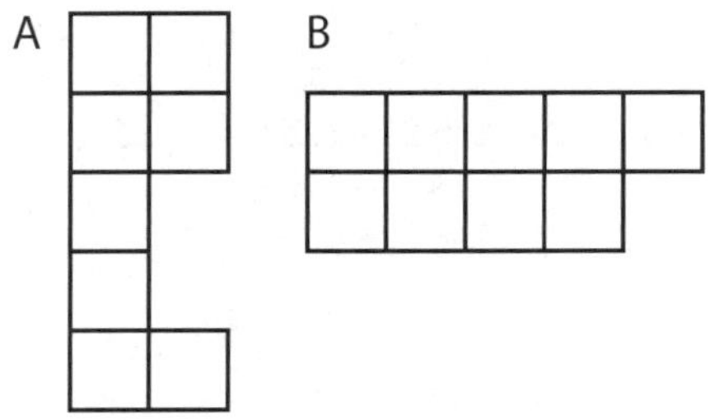

8. Which is longer: a yard or a meter?

____

9. How many lines of symmetry are there in a regular pentagon?

____

10. If a flagpole is 21 feet tall, how many yards tall is it?

____

NAME: ____________________

DIRECTIONS Solve each problem.

1.

$$\begin{array}{r} 25 \\ 52 \\ +\ 15 \\ \hline \end{array}$$

2. 4 x 80 = ☐

3. What is the product of 8 and 8?

____

4. 72 ÷ 8 = ☐

5. Write 2,304 in expanded notation.

____

6. Fill in the missing number.

550, 561, ________, 583

7. Which is longer: 2 hours or 100 minutes?

____

8. Does the palm of your hand have an area greater than or less than 1 m^2?

____

9. Name the lines.

____

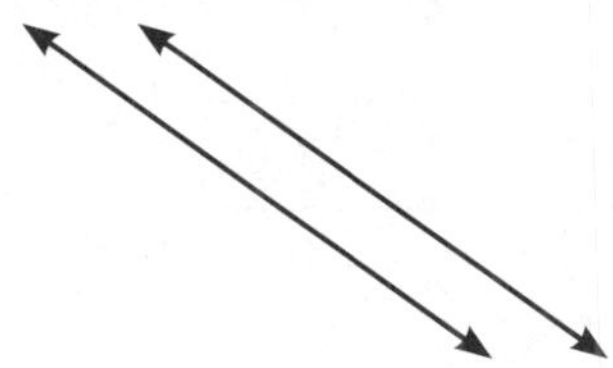

10. Gwen has a collection of 54 stuffed animals. Two-sixths are teddy bears. The rest are other types of animals. How many teddy bears does Gwen have?

____

SCORE

1. Ⓨ Ⓝ
2. Ⓨ Ⓝ
3. Ⓨ Ⓝ
4. Ⓨ Ⓝ
5. Ⓨ Ⓝ
6. Ⓨ Ⓝ
7. Ⓨ Ⓝ
8. Ⓨ Ⓝ
9. Ⓨ Ⓝ
10. Ⓨ Ⓝ

___ / 10

Total

DAY
148

NAME: ____________________

DIRECTIONS Solve each problem.

SCORE

1. Ⓨ Ⓝ
2. Ⓨ Ⓝ
3. Ⓨ Ⓝ
4. Ⓨ Ⓝ
5. Ⓨ Ⓝ
6. Ⓨ Ⓝ
7. Ⓨ Ⓝ
8. Ⓨ Ⓝ
9. Ⓨ Ⓝ
10. Ⓨ Ⓝ

___ / 10
Total

1.

$$\begin{array}{r} 79 \\ -\ 18 \\ \hline \end{array}$$

2. How many arms are there on 3 people?

____

3. 8 x 2 = ☐

4. What number follows 445?

____

5. What is the value of the digit 6 in the number 62?

____

6. 2 x 12 = 24 x ☐

7. How many minutes are there from 8:20 P.M. to 8:30 P.M.?

____

8. What is freezing on the Fahrenheit temperature scale?

____

9. Complete the chart.

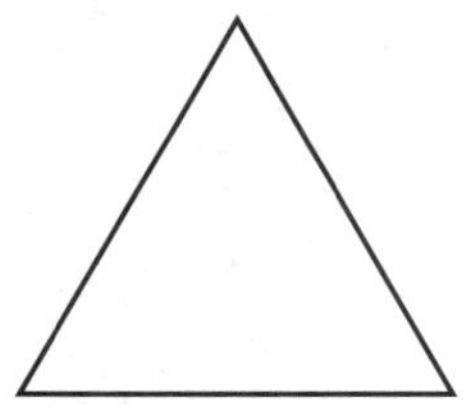

Number of Sides	
Number of Angles	
Number of Lines of Symmetry	
Name of Shape	

10. Can 5 cylinders be stacked on top of each other?

Circle: yes no

DAY
149

NAME: ______________________________

DIRECTIONS Solve each problem.

1. 25 + 25 = ☐

2.

$$\begin{array}{r} 9 \\ \times\ 4 \\ \hline \end{array}$$

3. Six times three is _______.

4. $4\overline{)32}$

5. 1 thousand + 3 tens =

____

6. 3 x ☐ = 18

7. $\frac{1}{2}$ foot = _______ inches

8. Write the line length.

____

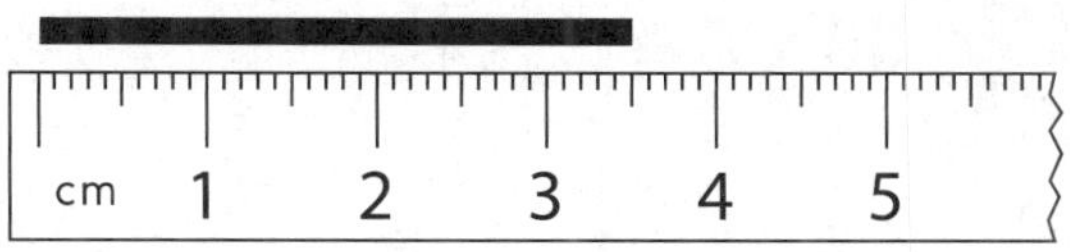

9. What shape forms the base of a cylinder?

____

10. Jack walks his dog for 20 minutes in the morning and 30 minutes at night. How many minutes does he walk his dog in a week?

____

SCORE

1. Ⓨ Ⓝ
2. Ⓨ Ⓝ
3. Ⓨ Ⓝ
4. Ⓨ Ⓝ
5. Ⓨ Ⓝ
6. Ⓨ Ⓝ
7. Ⓨ Ⓝ
8. Ⓨ Ⓝ
9. Ⓨ Ⓝ
10. Ⓨ Ⓝ

___ / 10
Total

DAY 150

NAME: ____________________

DIRECTIONS Solve each problem.

SCORE

1. Ⓨ Ⓝ
2. Ⓨ Ⓝ
3. Ⓨ Ⓝ
4. Ⓨ Ⓝ
5. Ⓨ Ⓝ
6. Ⓨ Ⓝ
7. Ⓨ Ⓝ
8. Ⓨ Ⓝ
9. Ⓨ Ⓝ
10. Ⓨ Ⓝ

___ / 10 Total

1. 100 – 25 = ☐

2. 8 x 6 = ☐

3. 80 x 6 = ☐

4. What is the odd number right before 721?

____

5. $7.00 + $2.00 + $1.50 =

____

6. 35 ☐ 14 = 21

7. Which is larger: $1\frac{1}{2}$ yards or 45 inches?

____

8. A train leaves at 8:05 A.M. It arrives at 10:10 A.M. How long does the trip take?

____

9. Is the shape below a prism, a pyramid, or a cylinder?

____

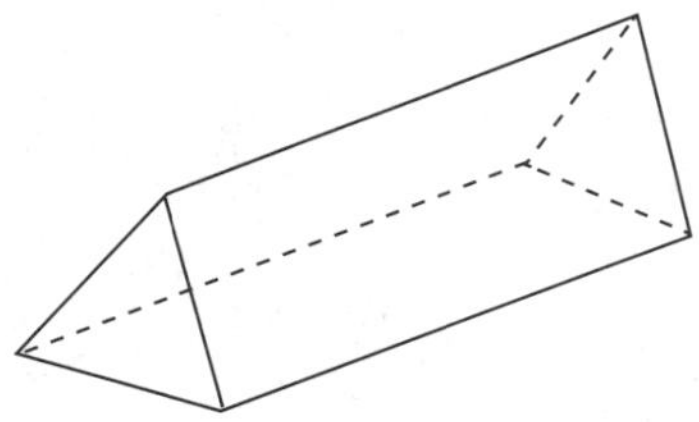

10. A teddy bear costs $12.50. Jack has $26.00. He wants to buy two teddy bears. Does Jack have enough money?

Circle: yes no

NAME: ____________________

DIRECTIONS Solve each problem.

1. $\begin{array}{r} 63 \\ +\ 19 \\ \hline \end{array}$

2. 9 x 9 = ☐

3. How many feet are there on 5 children?

____

4. 64 ÷ 8 = ☐

5. Which is smaller: $\frac{1}{4}$ or $\frac{7}{8}$?

____

6. ☐ x 6 = 30

7. Which is longer: 1 foot or 15 inches?

____

8. Would you use centimeters or meters to measure the height of a flag pole?

____

9. Circle the parallelogram.

10. If you divide me by 9 you get 7. What number am I?

____

SCORE

1. Ⓨ Ⓝ
2. Ⓨ Ⓝ
3. Ⓨ Ⓝ
4. Ⓨ Ⓝ
5. Ⓨ Ⓝ
6. Ⓨ Ⓝ
7. Ⓨ Ⓝ
8. Ⓨ Ⓝ
9. Ⓨ Ⓝ
10. Ⓨ Ⓝ

___ / 10

Total

DAY 152

NAME: ____________________

DIRECTIONS Solve each problem.

SCORE

1. Ⓨ Ⓝ
2. Ⓨ Ⓝ
3. Ⓨ Ⓝ
4. Ⓨ Ⓝ
5. Ⓨ Ⓝ
6. Ⓨ Ⓝ
7. Ⓨ Ⓝ
8. Ⓨ Ⓝ
9. Ⓨ Ⓝ
10. Ⓨ Ⓝ

___ / 10 Total

1. 50 – 25 = ______

2. 8 x 3 = ☐

3. Six times four is ______.

4. What is the numeral for five hundred thirty-four?

____

5. Write 3,562 in expanded notation.

____

____

6. Fill in the missing number.

339, 342, 345, 348, ______

7. ______ cups = 2 quarts

8. How many inches are there in a yard?

____

9. Name the shape of the cross-section.

____

10. Which letter is in the triangle, the circle, and the square?

____

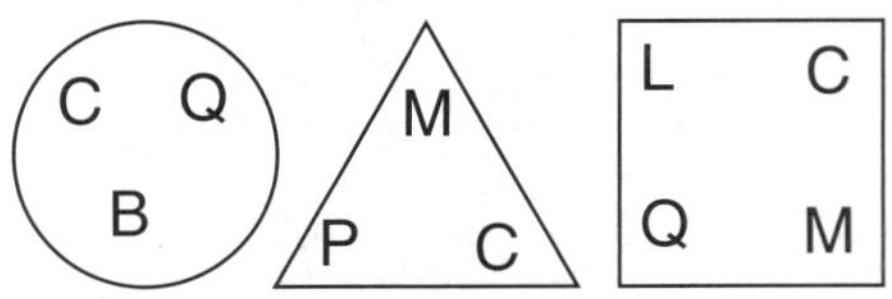

DAY 153

NAME: ______________________

DIRECTIONS Solve each problem.

1. 117 + 4 = ☐

2.
```
  26
x  2
----
```

3. 4 x 7 = ☐

4. How many groups of 10 are there in the number 100?

____

5. Write 2,094 in expanded notation.

____

6. ☐ ÷ 6 = 8

7. True or false? Your friend has a mass greater than 1 kg.

____

8. Write the line length.

____

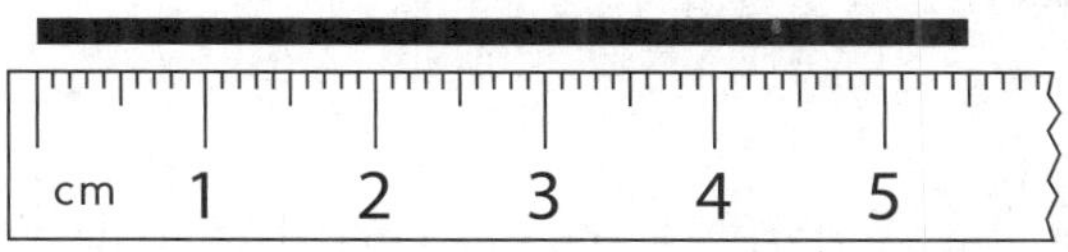

9. Which flavor do the children like best?

____

Favorite Flavors

Chocolate	Cherry	Lemon
248	127	68

10. How many inches are there in 4 feet?

____

SCORE

1. Ⓨ Ⓝ
2. Ⓨ Ⓝ
3. Ⓨ Ⓝ
4. Ⓨ Ⓝ
5. Ⓨ Ⓝ
6. Ⓨ Ⓝ
7. Ⓨ Ⓝ
8. Ⓨ Ⓝ
9. Ⓨ Ⓝ
10. Ⓨ Ⓝ

___ / 10
Total

DAY 154

NAME: ______________________________

DIRECTIONS Solve each problem.

SCORE

1. Ⓨ Ⓝ
2. Ⓨ Ⓝ
3. Ⓨ Ⓝ
4. Ⓨ Ⓝ
5. Ⓨ Ⓝ
6. Ⓨ Ⓝ
7. Ⓨ Ⓝ
8. Ⓨ Ⓝ
9. Ⓨ Ⓝ
10. Ⓨ Ⓝ

___ / 10 Total

1. 100 – 65 = ☐

2. What is the product of 8 and 7?

____

3. 6 x 5 = ☐

4. What is the ordinal number right after 683rd?

____

5. What is my change from $1.00 if I spend 45¢?

____

6. 18 ÷ 9 = 1 x ☐

7. Which has more mass: a pencil or a sheet of paper?

____

8. Would you use cups or gallons to measure lemonade for the whole class?

____

9. Look at the top, front, and side views. Is this a pyramid or prism?

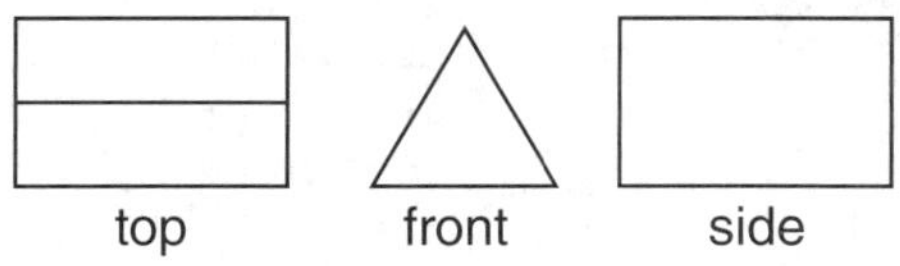

____

10. Write a question using the data from the graph.

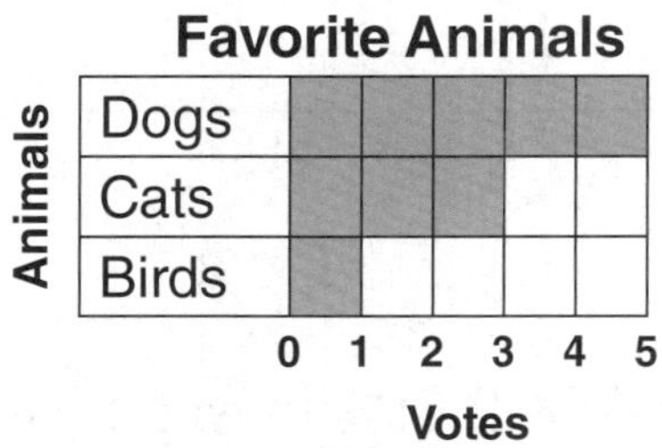

____

____

____

DAY 155

NAME: ______________________________

DIRECTIONS Solve each problem.

1. fifty + forty = ______

2. $\begin{array}{r} 30 \\ \times\ \ 4 \\ \hline \end{array}$

3. How many wheels are there on 6 tricycles?

____

4. $8\overline{)80}$

5. Write 5,270 in expanded notation.

____

6. 24 ☐ 66 = 90

7. True or false? A tissue has an area of more than 1 m^2.

____

8. Could it be 85°F on a cold day?

Circle: yes no

9. Circle the parallel lines on the capital H.

H

10. Manuel weighs 62 pounds. He can play football when he weighs 85 pounds. How many more pounds will Manuel have to gain in order to play on the football team?

____

SCORE

1. Ⓨ Ⓝ
2. Ⓨ Ⓝ
3. Ⓨ Ⓝ
4. Ⓨ Ⓝ
5. Ⓨ Ⓝ
6. Ⓨ Ⓝ
7. Ⓨ Ⓝ
8. Ⓨ Ⓝ
9. Ⓨ Ⓝ
10. Ⓨ Ⓝ

___ / 10
Total

DAY
156

NAME: ______________________

DIRECTIONS Solve each problem.

SCORE

1. Ⓨ Ⓝ
2. Ⓨ Ⓝ
3. Ⓨ Ⓝ
4. Ⓨ Ⓝ
5. Ⓨ Ⓝ
6. Ⓨ Ⓝ
7. Ⓨ Ⓝ
8. Ⓨ Ⓝ
9. Ⓨ Ⓝ
10. Ⓨ Ⓝ

___ / 10
Total

1. $17 + 43$

```
  17
+ 43
----
```

2. 7 x 5 = ☐

3. 7 x 50 = ☐

4. What number follows 592?

____

5. 50¢ + 15¢ + 5¢ =

____

6. 10 x ☐ = 5 x 6

7. What unit of time is used to measure how long it takes to wash your hands: minutes or hours?

____

8. What is the area of a square with 3-cm sides?

____

9. Draw all the lines of symmetry.

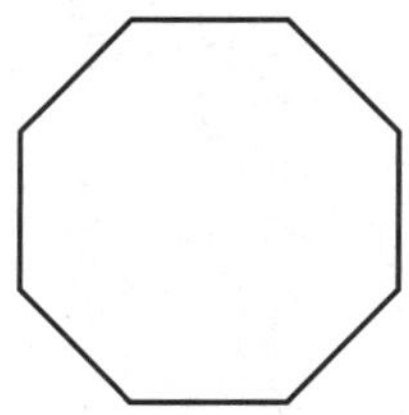

10. David has built 16 model airplanes. He builds two airplanes every month. How many months did it take him to build the 16 models?

____

NAME: ____________________

DIRECTIONS Solve each problem.

1. 37 – 28 = ☐

2. 15 x 5 = ____

3. 4 x 7 = ☐

4. 56 divided by 8 is ________.

5. Write 7,021 in expanded notation.

____

6. ☐ ÷ 3 = 6

7. How many minutes are there from 5:45 A.M. to 6:00 A.M.?

____

8. If each bottle holds 2 liters, what is the total capacity of all of the bottles?

____

9. Create a tally chart from the information below.

Minutes It Takes to Finish Homework

Mon.	Tue.	Wed.	Thurs.
35	30	45	20

10. Max has seen his favorite movie three more times than his best friend Tom. Tom has seen the movie two times. How many times has Max seen the movie?

____

SCORE

1. Ⓨ Ⓝ
2. Ⓨ Ⓝ
3. Ⓨ Ⓝ
4. Ⓨ Ⓝ
5. Ⓨ Ⓝ
6. Ⓨ Ⓝ
7. Ⓨ Ⓝ
8. Ⓨ Ⓝ
9. Ⓨ Ⓝ
10. Ⓨ Ⓝ

___ / 10 Total

DAY
158

NAME: ______________________

DIRECTIONS Solve each problem.

SCORE

1. Ⓨ Ⓝ
2. Ⓨ Ⓝ
3. Ⓨ Ⓝ
4. Ⓨ Ⓝ
5. Ⓨ Ⓝ
6. Ⓨ Ⓝ
7. Ⓨ Ⓝ
8. Ⓨ Ⓝ
9. Ⓨ Ⓝ
10. Ⓨ Ⓝ

___ / 10
Total

1. 18 + 44 = ☐

2. How many fingers are there on 3 hands?

____

3.

$$\begin{array}{r} 8 \\ \times\ 9 \\ \hline \end{array}$$

4. What number follows 180?

____

5. Add $1.25 to the coins below and write the total.

____

6. 3 x 6 = ☐ x 2

7. Tim painted these cupboards. Circle the one that needed the most paint.

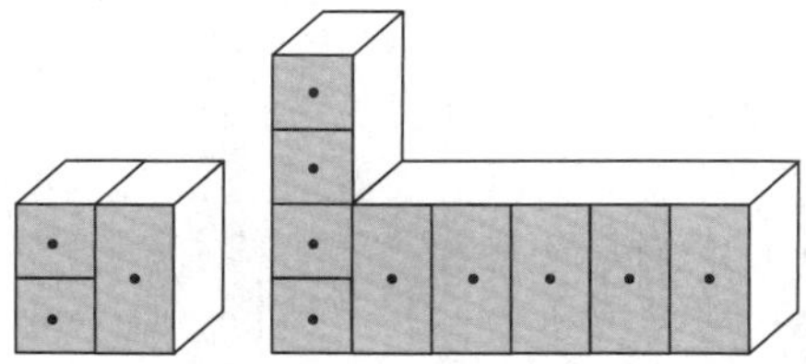

8. Could you live with a body temperature of 50°F?

Circle: yes no

9. How many lines of symmetry does a regular octagon have?

____

10. What is the largest even number that can be written using each of the digits 7, 2, and 3?

____

NAME: ____________________

DIRECTIONS Solve each problem.

1.

$$\begin{array}{r} 41 \\ -\ 19 \\ \hline \end{array}$$

2. 70 x 2 = ☐

3. Draw an array with two rows of nine.

4. How many groups of 7 are there in the number 56?

____

5.

$$\begin{array}{r} \$10.00 \\ \$5.00 \\ +\ \$1.50 \\ \hline \end{array}$$

6. 2 x ☐ = 12

7. These two floors are to be tiled. Circle the floor that needs less tile.

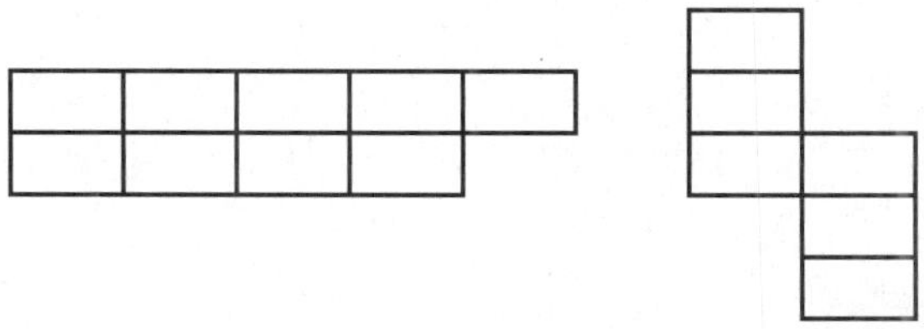

8. How many pints are there in a quart?

____

9. Are the lines below parallel or intersecting?

____

10. Sheldon loves movies and buys a new DVD each week. The DVDs cost $19.99 each. How much does Sheldon spend on DVDs in 4 weeks?

____

SCORE

1. Ⓨ Ⓝ
2. Ⓨ Ⓝ
3. Ⓨ Ⓝ
4. Ⓨ Ⓝ
5. Ⓨ Ⓝ
6. Ⓨ Ⓝ
7. Ⓨ Ⓝ
8. Ⓨ Ⓝ
9. Ⓨ Ⓝ
10. Ⓨ Ⓝ

___ / 10
Total

DAY

160

NAME: ______________________________

DIRECTIONS Solve each problem.

SCORE
1. Ⓨ Ⓝ
2. Ⓨ Ⓝ
3. Ⓨ Ⓝ
4. Ⓨ Ⓝ
5. Ⓨ Ⓝ
6. Ⓨ Ⓝ
7. Ⓨ Ⓝ
8. Ⓨ Ⓝ
9. Ⓨ Ⓝ
10. Ⓨ Ⓝ
___ / 10 Total

1. 11 + 5 + 29 = ☐

2. 9 x 6 = ☐

3.

$$\begin{array}{r} 16 \\ \times\ \ 4 \\ \hline \end{array}$$

4. Is 573 an even or an odd number?

____

5. What is the value of 2 in 263?

____

6. Fill in the missing number.

312, 317, 322, ______, 332

7. How many full pitchers will it take to fill the bucket?

____

8. How many hours are there in 2 days?

____

9. How many angles are there in an octagon?

____

10. Ninety-nine people show up to a school fund-raiser. Fifty people each donate \$25.00 to the school. Thirty-three people donate \$50.00 each. The rest donate \$100.00 each. How many people donate \$100.00 to the school?

____

DAY 161

NAME: ____________________

DIRECTIONS Solve each problem.

1. 202 + 37 = ☐

2. 4 x 8 = ☐

3. 4 x 80 = ☐

4. 27 ÷ 3 = ☐

5. Write 264 in expanded notation.

____

6. 2,000 + ☐ + 6 = 2056

7. True or false? A playground has an area of more than 1 m^2.

____

8. Write 9 minutes past 10 on the clock.

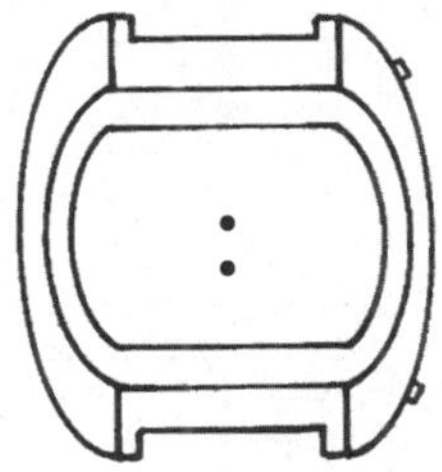

9. Complete the chart.

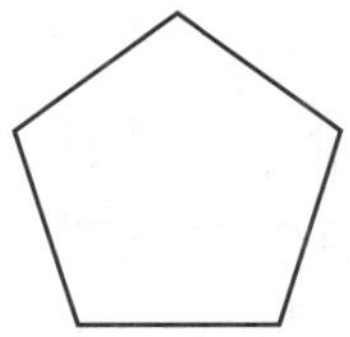

Number of Sides	
Number of Angles	
Number of Lines of Symmetry	
Name of Shape	

10. If you multiply me by 10, you get 120. What number am I?

____

SCORE

1. Ⓨ Ⓝ
2. Ⓨ Ⓝ
3. Ⓨ Ⓝ
4. Ⓨ Ⓝ
5. Ⓨ Ⓝ
6. Ⓨ Ⓝ
7. Ⓨ Ⓝ
8. Ⓨ Ⓝ
9. Ⓨ Ⓝ
10. Ⓨ Ⓝ

___ / 10 Total

DAY
162

NAME: ______________________

DIRECTIONS Solve each problem.

SCORE

1. Ⓨ Ⓝ
2. Ⓨ Ⓝ
3. Ⓨ Ⓝ
4. Ⓨ Ⓝ
5. Ⓨ Ⓝ
6. Ⓨ Ⓝ
7. Ⓨ Ⓝ
8. Ⓨ Ⓝ
9. Ⓨ Ⓝ
10. Ⓨ Ⓝ

___ / 10
Total

1.
$$\begin{array}{r} 47 \\ -\ 24 \\ \hline \end{array}$$

2. Six times ten is _______.

3. 82 x 0 = ☐

4. What is the next even number after 680?

____

5. True or false? $\frac{1}{8}$ is less than $\frac{3}{8}$.

____

6. Fill in the missing number.

227, 231, _______, 239, 243

7. Name the first month of the year.

____

8. A movie starts at 7:20 P.M. It lasts for 2 hours and 10 minutes. What time will the movie end?

____

9. Is the object below a prism, a pyramid, or a cylinder?

____

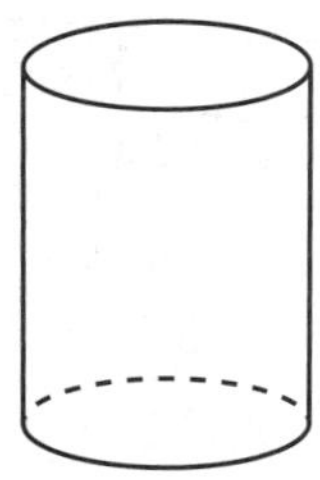

10. There are 42 crackers in a box. There are 6 people at a party. If the crackers are shared equally, how many will each person get?

____

NAME: ______________________________

DIRECTIONS Solve each problem.

1. 3 + 4 + 6 = ☐

2.
```
  17
x  3
----
```

3. What is the product of 4 and 10?

____

4. 8 ⟌ 40

5. Write 4,512 in expanded notation.

____

6. True or false? 10 x 3 = 6 x 5

____

7. True or false? A ruler has a mass greater than 1 kg.

____

8. What is the perimeter of a hexagon with six 2-inch sides?

____

9. What is the name for the part of the solid that is shaded?

____

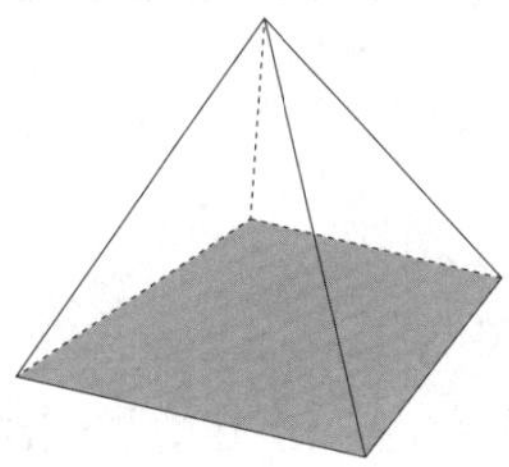

10. Seventy-two students from Sharp Elementary School, eighty-five students from Lee Elementary School, and seventy-four students from Kennedy Elementary School go on a field trip to a museum. How many students go on the field trip?

____

SCORE

1. Ⓨ Ⓝ
2. Ⓨ Ⓝ
3. Ⓨ Ⓝ
4. Ⓨ Ⓝ
5. Ⓨ Ⓝ
6. Ⓨ Ⓝ
7. Ⓨ Ⓝ
8. Ⓨ Ⓝ
9. Ⓨ Ⓝ
10. Ⓨ Ⓝ

___ / 10 Total

DAY
164

NAME: ____________________

DIRECTIONS Solve each problem.

SCORE

1. Ⓨ Ⓝ
2. Ⓨ Ⓝ
3. Ⓨ Ⓝ
4. Ⓨ Ⓝ
5. Ⓨ Ⓝ
6. Ⓨ Ⓝ
7. Ⓨ Ⓝ
8. Ⓨ Ⓝ
9. Ⓨ Ⓝ
10. Ⓨ Ⓝ

___ / 10
Total

1. $24 - 12 = \square$

2.
$$\begin{array}{r} 6 \\ \times\ 8 \\ \hline \end{array}$$

3. Seven times one is

____________________.

4. What is the numeral for seven hundred twenty?

____

5. What is my change from $2.35 if I spend 45¢?

____

6. $36 \square 9 = 27$

7. Which is longer: 7 feet or 2 yards?

____

8. Write the line length.

____

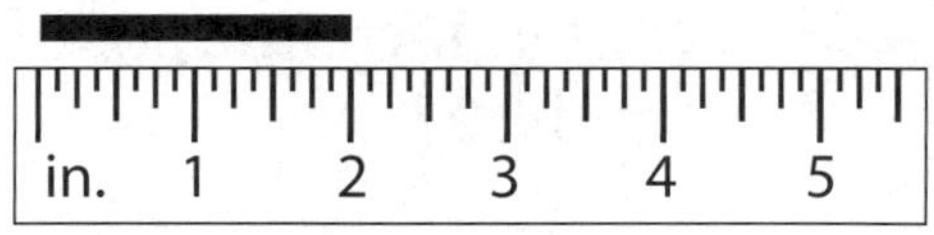

9. Name the shape of the cross-section.

____

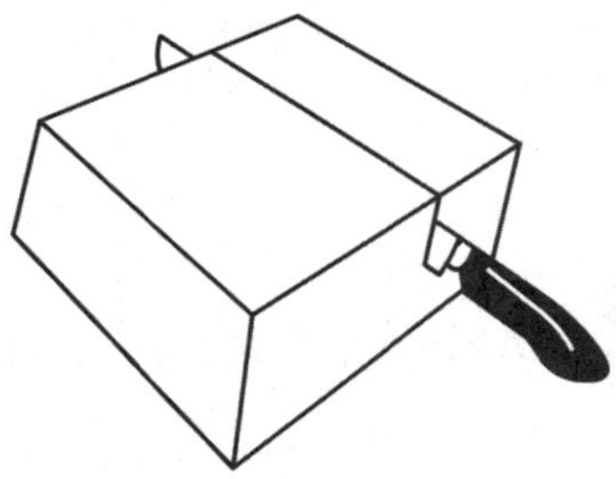

10. Sue invites 40 people to a party. Only half of those she invites can come. How many people can come to Sue's party?

____

NAME: ______________________________

DIRECTIONS Solve each problem.

1.

$$\begin{array}{r} 79 \\ +\ 81 \\ \hline \end{array}$$

2. 9 x 1 = ☐

3. 9 x 10 = ☐

4. What is 48 divided by 8?

____

5. Make the smallest 4-digit number possible using each of the digits 0, 1, 2, and 3.

____

6. 3 x 3 = 8 + ☐

7. Is a pen longer or shorter than a meter?

____

8. Could it be 92°F on a hot day?

Circle: yes no

9. Circle the parallelogram.

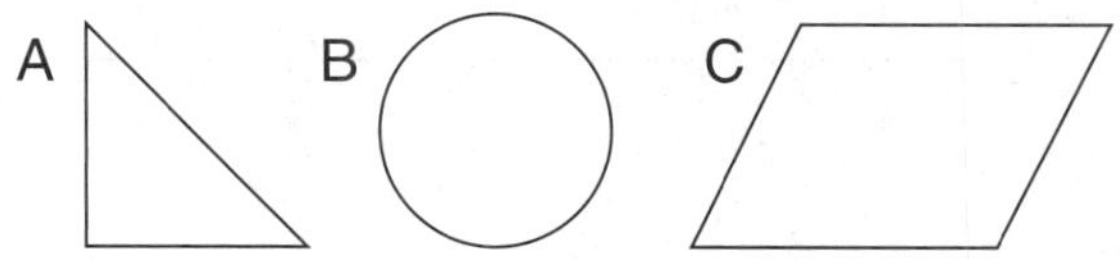

10. How many cups are there in 2 gallons?

____

SCORE

1. Ⓨ Ⓝ
2. Ⓨ Ⓝ
3. Ⓨ Ⓝ
4. Ⓨ Ⓝ
5. Ⓨ Ⓝ
6. Ⓨ Ⓝ
7. Ⓨ Ⓝ
8. Ⓨ Ⓝ
9. Ⓨ Ⓝ
10. Ⓨ Ⓝ

___ / 10
Total

DAY
166

NAME: ____________________

DIRECTIONS Solve each problem.

SCORE

1. Ⓨ Ⓝ
2. Ⓨ Ⓝ
3. Ⓨ Ⓝ
4. Ⓨ Ⓝ
5. Ⓨ Ⓝ
6. Ⓨ Ⓝ
7. Ⓨ Ⓝ
8. Ⓨ Ⓝ
9. Ⓨ Ⓝ
10. Ⓨ Ⓝ

___ / 10
Total

1. 20 – 18 = ☐

2. 8 x 5 = ☐

3. Seven times twenty is

____________________.

4. What number follows 495?

____

5. $12.00 + $8.00 + $2.50 =

____

6. 32 + ☐ = 51

7. ______ gallon(s) = 4 quarts

8. It will be 9:00 in ten minutes. Write the current time.

____

9. Are these lines perpendicular?

Circle: yes no

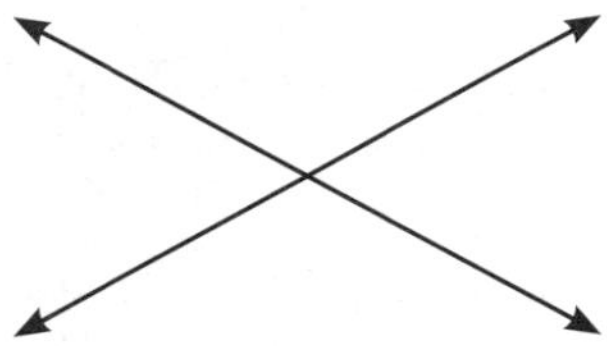

10. A pizza parlor sold 72 pizzas one night. One-third of the pizzas were pepperoni. How many pepperoni pizzas were sold?

____

DAY 167

NAME: ____________________________

DIRECTIONS Solve each problem.

1. $104 - 36 = \square$

2. $3 \times 12 = \square$

3.
$$\begin{array}{r} 40 \\ \times \quad 4 \\ \hline \end{array}$$

4. How many 2s are in 18?

____

5. If you subtract 3 dimes from the coins below, how much money will be left?

____

6. Fill in the missing number.

61, ________, 55, 52, 49

7. Which is shorter: 5 inches or $\frac{1}{2}$ foot?

____

8. How many weeks are there in a year?

____

9. Circle the rhombus.

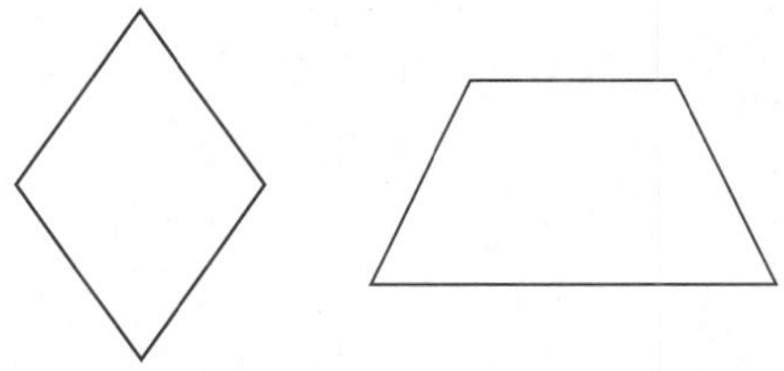

10. A good reader should recognize 99 out of every 100 words when reading. How many words should a good reader recognize out of every 1,000 words?

____

SCORE

1. Ⓨ Ⓝ
2. Ⓨ Ⓝ
3. Ⓨ Ⓝ
4. Ⓨ Ⓝ
5. Ⓨ Ⓝ
6. Ⓨ Ⓝ
7. Ⓨ Ⓝ
8. Ⓨ Ⓝ
9. Ⓨ Ⓝ
10. Ⓨ Ⓝ

___ / 10 Total

DAY
168

NAME: ______________________________

DIRECTIONS Solve each problem.

SCORE

1. Ⓨ Ⓝ
2. Ⓨ Ⓝ
3. Ⓨ Ⓝ
4. Ⓨ Ⓝ
5. Ⓨ Ⓝ
6. Ⓨ Ⓝ
7. Ⓨ Ⓝ
8. Ⓨ Ⓝ
9. Ⓨ Ⓝ
10. Ⓨ Ⓝ

___ / 10
Total

1.
$$\begin{array}{r} 47 \\ 14 \\ +\ 23 \\ \hline \end{array}$$

2. 80 x 1 = ☐

3. Eighty-two times one is

______________________.

4. What is the odd number right before 720?

____

5. Is 1 greater than, less than, or equal to $\frac{9}{10}$?

____

6. 2,500 + ☐ = 2,534

7. How many minutes are there from 7:10 A.M. to 7:30 A.M.?

____

8. What month has the fewest number of days?

____

9. Flip this shape across the line of symmetry.

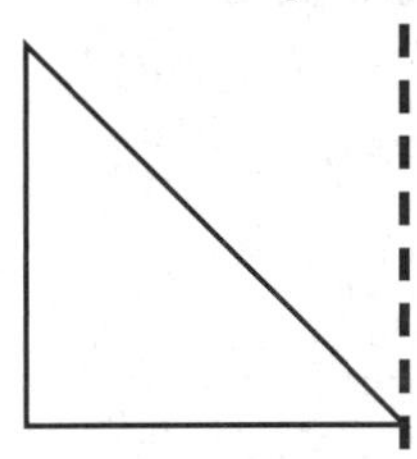

10. I want to double a recipe that calls for 2 $\frac{1}{2}$ cups of flour. How much flour will I need to add?

____

DAY 169

NAME: ____________________

DIRECTIONS Solve each problem.

1. 47 – 16 = ☐

2. If there are 5 boxes with 6 cans per box, what is the total number of cans?

____

3.
```
  18
x  5
----
```

4. If 15 bones are shared equally between 3 dogs, how many bones will each dog get?

____

5. What is the value of the digit 3 in the number 2,443?

____

6. ☐ ÷ 12 = 3

7. Write the line length.

____

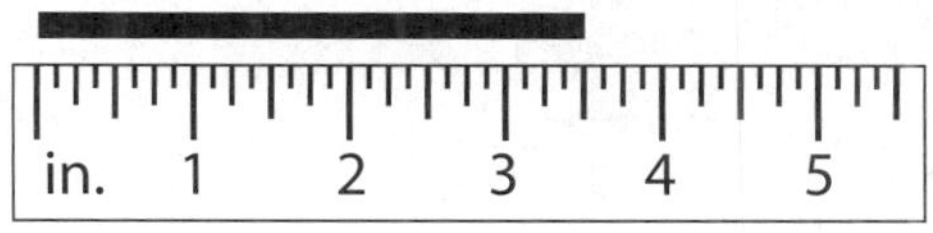

8. Which is longer: a centimeter or an inch?

____

9. Draw all the lines of symmetry.

10. Timothy has $15.45 in his wallet. He earns $6.75 by helping his mom with chores. He buys a toy car at the store for $5.15. How much money does Timothy have now?

____

SCORE

1. Ⓨ Ⓝ
2. Ⓨ Ⓝ
3. Ⓨ Ⓝ
4. Ⓨ Ⓝ
5. Ⓨ Ⓝ
6. Ⓨ Ⓝ
7. Ⓨ Ⓝ
8. Ⓨ Ⓝ
9. Ⓨ Ⓝ
10. Ⓨ Ⓝ

___ / 10
Total

DAY
170

NAME: ______________________________

DIRECTIONS Solve each problem.

SCORE

1. Ⓨ Ⓝ
2. Ⓨ Ⓝ
3. Ⓨ Ⓝ
4. Ⓨ Ⓝ
5. Ⓨ Ⓝ
6. Ⓨ Ⓝ
7. Ⓨ Ⓝ
8. Ⓨ Ⓝ
9. Ⓨ Ⓝ
10. Ⓨ Ⓝ

___ / 10
Total

1. 34 + 56 = ☐

2.
$$\begin{array}{r} 50 \\ \times\ 3 \\ \hline \end{array}$$

3. Eighty times zero is

______________________.

4. What number follows 593?

____

5. What is my change from $1.85 if I spend 75¢?

____

6. 45 ÷ 5 = 3 x ☐

7. Which has more mass: a rooster or a feather?

____

8. What is the perimeter of a rectangular room that is 10 ft. x 12 ft.?

____

9. How many fewer people like watching baseball than basketball?

____

Favorite Sport to Watch

Soccer	Basketball	Baseball
237	475	362

10. Draw lines to divide the hexagon into 3 equal parts.

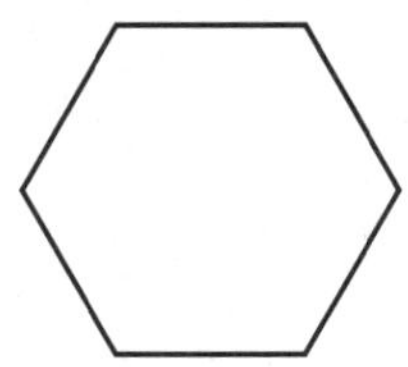

NAME: ____________________

DIRECTIONS Solve each problem.

1.

$$\begin{array}{r} 18 \\ 6 \\ +\ 32 \\ \hline \end{array}$$

2. 8 x 4 = ☐

3. 30 x 8 = ☐

4. 42 ÷ 6 = ☐

5. 2000 + 300 + 70 + 4 =

____

6. 10 x ☐ = 5 x 4

7. Jose painted these cupboards. Circle the one that needed the most paint.

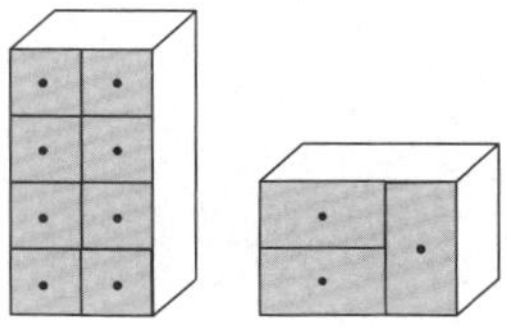

8. How many cups are there in a quart?

____

9. How many lines of symmetry does an equilateral triangle have?

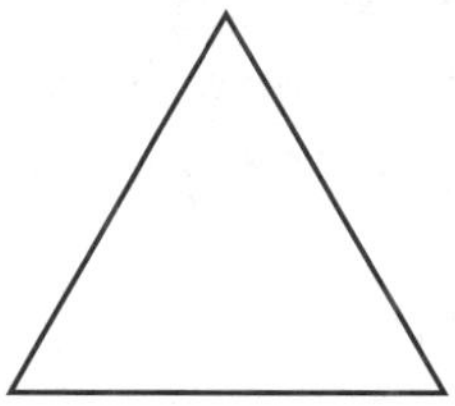

____

10. Hector wants to buy a new MP3 player that costs $84.00. He washes his dad's car every weekend and his dad gives him $6.00 each time. How many times will Hector have to wash his dad's car before he can afford the MP3 player?

____

SCORE

1. Ⓨ Ⓝ
2. Ⓨ Ⓝ
3. Ⓨ Ⓝ
4. Ⓨ Ⓝ
5. Ⓨ Ⓝ
6. Ⓨ Ⓝ
7. Ⓨ Ⓝ
8. Ⓨ Ⓝ
9. Ⓨ Ⓝ
10. Ⓨ Ⓝ

___ / 10 Total

NAME: ______________________________

DIRECTIONS Solve each problem.

SCORE

1. Ⓨ Ⓝ
2. Ⓨ Ⓝ
3. Ⓨ Ⓝ
4. Ⓨ Ⓝ
5. Ⓨ Ⓝ
6. Ⓨ Ⓝ
7. Ⓨ Ⓝ
8. Ⓨ Ⓝ
9. Ⓨ Ⓝ
10. Ⓨ Ⓝ

___ / 10 Total

1. 97 – 24 = ☐

2. 70 x 100 = ________

3. 8 x 4 = ☐

4. What is the ordinal number right after 471st?

____

5. $2.00 – $1.50 = ________

6. ________ + 300 + 4 = 1,304

7. Write a quarter past three on the clock.

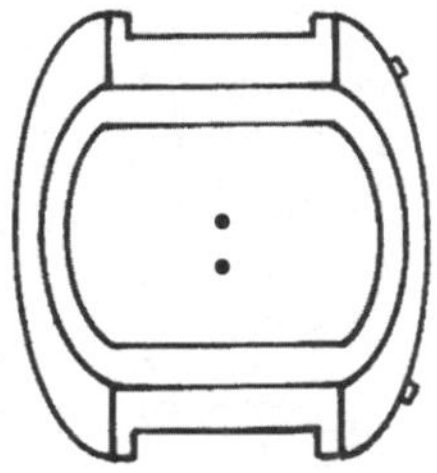

8. Is the palm of your hand greater than, less than, or equal to 1 square inch?

____

9. How many vertices does a cylinder have?

____

10. Dog biscuits come in boxes of 56. If you give your dog 2 biscuits each day of the week, how many days until you run out of biscuits?

____

NAME: ______________________________

DIRECTIONS Solve each problem.

1. 46 + 24 = ☐

2. What is the product of 10 and 10?

____

3. $\begin{array}{r} 5 \\ \times\ 8 \\ \hline \end{array}$

4. $9\overline{)18}$

5. Shade $\frac{42}{100}$.

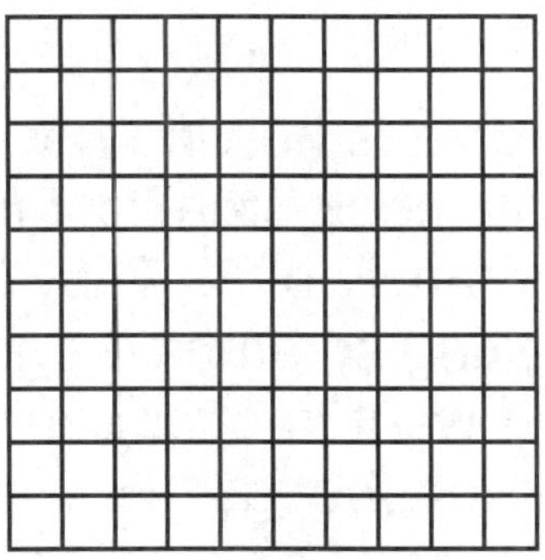

6. Fill in the missing number.

124, 128, ________, 136, 140

7. Would you more likely use inches or feet to measure the distance from your kitchen to the front door?

____

8. Could your body have a temperature of 98°F?

Circle: yes no

9. Name the solid below.

____

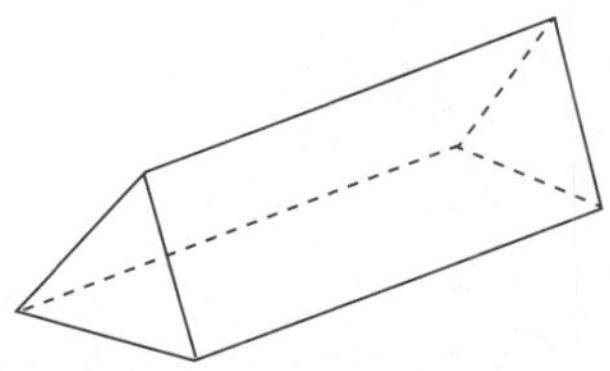

10. A scout troop of 6 girls sells 535 boxes of cookies. Each box of cookies costs $3.50. Samantha sells 154 boxes of cookies. How many boxes did the rest of the girls sell?

____

SCORE

1. Ⓨ Ⓝ
2. Ⓨ Ⓝ
3. Ⓨ Ⓝ
4. Ⓨ Ⓝ
5. Ⓨ Ⓝ
6. Ⓨ Ⓝ
7. Ⓨ Ⓝ
8. Ⓨ Ⓝ
9. Ⓨ Ⓝ
10. Ⓨ Ⓝ

___ / 10
Total

DAY
174

NAME: ____________________

DIRECTIONS Solve each problem.

SCORE

1. Ⓨ Ⓝ
2. Ⓨ Ⓝ
3. Ⓨ Ⓝ
4. Ⓨ Ⓝ
5. Ⓨ Ⓝ
6. Ⓨ Ⓝ
7. Ⓨ Ⓝ
8. Ⓨ Ⓝ
9. Ⓨ Ⓝ
10. Ⓨ Ⓝ

___ / 10
Total

1. $\begin{array}{r} 38 \\ -\ 23 \\ \hline \end{array}$

2. 10 times 8 is ________.

3. $\begin{array}{r} 17 \\ \times\ \ 2 \\ \hline \end{array}$

4. Make tally marks for the number 16.

5. Subtract 4 nickels from $1.35.

____

6. ☐ x 3 = 6 x 4

7. What unit of time is used to measure how long it takes to eat your lunch?

____

8. What is the perimeter of the triangle?

____

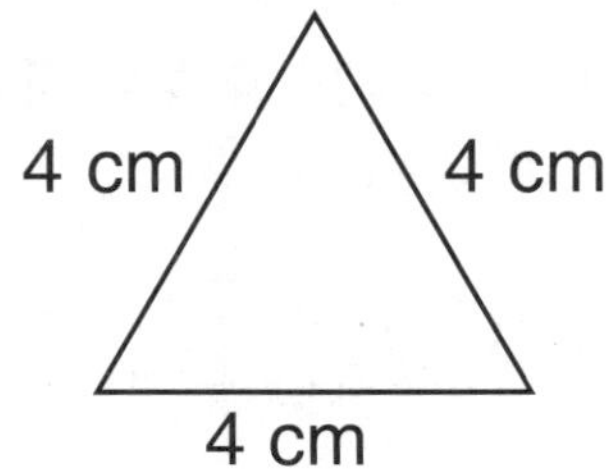

9. What polygon is shaded on the figure below?

____

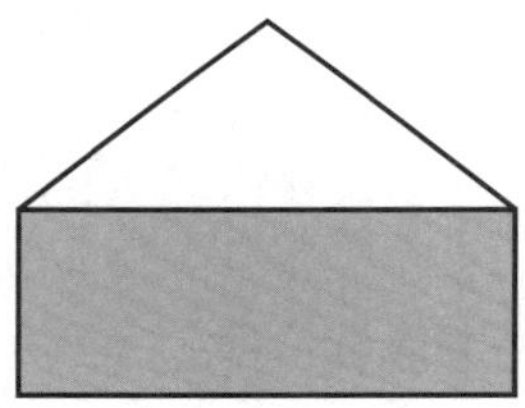

10. Sophia is helping her mom cook breakfast for her family of 5. They are making scrambled eggs and want to offer each person 2 eggs. How many cartons of one-dozen eggs are needed?

____

NAME: ______________________________

DIRECTIONS Solve each problem.

1. 25 – 11 = ☐

2.
```
   62
x   3
-----
```

3. 8 x 8 = ☐

4. Is 828 an even or odd number?

____

5. Add 4 tens to 126.

____

6. 14 + 2 = ☐ x 8

7. These two floors are to be tiled. Circle the floor that needs more tile.

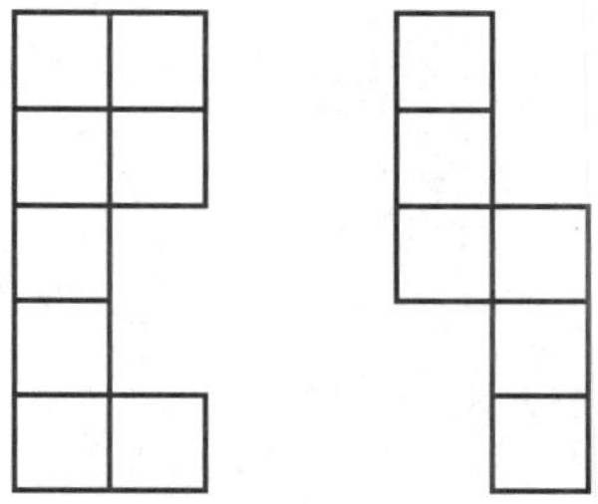

8. How many feet are in two yards?

____

9. Circle the parallel lines on the capital I.

10. Draw the mirror image of the shape.

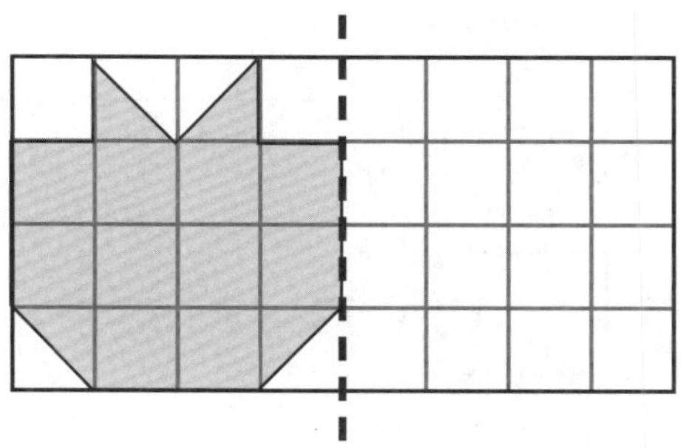

SCORE

1. Ⓨ Ⓝ
2. Ⓨ Ⓝ
3. Ⓨ Ⓝ
4. Ⓨ Ⓝ
5. Ⓨ Ⓝ
6. Ⓨ Ⓝ
7. Ⓨ Ⓝ
8. Ⓨ Ⓝ
9. Ⓨ Ⓝ
10. Ⓨ Ⓝ

___ / 10 Total

DAY
176

NAME: ____________________

DIRECTIONS Solve each problem.

SCORE

1. Ⓨ Ⓝ
2. Ⓨ Ⓝ
3. Ⓨ Ⓝ
4. Ⓨ Ⓝ
5. Ⓨ Ⓝ
6. Ⓨ Ⓝ
7. Ⓨ Ⓝ
8. Ⓨ Ⓝ
9. Ⓨ Ⓝ
10. Ⓨ Ⓝ

___ / 10
Total

1.
$$\begin{array}{r} 33 \\ 15 \\ +\ 27 \\ \hline \end{array}$$

2. 10 x 5 = ☐

3. How many tires are there on 3 bicycles?

____

4. 45 shared equally among 9 groups is

____________________.

5. What is the value of the digit 5 in the number 453?

____

6. ☐ + 40 + 7 = 347

7. True or false? A grape has a mass greater than 1 kg.

____

8. I start watching TV at 6:15 P.M. The show ends at 6:30 P.M. How long did I watch TV?

____

9. Complete the chart about the figure below.

Number of Sides	
Number of Angles	
Number of Lines of Symmetry	
Name of Shape	

10. Terri reads 1 book every 2 weeks. How long will it take her to read 6 books?

____

DAY 177

NAME: ______________________________

DIRECTIONS Solve each problem.

SCORE

1. $39 - 17 = \square$

2. Nine times ten is _______.

3.
$$\begin{array}{r} 14 \\ \times\ 3 \\ \hline \end{array}$$

4. What is the numeral for eight hundred thirty-three?

____

5. Write 1,256 in expanded notation.

____

6. $34 + \square = 61$

7. Is a car longer or shorter than a meter?

____

8. What is the total capacity of the cups below?

____

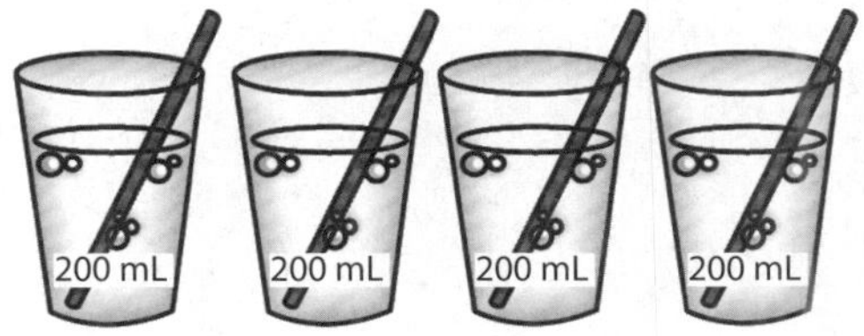

9. Name the shape of the cross-section.

____

10. Which 2 letters are in the square and the circle, but not in the triangle?

____

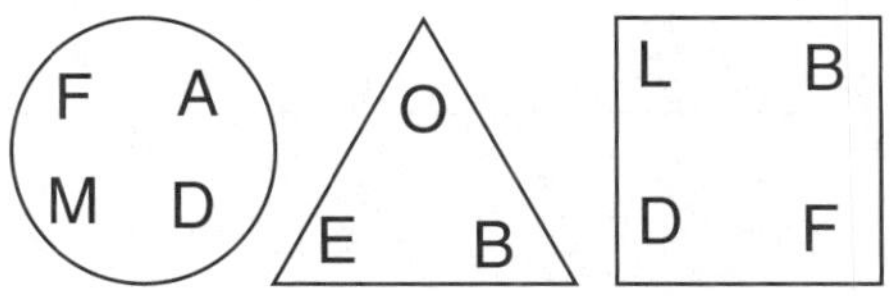

1. Ⓨ Ⓝ
2. Ⓨ Ⓝ
3. Ⓨ Ⓝ
4. Ⓨ Ⓝ
5. Ⓨ Ⓝ
6. Ⓨ Ⓝ
7. Ⓨ Ⓝ
8. Ⓨ Ⓝ
9. Ⓨ Ⓝ
10. Ⓨ Ⓝ

___ / 10 Total

DAY
178

NAME: ____________________

DIRECTIONS Solve each problem.

SCORE

1. Ⓨ Ⓝ
2. Ⓨ Ⓝ
3. Ⓨ Ⓝ
4. Ⓨ Ⓝ
5. Ⓨ Ⓝ
6. Ⓨ Ⓝ
7. Ⓨ Ⓝ
8. Ⓨ Ⓝ
9. Ⓨ Ⓝ
10. Ⓨ Ⓝ

___ / 10 Total

1. 25 + 27 = ☐

2. 8 x 9 = ☐

3. What is the product of 6 and 8?

____

4. How many rows of 8 are there in 16?

____

5. What is my change from $5.50 if I spend $2.75?

____

6. 9 x 2 = 6 x ☐

7. True or false? The classroom door has an area of more than 1 m^2.

____

8. What temperature is freezing on the Celsius scale?

____

9. Which solid figure has only one face?

____

10. What is the smallest odd number that can be written using each of the digits 5, 6, and 9?

____

NAME: ____________________

DIRECTIONS Solve each problem.

1.

$$\begin{array}{r} 42 \\ -\ 31 \\ \hline \end{array}$$

2. 6 x 8 = ☐

3. 60 x 8 = ________

4. What number follows 726?

____

5. $\frac{3}{3}$ of 24 = ☐

6. 200 + 50 + ☐ = 256

7. ________ cups = 1 gallon

8. Write the line length.

____

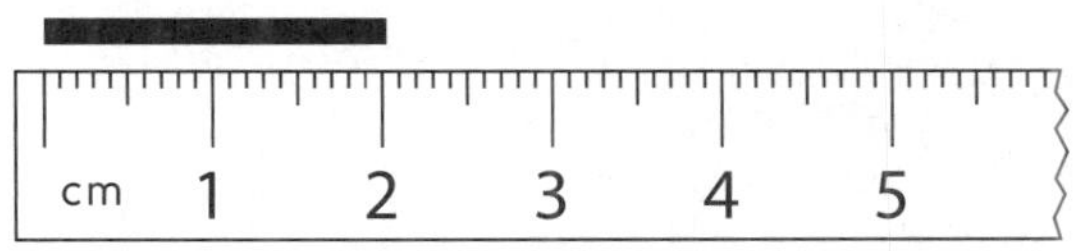

9. Draw all the lines of symmetry.

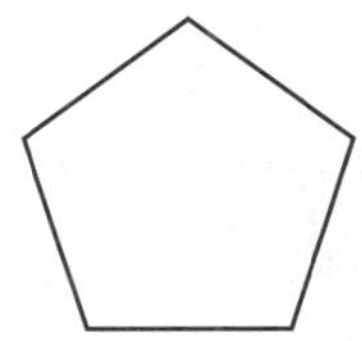

10. Write a subtraction question using the data from the graph below.

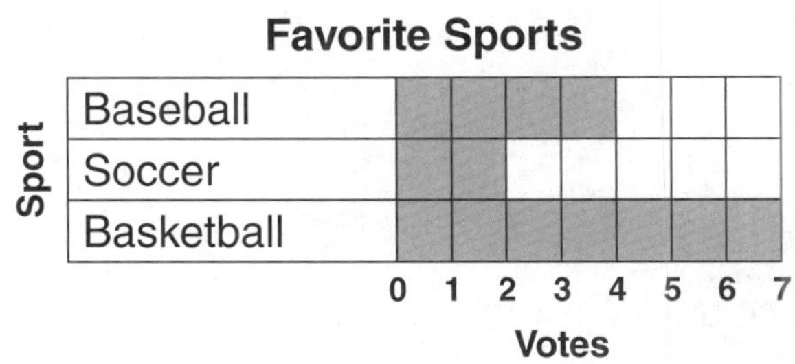

____

____

____

____

SCORE

1. Ⓨ Ⓝ
2. Ⓨ Ⓝ
3. Ⓨ Ⓝ
4. Ⓨ Ⓝ
5. Ⓨ Ⓝ
6. Ⓨ Ⓝ
7. Ⓨ Ⓝ
8. Ⓨ Ⓝ
9. Ⓨ Ⓝ
10. Ⓨ Ⓝ

___ / 10 Total

DAY 180

NAME: ______________________________

DIRECTIONS Solve each problem.

SCORE

1. Ⓨ Ⓝ
2. Ⓨ Ⓝ
3. Ⓨ Ⓝ
4. Ⓨ Ⓝ
5. Ⓨ Ⓝ
6. Ⓨ Ⓝ
7. Ⓨ Ⓝ
8. Ⓨ Ⓝ
9. Ⓨ Ⓝ
10. Ⓨ Ⓝ

___ / 10 Total

1. 10 more than 23 is

____

2. 80 x 1 = ☐

3. How many feet are there on 7 people?

____

4. $5\overline{)35}$

5. What is 3 hundred more than 2,568?

____

6. Fill in the missing number.

1,216; 1,116; 1,016; _______

7. Label the prism with the words *width, length,* and *height.*

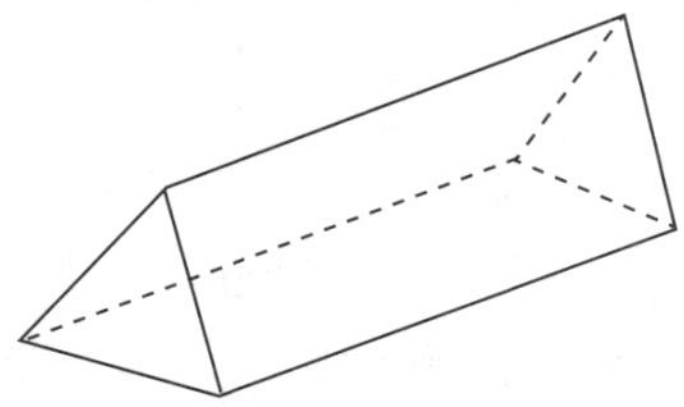

8. Write 30 minutes after 8 on the clock.

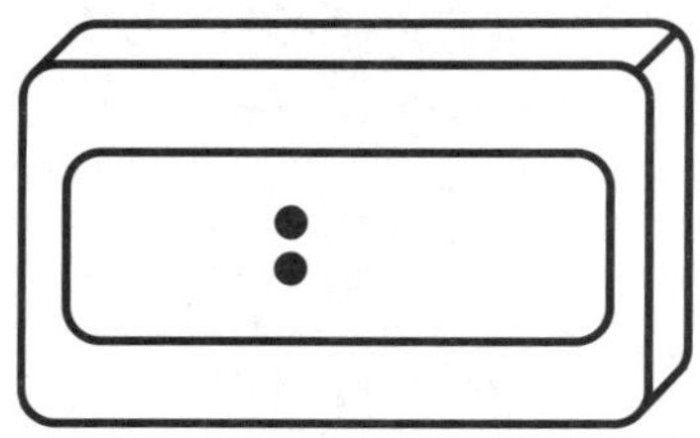

9. Circle the pentagon.

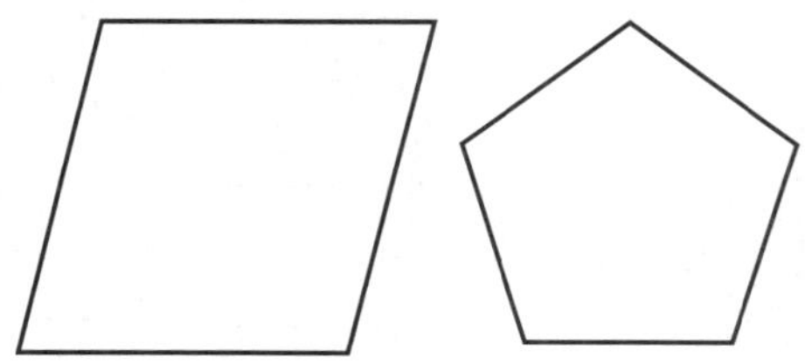

10. Mark spends one-third of the day sleeping. He spends 8 hours at school and one-sixth of his day at soccer practice. How much free time does Mark have?

____

ANSWER KEY

Day 1
1. 9
2. 10
3. 3 rows of 5 circles should be drawn.
4. 7 rows
5. 56
6. 44
7. 7 days
8. The bottom pencil should be circled.
9. square or rhombus
10. 28 children

Day 2
1. 5
2. 45
3. 40
4. 42
5. $\frac{1}{4}$
6. 5
7. 30 days
8. six o'clock
9. slide
10. 7 cookies

Day 3
1. 19
2. 100
3. 9 rows of 2 squares should be drawn.
4. 3 monkeys should be circled.
5. 10
6. 14
7. Saturday and Sunday
8. 5 cm
9. The first two shapes should be circled.
10. 2 outfits

Day 4
1. 24
2. 6 rows of 5 triangles should be drawn.
3. 80
4. thirty-seven
5. 10
6. 4
7. The second group of tables should be circled.
8. seven-thirty
9. triangle
10. 14

Day 5
1. 15
2. 60
3. 24
4. no
5. 16 quarters
6. 20
7. December
8. The book should be circled.
9. 5 children
10. 65

Day 6
1. 21
2. 15
3. 4, 6, 8
4. 8
5. 75¢
6. 8
7. sheet of paper
8. 2:15
9. no
10. 34, 43, 345, 534, 543

Day 7
1. 22
2. 4 rows of 3 circles should be drawn.
3. 25
4. 4
5. one whole
6. true
7. 31 days
8. Alli's toys should be circled.
9. cylinder
10. 79 stickers

Day 8
1. 79
2. 28
3. 4 rows of 2 girls should be drawn.
4. 80
5. 7
6. +
7. Wednesday
8.

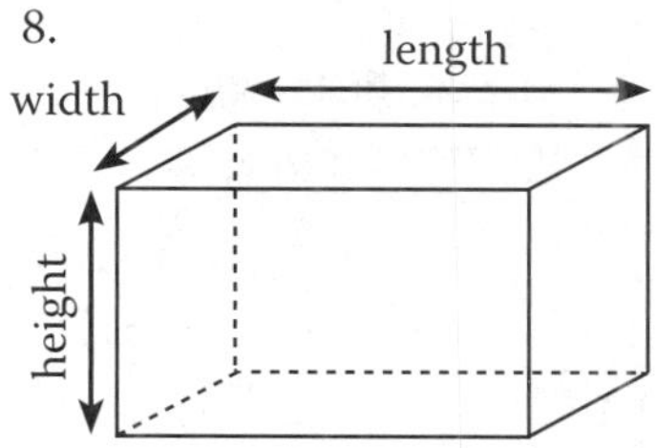

9. A circle or oval should be drawn.
10. twelve o'clock

Day 9
1. 14
2. 27
3. Two rows of 8 circles should be drawn.
4. 4 lines of 5
5. 6 dimes
6. 30
7. eight thirty
8. mouse
9. The same triangle should be drawn.
10. The box with 2 rocks and the box with 5 rocks should be circled.

Day 10
1. 19
2. 32
3. 9 rows of 10 dots should be drawn.
4. 2 digits
5. 3
6. 5
7. 8:15 should be drawn.
8. 12-inch ruler
9. Heads: 6 tally marks should be drawn
   Tails: 4 tally marks should be drawn.
10. 2 more students

Day 11
1. 21
2. 20 legs
3. 36

ANSWER KEY *(cont.)*

4. Groups of 3 circles should be colored the same.
5. 328
6. 44, 55, 66
7. eleven thirty
8. 11 inches
9. 3, 3
10. 1:00

Day 12

1. 24
2. 40
3. 6
4. 8
5. $\frac{2}{4}$ or $\frac{1}{2}$
6. –
7. May
8. The lion should be circled.
9. A square should be drawn.
10. The fifth pencil from the left should be circled.

Day 13

1. 6
2. 25
3. 4 rows of 2 sticks should be drawn.
4. 5 rows
5. 45¢
6. +
7. 14 days
8. 10:30
9. true
10. a quarter and a dime

Day 14

1. 58
2. 28
3. 9 piles of 4 books should be drawn.
4. 160
5. 45¢
6. 32
7. 8:45
8. house
9. hexagon
10. 40 eyes

Day 15

1. 6
2. 45
3. 3 rows of 10 oranges should be drawn.
4. Circles around every 2 pumpkins should be drawn.
5. 30 + 1
6. 13
7. Saturday
8. 2:45 should be drawn.
9. 2 kids
10. 2:00 A.M.

Day 16

1. 31
2. 40
3. 60
4. 19 tally marks should be drawn.
5. $\frac{3}{4}$
6. 44
7. seven-thirty
8. toothpick
9. triangle
10. 6 slices

Day 17

1. 10
2. 10, 15, 20
3. 18
4. 9 rows
5. 150
6. 5
7. 6:30
8. 31 days
9. rectangular prism or cube
10. 105

Day 18

1. 10
2. 24
3. 7 rows of 5 books should be drawn.
4. 19
5. 2 tens or 20
6. 7
7. April
8. 12:00
9. triangles
10. 145 cm

Day 19

1. 12
2. 60 fingers
3. 8
4. 1 lollipop each
5. One box should be colored.
6. –
7. 12:00 A.M.
8. 10:15 should be drawn.
9. 1, 1, 1
10. 8 should be colored.

Day 20

1. 56
2. 12
3. 8, 12, 16
4. four hundred fifty-six
5. 4
6. 4
7. four forty-five
8. Thursday
9. pizza
10. C

Day 21

1. 30
2. 32
3. 40
4. 3 groups of 2 should be circled.
5. 100
6. + or –
7. 7:15
8. 8
9. 4 angles
10. 41

Day 22

1. 59
2. 70
3. 8
4. 80
5. 3 apples should be colored.
6. 25
7. April

ANSWER KEY *(cont.)*

8. The pumpkin should be circled.
9. cone
10. cube

Day 23

1. 21
2. 12
3. 32
4. 5 rows
5. 10
6. 40
7. nine fifteen
8. car
9. flip
10. 2 bags

Day 24

1. 10
2. 36
3. 40
4. 151st
5. 55¢
6. 12
7. 30 days
8. 2:30
9. A rectangle should be drawn.
10. $2.30

Day 25

1. 7
2. 14
3. 9 rows of 5 dots should be drawn.
4. 8 birds
5. $0.60
6. 9
7. Wednesday
8. 9:00 should be drawn.
9.

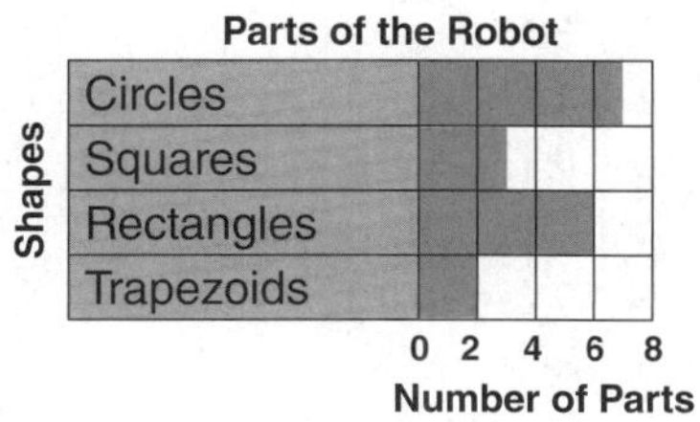

10. 28

Day 26

1. 89
2. 50
3. 8 rows of 3 stars should be drawn.
4. 81
5. $\frac{1}{2}$
6. 32
7. Sunday
8. 1:30 should be drawn.
9.

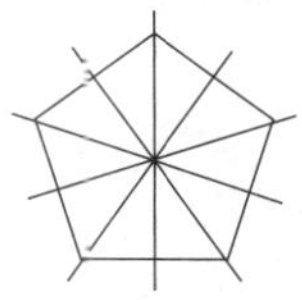

Any one line may be drawn.

10. 85¢

Day 27

1. 21
2. 25
3. 18
4. 3 groups of 3 should be circled.
5. 6 tens
6. 4
7. 4:30
8. a big jug
9. A robot should be drawn with 1 square, 4 rectangles, and 3 circles.
10. 21 cm

Day 28

1. 21
2. 21
3. 16 sides
4. 31
5. 7 tens
6. –
7. July
8. 8:45
9. squares
10. 15¢

Day 29

1. 5
2. 36
3. 40
4. 6 snakes
5. 1
6. 4
7. 31 days
8. The matches box should be colored.
9. 6 sides, 6 angles
10. third

Day 30

1. 70
2. 32
3. 5 rows of 10 cups should be drawn.
4. one hundred forty-seven
5. 8 ones or 8
6. 6
7. three o'clock
8. path
9. 2 rectangles and 1 square
10. 7 kids

Day 31

1. 10
2. 28
3. 8 rows of 4 books should be drawn.
4. 4 groups of 2 should be circled.
5. 19
6. 100, 50, 0
7. July
8. 3:30
9. triangular prism
10. 38

Day 32

1. 31
2. 24
3. 12
4. 73rd
5. One box should be colored.
6. 15
7. 28 or 29 days
8. 12:00 P.M.
9. A circle or oval should be drawn.
10. 83

ANSWER KEY *(cont.)*

Day 33

1. 22
2. 18 flowers
3. 56
4. 5 rows
5. 20 dimes
6. 10 candies
7. 5:15
8. ruler
9. cylinder
10. 13 nickles

Day 34

1. 19
2. 80
3. 2 groups of 4 baseballs should be drawn.
4. 20 tally marks should be drawn.
5. 45¢
6. x
7. Saturday
8. milk jug
9. 4 inches
10. The knife should be circled.

Day 35

1. 12
2. 40
3. 24
4. 5 faces
5. $3.00
6. 4
7. 12:00 should be drawn.
8. 24 hours
9. turn
10. 5 red and green cars

Day 36

1. 22
2. true
3. 72
4. 64
5. $2.75
6. 21
7. 8:00
8. The right group of tables should be circled.
9. 12 edges
10. 352

Day 37

1. 20
2. 6 piles of 4 logs should be drawn.
3. 0
4. Three groups of three should be circled.
5. 0.05
6. 15
7. February
8. 5:45
9. face
10. 13 pieces

Day 38

1. 8
2. 6
3. 8 rows of 5 items should be drawn.
4. 543
5. 4 hundreds
6. 5
7. two forty-five
8. classroom floor
9. 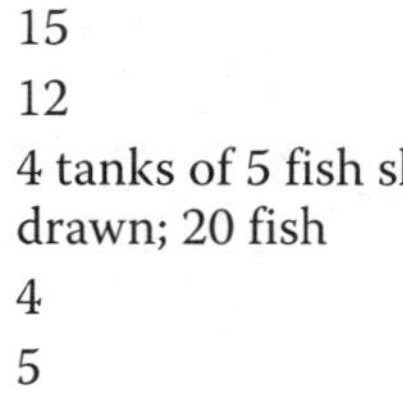
10. 3 flowers

Day 39

1. 15
2. 12
3. 4 tanks of 5 fish should be drawn; 20 fish
4. 4
5. 5
6. x
7. 30 days
8. pool
9. yellow
10. Friday

Day 40

1. 374
2. 48
3. 24
4. 64
5. 33¢
6. 350
7. Wednesday
8. 6:15 should be drawn.
9. hexagon
10. 9 cars

Day 41

1. 50
2. 36
3. 4 legs on 5 cats should be drawn.
4. 4 groups of 2 should be circled.
5. 5 ones or 5
6. 40
7. one fifteen
8. house
9. true
10. $3.11

Day 42

1. 30
2. 72
3. 6 bunches of 4 flowers should be drawn.
4. 13 tally marks should be drawn.
5. 99
6. 2
7. 30 days
8. 5:30 should be drawn.
9. 3 angles
10. C

Day 43

1. 30
2. 18
3. 24
4. 7 pencils per student
5. 1 ten or 10
6. +
7. 6:45

ANSWER KEY *(cont.)*

8. mug
9. C, B, A
10. 685

Day 44

1. 22
2. 35
3. 10
4. 71
5. one quarter
6. 7
7. October
8. 7:00
9. 13
10. one dollar

Day 45

1. 100
2. 42
3. 20
4. 7 birds
5. 5 quarters
6. –
7. Tuesday
8. The banana should be circled.
9. pentagon
10. 7 and 8

Day 46

1. 60
2. 14
3. 100
4. 77
5. 50 or 5 tens
6. 4
7. March 18th
8. clock, watch, or stopwatch
9.

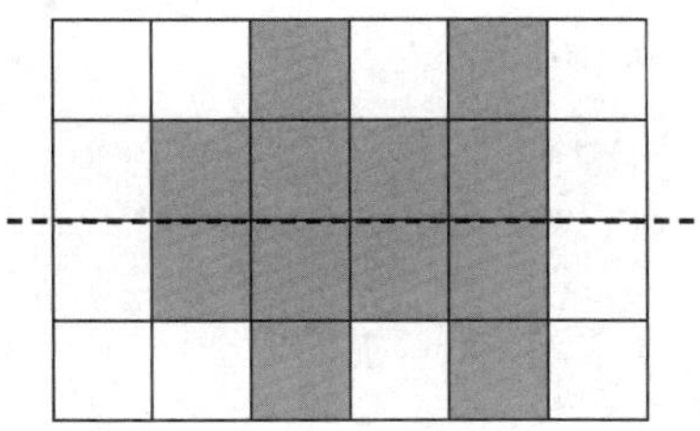

10. 80¢

Day 47

1. 12
2. 72
3. 0
4. Corn should be circled into 4 groups of 4.
5. $0.60
6. 7
7. 31 days
8. teaspoon
9. right angle
10. The star should look symmetrical.

Day 48

1. 32
2. 81
3. 0
4. 406
5. 41¢
6. 52
7. 7
8. 10:00
9. Vertices: 6
   Edges: 9
   Faces 5
10. square pyramid

Day 49

1. 5
2. 36
3. 20 fingers
4. 3
5. 42
6. 28
7. 4 hours
8. 1
9. C and D
10. 4 outfits

Day 50

1. 25
2. 72
3. 60
4. even
5. $\frac{5}{8}$
6. 24
7. 60 minutes
8. The solid on the left should be circled.
9. false
10.

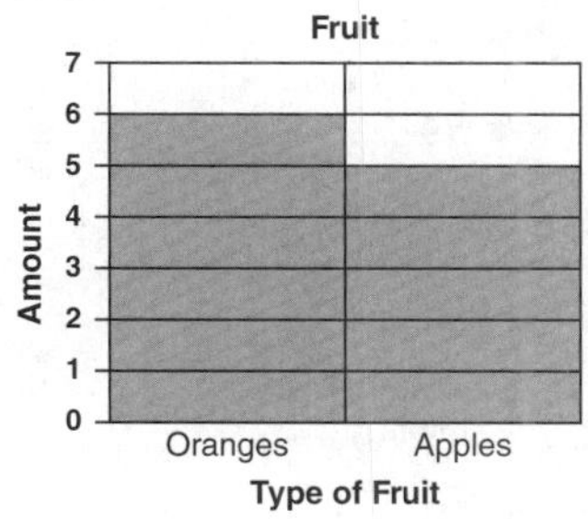

Day 51

1. 11
2. 32
3. 24
4. 5 chairs
5. 0.50
6. 297
7. June 7th
8. 9
9.

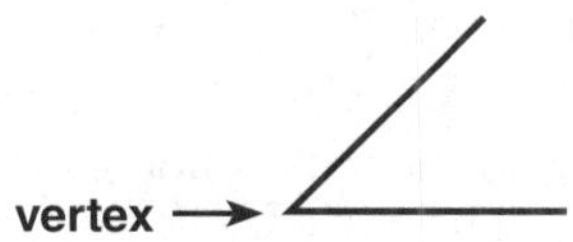

10. 131

Day 52

1. 59
2. twenty-eight
3. 18
4. 97
5. 2 hundreds or 200
6. 10
7. adult, child, baby
8. 5
9. The tea and apple juice containers should be circled.
10. 9:00

Day 53

1. 42
2. 48
3. 64
4. 9 toys
5. 5 circles should be colored
6. 5
7. meters

ANSWER KEY *(cont.)*

8. The $1 stamp should be circled.
9. science
10. 45¢

Day 54

1. 36
2. 35
3. 63
4. even number
5. 300 or 3 hundreds
6. 9
7. 6 hours
8. shorter
9. 12 edges
10. Sue, Jody, Eric

Day 55

1. 60
2. 40
3. 0
4. 3 groups
5. $3.77
6. 10 stickers
7. The milk container should be circled.
8. 8:15
9. true
10. $2.10

Day 56

1. 89
2. An array of 6 rows by 5 columns should be drawn.
3. 27
4. 90th
5. 80¢
6. ÷
7. 8:30
8. 1 hour
9. A and B
10. 7 cars

Day 57

1. 22
2. true
3. 28
4. 4 cars
5. 357
6. 95
7. ruler
8. 16 cm
9. obtuse angle
10. 8 insects

Day 58

1. 80
2. 4 boxes of 9 pencils should be drawn; 4 x 9 = 36
3. 15
4. 67
5. $\frac{5}{8}$
6. 3
7. minute
8. December 6th
9. 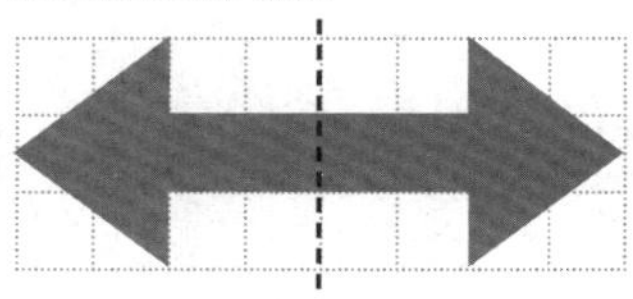
10. a lollipop and a chocolate

Day 59

1. 16
2. 42
3. 24
4. 3
5. $0.60
6. 4
7. January 1
8. 60 pounds
9. edge
10. 4, 7, 10, 13, 16

Day 60

1. 81
2. 7 groups of 4 lines should be drawn; 7 x 4 = 28
3. 50
4. 74
5. $0.50
6. 8
7. 31 days
8. 5 in.
9. 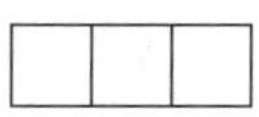
10. a quarter

Day 61

1. 81
2. 18
3. 40 toes
4. 11 flowers per vase
5. $8.70
6. 6 candies
7. 4 hours
8. 5
9. Comics – 3 tally marks
   Fairy Tales – 8 tally marks
   Mysteries – 12 tally marks
10. 134

Day 62

1. 15
2. 42
3. 36
4. 64
5. true
6. 2
7. frog, cat, horse
8. 9:45
9. Arrow should be pointing to the right.
10. $1.47

Day 63

1. 61
2. 21
3. 8
4. 10
5. 51
6. 125
7. 31 days
8. 12 cm
9. 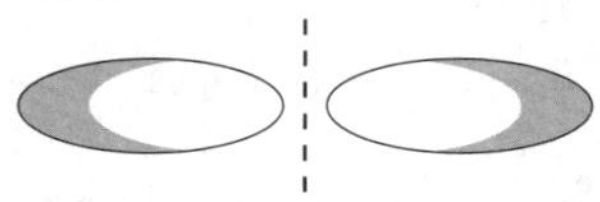
10. 6 times

Day 64

1. 45
2. 25
3. 50
4. 42
5. 24
6. x
7. February 27th

8. $1\frac{1}{2}$ hours
9. true
10. 40

Day 65

1. 61
2. 27
3. 0
4. 5 pairs
5. 4 ones or 4
6. 3
7. mug
8. 21 days
9. sphere
10. $1.90

Day 66

1. 13
2. 20
3. 200
4. 74
5. 2 circles should be colored.
6. 500
7. day
8. 15 hours
9. A
10. 90 years old

Day 67

1. 20
2. 90
3. 42
4. 5 apples per box
5. 467
6. 9
7. 365 days
8. taller
9. 27 years older
10. $2.61

Day 68

1. 60
2. 18
3. 20 fingers
4. 835
5. $4.31
6. 7 apples
7. scale
8. 3:15
9. pentagon
10. January

Day 69

1. 17
2. 36
3. 35
4. 5 pencils
5. 23¢
6. ÷
7. The laundry detergent should be circled.
8. 1 minute
9. square
10. 8 days

Day 70

1. 23
2. 80
3. 160
4. 244
5. $10.14
6. 10
7. 25 cm
8. gallon of juice
9. The ball and orange should be circled.
10. 58

Day 71

1. 21
2. 24
3. 36
4. 2
5. 964
6. 4
7. $1\frac{1}{2}$ hours
8. year
9. 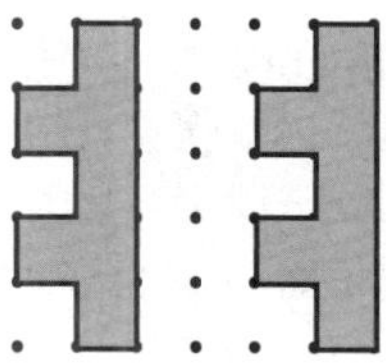
10. 4 days

Day 72

1. 10
2. 18 sides
3. 21
4. 35
5. 20 quarters
6. 36
7. June 27th
8. 4 hours
9. C, A, B
10. $\frac{1}{4}$ of the circle should be green. $\frac{1}{2}$ of the circle should be red. $\frac{1}{4}$ of the circle should be blue.

Day 73

1. 70
2. An array of 7 rows by 2 columns should be drawn.
3. 15
4. 3 rows
5. yes
6. 390
7. paper clip, pencil, book
8. thermometer
9. 8:30
10. a dime and a nickel

Day 74

1. 21
2. 0
3. 100
4. odd number
5. 1 one or 1
6. 10
7. August
8. The solid on the right should be circled.
9. 6 faces
10. 6:10 A.M.

Day 75

1. 60
2. 36
3. 20
4. 7
5. $0.66
6. x
7. can of soda

ANSWER KEY *(cont.)*

8. 11 inches
9. A should be circled.
10. 4 bags

Day 76
1. 62
2. 48
3. 24
4. 67th
5. $6.97
6. 26, 24
7. September
8. 3
9. 23 times
10. 460

Day 77
1. 4
2. 17
3. 30
4. 8 rows
5. $0.60
6. 8 pencils
7. July 2nd
8. a person
9. cone
10. $\frac{3}{4}$

Day 78
1. 25
2. 56
3. 3 rows of 5 flowers should be drawn; 15.
4. 79
5. 4 quarters
6. 7
7. 9:00
8. The cup should be circled.
9. obtuse angle
10. $11.43

Day 79
1. 8
2. 20
3. 24
4. 5 pencils
5. no
6. 400
7. 4 hours
8. 16 cm
9. cube
10. 132

Day 80
1. 61
2. 12 ears
3. 56
4. 253
5. 88
6. +
7. 31 days
8. shorter
9. 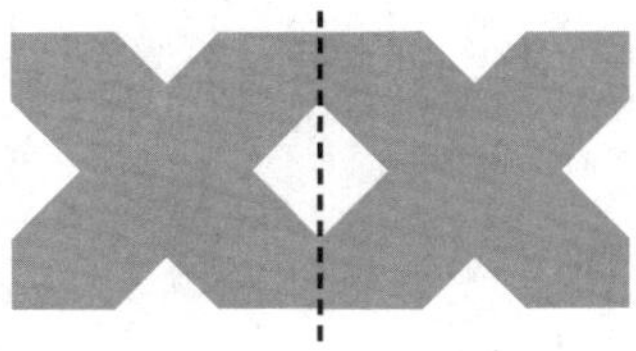
10. 24 players

Day 81
1. 129
2. 70
3. 21
4. 9
5. $\frac{1}{7}$
6. –
7. 3 hours
8. 7 feet
9. none
10. 45, 46, 54, 56, 64, 65

Day 82
1. 74
2. 72
3. 63
4. 157
5. no
6. 535
7. centimeter
8. 12:45
9. Vertices: 12
   Edges: 18
   Faces: 8
10. $1.00

Day 83
1. 25
2. 48
3. 25
4. 5 stars
5. $0.30
6. 3
7. April 15th
8. 20 feet
9. right angle
10. sphere

Day 84
1. 19
2. 0
3. 48
4. 6
5. $0.29
6. 6
7. calendar
8. 12 months
9. 

10. $4 \times 5 = 20$
    $5 \times 4 = 20$
    $20 \div 4 = 5$
    $20 \div 5 = 4$

Day 85
1. 46
2. 21
3. 5 groups of 7 hats should be drawn; 35.
4. 4
5. 30
6. 9
7. desk, chair, book
8. 5
9. 2 edges
10. 80 pages

Day 86
1. 27
2. 4 noses
3. 45
4. 54
5. $6.61
6. 29

ANSWER KEY *(cont.)*

7. 12 hours
8. 13
9. 1 person fewer
10. $\frac{1}{4}$ of the cake

Day 87

1. 12
2. 32
3. 24
4. 9 crackers
5. 4 thousand or 4,000
6. 9
7. November
8. The detergent container should be circled.
9. yes
10. $9.00

Day 88

1. 181
2. 14
3. 81
4. 32 tally marks should be drawn; 4.
5. Possible answers $\frac{1}{1}$, $\frac{2}{2}$, $\frac{3}{3}$, etc.
6. ÷
7. 10 cm
8. 5 cm
9. true
10. 13 red and green marbles

Day 89

1. 19
2. 80
3. 16 ears
4. 5
5. 3 hundreds
6. 4
7. Sunday
8. toothpick, pencil, ruler
9. 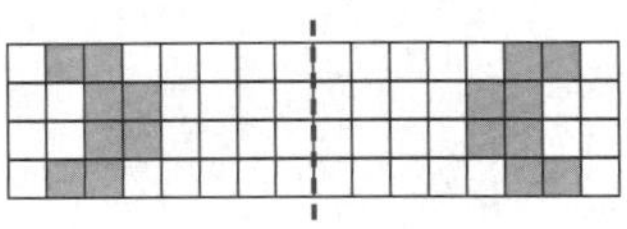
10. 49

Day 90

1. 21
2. 100
3. 36
4. 480
5. yes
6. –
7. December 31st
8. 6:30
9. face
10. 6

Day 91

1. 70
2. An array of 7 rows by 8 columns should be drawn.
3. 48
4. 6
5. $\frac{2}{4}$ or $\frac{1}{2}$
6. 55
7. The flower stamp should be circled.
8. 2:15
9. 4
10. A

Day 92

1. 22
2. 24
3. 30
4. 197
5. 145 should be circled.
6. 40
7. 100
8. 5:20
9. 14
10. 65¢

Day 93

1. 42
2. 48
3. 60
4. 2
5. 43
6. 7
7. 9:45 should be drawn.
8. The ball should be circled.
9. C
10. 4 cups

Day 94

1. 700
2. 64
3. 20 legs
4. 382
5. 16
6. 6
7. 10
8. inches
9. triangle
10. 548

Day 95

1. 20
2. 40
3. An array of 6 rows by 1 column should be drawn.
4. 3
5. 65¢
6. ÷
7. B
8. shorter
9. cylinder
10. 2 parts should be blue; 1 part should be red; 1 part should be yellow; 1 part should be orange

Day 96

1. 70
2. 55
3. 8 tails
4. 381
5. yes
6. 7
7. five twenty
8. true
9. 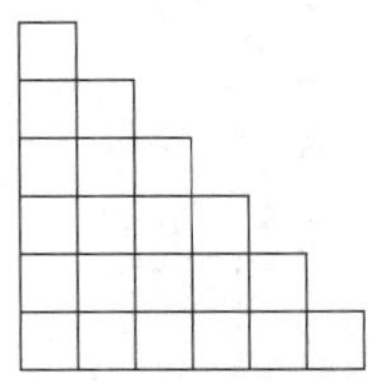
10. 3 quarters and 4 dimes

ANSWER KEY *(cont.)*

Day 97

1. 45
2. 90
3. 80
4. 4 markers
5. $1.85
6. 38
7. Soda bottle should be circled.
8. 7:10
9. 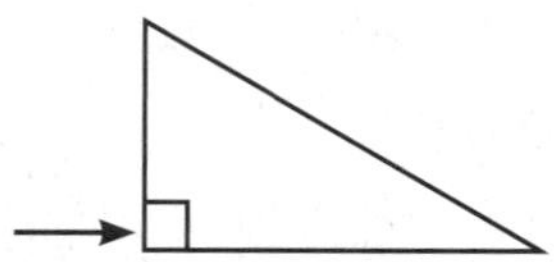
10. 9 bows

Day 98

1. 50
2. 50
3. 20 fingers
4. 100th
5. 5 tens
6. ÷
7. C
8. 7:40
9. 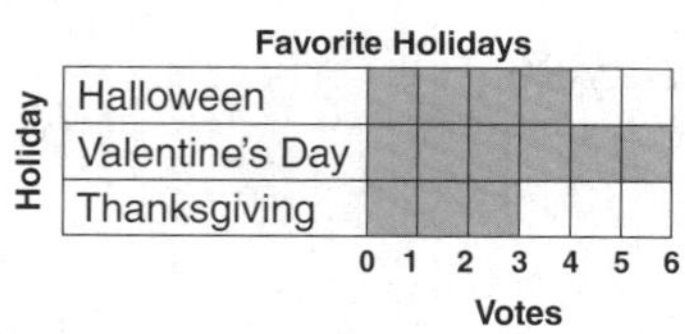

10. 1 ball

Day 99

1. 62
2. 40
3. 28
4. 6
5. true
6. 10
7. 7:40
8. The bag of potatoes should be circled.
9. none
10. 128 stickers

Day 100

1. 45
2. 8
3. 80
4. 527
5. 6
6. 4
7. 12
8. 2:45
9. no
10. 2 cars

Day 101

1. 61
2. 112
3. An array of 7 rows by 10 columns should be drawn.
4. 8 blocks
5. 54
6. 35
7. 4:45 should be drawn.
8. 8
9. circle
10. 84 newspapers

Day 102

1. 47
2. 0
3. 27
4. even number
5. 3 of the diamonds should be colored.
6. 2
7. five fifty
8. 10 times
9. 
10. 2 quarters, 1 dime, 1 nickel; or 1 half-dollar, 3 nickels

Day 103

1. 27
2. 320
3. 54
4. 5
5. yes
6. ÷
7. The right solid should be circled.
8. less
9. 35 children
10. 749, 794, 746, 764, 769, 796

Day 104

1. 40
2. 30
3. 70
4. 674
5. 25 dimes
6. 7
7. inches
8. A
9. 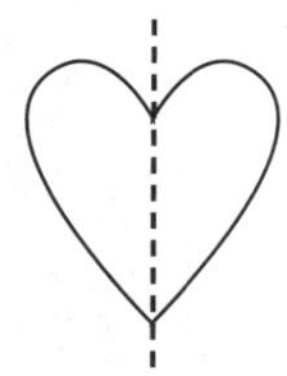
10. 8:10

Day 105

1. 45
2. 72
3. 0
4. 10
5. 248
6. 36
7. 14
8. 10:50
9. acute angle
10. 2 markers

Day 106

1. 267
2. 30 toes
3. 42
4. 629
5. yes
6. 6
7. 6:50
8. The soda bottle should be circled.
9. Reading: 17 tally marks
   Video games: 11 tally marks
   Toys: 22 tally marks
10. no

ANSWER KEY *(cont.)*

Day 107
1. 41
2. 4
3. 40
4. 12 crayons
5. The right figure should be circled.
6. 27
7. The laundry detergent should be circled.
8. shorter
9. The parallelogram (left shape) should be circled.
10. February

Day 108
1. 70
2. 0
3. 108
4. 322
5. 1 thousand, 5 hundreds, 0 tens, 6 ones
6. ÷
7. The glue should be circled.
8. 10:15
9. 4
10. 17 faces

Day 109
1. 200
2. 14
3. 56
4. 4
5. $\frac{3}{4}$, $\frac{4}{4}$ or 1
6. 1
7. The left solid should be circled.
8. 12:15
9. acute angle
10. 2 pizzas

Day 110
1. 500
2. 144
3. 76
4. 453
5. 75¢
6. 10
7. 2:30 should be drawn.
8. A and B
9. no
10. 27 leaves

Day 111
1. 89
2. 16
3. 60
4. 4 apples
5. 3 sections should be colored.
6. 301
7. more
8. 8:20
9. A square should be drawn for the front and top views.
10. 3 boxes

Day 112
1. 9
2. 40
3. 105
4. 90
5. 691 should be circled.
6. 3
7. 11:06
8. The right shape should be circled.
9. 36
10. $\frac{4}{12}$ or $\frac{1}{3}$

Day 113
1. 24
2. 50
3. 60
4. 9
5. $\frac{8}{100}$ or $\frac{2}{25}$
6. 85
7. The right solid should be circled.
8. 22 cm
9. false
10. 10 minutes

Day 114
1. 200
2. 33
3. 28
4. 452
5. 5 thousand or 5,000
6. –
7. 2:45 should be drawn.
8. 8
9. circle
10. 159

Day 115
1. 33
2. 20
3. 60
4. 9
5. 20 quarters
6. 7
7. 9:30 should be drawn.
8. inches
9. 15 edges
10. 59, 62, 65, 68, 71

Day 116
1. 60
2. 20
3. 22
4. 80
5. $\frac{3}{10}$ should be circled.
6. 6
7. 1
8. taller
9. face
10. 70'

Day 117
1. 71
2. 10 points
3. 48
4. 5
5. 538
6. ÷
7. The apple should be circled.
8. 2:40
9. parallel
10. no

Day 118
1. 10
2. 15
3. 0
4. 830
5. 298 should be circled.
6. 270
7. nine ten

ANSWER KEY *(cont.)*

8. The cookies should be circled.
9. 
10. 465

Day 119
1. 229
2. 24
3. 240
4. 5
5. 55¢
6. 26
7. B and C
8. 2:30
9. B
10. $5.00

Day 120
1. 27
2. 30
3. 21
4. 730
5. $1.25
6. 3
7. The cup should be circled.
8. 28
9. Beach: 32 tally marks
   Mountains: 17 tally marks
   Desert: 23 tally marks
10. 12 steps

Day 121
1. 24
2. 120
3. 12 paws
4. 5 triangles
5. $\frac{27}{100}$
6. 7
7. less
8. 7:40
9. B, C, A
10. 29

Day 122
1. 6
2. An array of 6 rows by 4 columns should be drawn.
3. 20
4. 236th
5. 2,147 should be circled.
6. 26
7. 8:15
8. The left figure should be circled.
9. parallel lines
10. $97.45

Day 123
1. 54
2. 60
3. 54
4. 5
5. 7 hundred or 700
6. 503
7. 8
8. 1
9. circle
10.

6	1	8
7	5	3
2	9	4

Day 124
1. 62
2. 78
3. 40 toes
4. $2 per person
5. 518
6. 6
7. 1:30
8. 2:45
9. 
10. G

Day 125
1. 52
2. An array of 7 rows by 3 columns should be drawn.
3. 98
4. 9 stickers
5. 3 hundred or 300
6. ÷
7. 11:30 should be drawn.
8. 10 milk jugs
9. Answers will vary but should include two of the following: square, rectangle, rhombus, trapezoid, or parallelogram.
10. Answers will vary, but the sum of the two numbers should be 56.

Day 126
1. 14
2. 30
3. 300
4. odd number
5. 1 thousand, 4 hundreds, 0 tens, 9 ones
6. 4 kids
7. 6:45 should be drawn.
8. 24"
9. front: triangle,
   top: circle
10. 8 pieces

Day 127
1. 61
2. 18
3. 48
4. 5
5. The left hundred grid should be circled.
6. 540
7. six twenty
8. The left solid should be circled.
9. The angle on the right should be circled.
10. 2 buses

ANSWER KEY *(cont.)*

Day 128

1. 7
2. 63
3. 246
4. 366
5. $0.25
6. 12
7. 12
8. C, B, A
9. The right shape should be circled.
10. 42 people

Day 129

1. 80
2. 80
3. 24
4. 9
5. 15¢
6. 9
7. 1:30
8. 3 in.
9. Pepperoni: 5 faces
Pineapple: 2 faces
Cheese: 4 faces
10. 113 students

Day 130

1. 51
2. 48
3. 8
4. 693
5. 35¢
6. 54
7. The bat should be circled.
8. less
9. perpendicular lines
10. 7 stickers

Day 131

1. 53
2. 160
3. 180
4. 9
5. 2
6. ÷
7. 11:40
8. 5
9. triangle
10. 2,368

Day 132

1. 28
2. 14
3. 140
4. 436
5. 42¢
6. 272
7. 120 minutes
8. The bucket should be circled.
9. 5 angles
10. $32.00

Day 133

1. 16
2. 12 wheels
3. 72
4. 10
5. 72
6. 34
7. inches
8. 9
9. false
10. 84

Day 134

1. 45
2. 20 fingers
3. 54
4. 6 tally marks should be drawn.
5. $0.35
6. 8¢
7. 2:15
8. less than
9. B
10. 27 marbles

Day 135

1. 19
2. 90
3. An array of 5 rows by 9 columns should be drawn.
4. 3
5. 25¢
6. 10
7. false
8. The right shape should be circled.
9. 49 more people
10. 9 steps

Day 136

1. 3
2. 210
3. 36
4. 725
5. yes
6. 6
7. 1:30 should be drawn.
8. 20 minutes
9. no
10. 12 pairs of shoes

Day 137

1. 56
2. twenty-seven
3. 270
4. 9
5. 9 hundred or 900
6. +
7. 4
8. minutes
9. The square (left shape) should be circled.
10. 16 cups

Day 138

1. 12
2. 16 hands
3. 72
4. 720
5. 200 + 40 + 8
6. 302
7. false
8. 1
9. 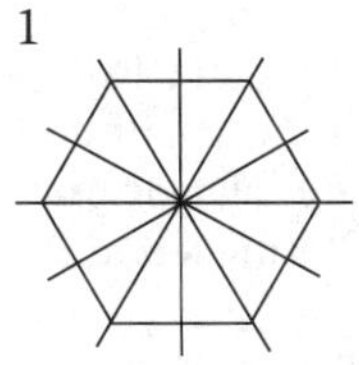
10. 5 outfits

ANSWER KEY *(cont.)*

Day 139

1. 60
2. 21
3. 210
4. 6
5. 165
6. 4
7. 12 times
8. 3 cm
9. 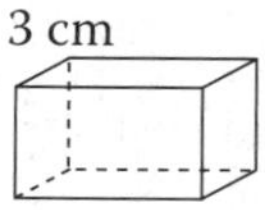
10. 554

Day 140

1. 16
2. 56
3. 560
4. 97
5. $1.50
6. 18
7. 16 cm²
8. pencil
9. 4 triangles should be drawn.
10. 9 pages

Day 141

1. 13
2. 10
3. 90
4. 8
5. 4
6. 483
7. $\frac{1}{2}$
8. a bag of rocks
9. circle
10. 5 quarters and 1 dime; or 3 quarters, 1 half dollar, and 2 nickels; or one dollar coin, 2 dimes, and 3 nickels

Day 142

1. 4
2. 13
3. 81
4. 737
5. 198
6. 3
7. The cupboard on the right should be circled.
8. longer
9. 46 fewer people
10. 9 minutes

Day 143

1. 456
2. 32
3. 6 eyes
4. 10
5. one fourth
6. 8
7. The pasta should be circled.
8. 9 cm
9. 
10. 12 dogs

Day 144

1. 400
2. 0
3. 0
4. 528
5. 45¢
6. ÷
7. December
8. yes
9. cube
10. 84 bananas

Day 145

1. 15
2. 49
3. 120
4. 8
5. $6.50
6. 43
7. 2 cups
8. centimeters
9. surfaces: 3
   edges: 2
   vertices: 0
10. 765

Day 146

1. 24
2. 42
3. 13
4. 5
5. 1,606
6. 6
7. B
8. meter
9. 5 lines of symmetry
10. 7 yards

Day 147

1. 92
2. 320
3. 64
4. 9
5. 2,000 + 300 + 4
6. 572
7. 2 hours
8. less than
9. parallel lines
10. 18 teddy bears

Day 148

1. 61
2. 6 arms
3. 16
4. 446
5. 6 tens or 60
6. 1
7. 10 minutes
8. 32° F
9. Number of Sides: 3
   Number of Angles: 3
   Number of Lines of Symmetry: 3
   Name of Shape: triangle
10. yes

Day 149

1. 50
2. 36
3. 18
4. 8
5. 1,030
6. 6
7. 6
8. 3.5 cm
9. circle
10. 350 minutes

ANSWER KEY *(cont.)*

Day 150

1. 75
2. 48
3. 480
4. 719
5. $10.50
6. –
7. $1\frac{1}{2}$ yards
8. 2 hours 5 minutes
9. prism
10. yes

Day 151

1. 82
2. 81
3. 10 feet
4. 8
5. $\frac{1}{4}$
6. 5
7. 15 inches
8. meters
9. The left figure should be circled.
10. 63

Day 152

1. 25
2. 24
3. 24
4. 534
5. 3,000 + 500 + 60 + 2
6. 351
7. 8
8. 36 inches
9. hexagon
10. C

Day 153

1. 121
2. 52
3. 28
4. 10
5. 2,000 + 90 + 4
6. 48
7. true
8. 5.5 cm
9. chocolate
10. 48 inches

Day 154

1. 35
2. 56
3. 30
4. 684th
5. $0.55
6. 2
7. a pencil
8. gallons
9. prism
10. Answers will vary.

Day 155

1. 90
2. 120
3. 18 wheels
4. 10
5. 5,000 + 200 + 70
6. +
7. false
8. no
9. 
10. 23 pounds

Day 156

1. 60
2. 35
3. 350
4. 593
5. 70¢
6. 3
7. minutes
8. 9 cm²
9. 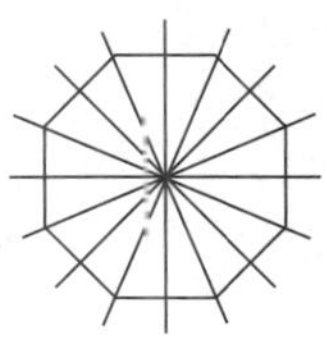
10. 8 months

Day 157

1. 9
2. 75
3. 28
4. 7
5. 7,000 + 20 + 1
6. 18
7. 15 minutes
8. 6 L
9. Mon.: 35 tally marks
Tue.: 30 tally marks
Wed.: 45 tally marks
Thur.: 20 tally marks
10. 5 times

Day 158

1. 62
2. 15 fingers
3. 72
4. 181
5. $1.55
6. 9
7. The right cupboard should be circled.
8. no
9. 8
10. 732

Day 159

1. 22
2. 140
3. An array of 2 rows by 9 columns should be drawn.
4. 8
5. $16.50
6. 6
7. The right floor should be circled.
8. 2 pints
9. intersecting lines
10. $79.96

Day 160

1. 45
2. 54
3. 64
4. odd number
5. 2 hundred or 200
6. 327
7. 3 pitchers
8. 48 hours
9. 8 angles
10. 16 people

ANSWER KEY *(cont.)*

Day 161

1. 239
2. 32
3. 320
4. 9
5. 200 + 60 + 4
6. 50
7. true
8. 10:09
9. Number of Sides: 5
   Number of Angles: 5
   Number of Lines of Symmetry: 5
   Name of Shape: pentagon
10. 12

Day 162

1. 23
2. 60
3. 0
4. 682
5. true
6. 235
7. January
8. 9:30
9. cylinder
10. 7 crackers

Day 163

1. 13
2. 51
3. 40
4. 5
5. 4,000 + 500 + 10 + 2
6. true
7. false
8. 12 inches
9. base
10. 231 students

Day 164

1. 12
2. 48
3. 7
4. 720
5. $1.90
6. –
7. 7 feet
8. 2 in.
9. rectangle
10. 20 people

Day 165

1. 160
2. 9
3. 90
4. 6
5. 1,023
6. 1
7. shorter
8. yes
9. C
10. 32 cups

Day 166

1. 2
2. 40
3. 140
4. 496
5. $22.50
6. 19
7. 1
8. 8:50
9. no
10. 24 pizzas

Day 167

1. 68
2. 36
3. 160
4. 9 twos
5. $0.80
6. 58
7. 5 inches
8. 52 weeks
9. The left shape should be circled.
10. 990 words

Day 168

1. 84
2. 80
3. 82
4. 719
5. greater than
6. 34
7. 20 minutes
8. February
9. 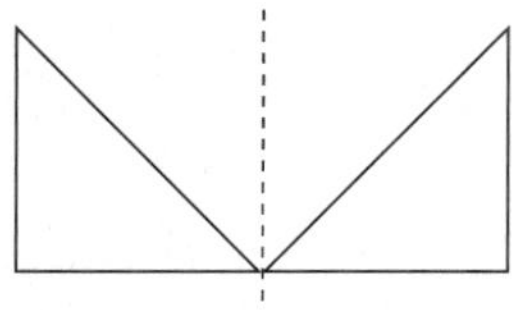
10. 5 cups

Day 169

1. 31
2. 30 cans
3. 90
4. 5
5. 3 ones or 3
6. 36
7. $3\frac{1}{2}$ in.
8. inch
9. 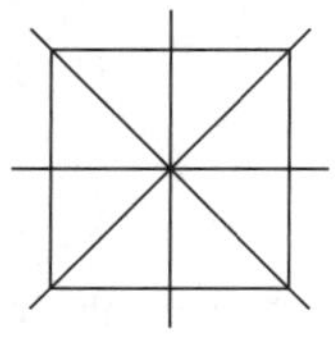
10. $17.05

Day 170

1. 90
2. 150
3. 0
4. 594
5. $1.10
6. 3
7. rooster
8. 44 feet
9. 113 fewer people
10. 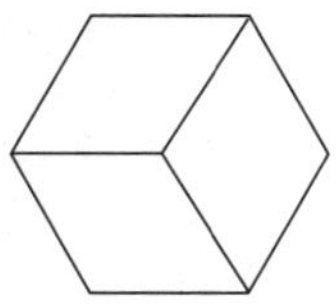

ANSWER KEY *(cont.)*

Day 171

1. 56
2. 32
3. 240
4. 7
5. 2,374
6. 2
7. The left cupboard should be circled.
8. 4 cups
9. 3
10. 14 times

Day 172

1. 73
2. 7,000
3. 32
4. 472nd
5. $.50
6. 1,000
7. 3:15
8. greater than
9. none
10. 28 days

Day 173

1. 70
2. 100
3. 40
4. 2
5. 42 boxes should be shaded.
6. 132
7. feet
8. yes
9. triangular prism
10. 381 boxes

Day 174

1. 15
2. 80
3. 34
4. 16 tally marks should be drawn.
5. $1.15
6. 8
7. minutes
8. 12 cm
9. rectangle
10. 1 dozen

Day 175

1. 14
2. 186
3. 64
4. even number
5. 166
6. 2
7. The left floor should be circled.
8. 6 feet
9. 
10. 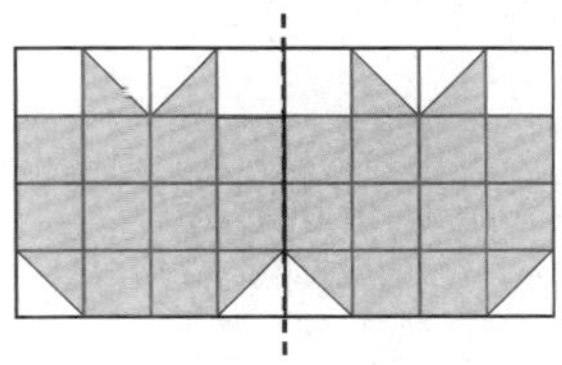

Day 176

1. 75
2. 50
3. 6 tires
4. 5
5. 5 tens or 50
6. 300
7. false
8. 15 minutes
9. Number of Sides: 4
   Number of Angles: 4
   Number of Lines of Symmetry: 4
   Name of Shape: square
10. 12 weeks

Day 177

1. 22
2. 90
3. 42
4. 833
5. 1,000 – 200 + 50 + 6
6. 27
7. longer
8. 800 mL
9. triangle
10. D and E

Day 178

1. 52
2. 72
3. 48
4. 2 rows
5. $2.75
6. 3
7. true
8. 0° C
9. sphere
10. 569

Day 179

1. 11
2. 48
3. 480
4. 727
5. 24
6. 6
7. 16
8. 2 cm
9. 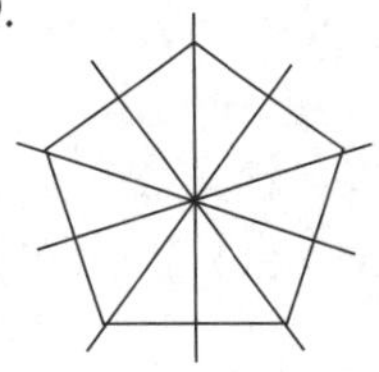
10. Answers will vary.

Day 180

1. 33
2. 80
3. 14
4. 7
5. 2,868
6. 916
7. 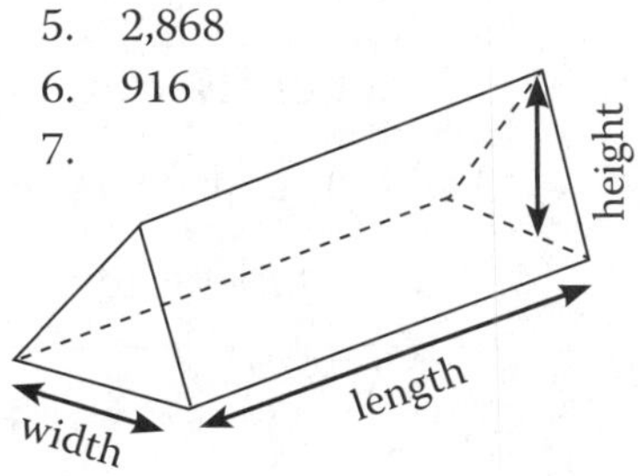

8. 8:30
9. The shape on the right should be circled.
10. 4 hours

DIGITAL RESOURCES

Accessing the Digital Resources

The digital resources can be downloaded by following these steps:

1. Go to www.tcmpub.com/digital
2. Use the ISBN number to redeem the digital resources.
3. Respond to the question using the book.
4. Follow the prompts on the Content Cloud website to sign in or create a new account.
5. The content redeemed will now be on your My Content screen. Click on the product to look through the digital resources. All resources are available for download. Select files can be previewed, opened, and shared. For questions and assistance with your license key card, or to report a lost card, please contact Shell Education.

   mail: customerservice@tcmpub.com
   phone: 800-858-7339

CONTENTS OF THE DIGITAL RESOURCES

Teacher Resources

- Practice Page Item Analysis Chart
- Student Item Analysis Chart

Student Resources

- Practice Pages